BYPASS

BYPASS

A CARDIOLOGIST REVEALS WHAT EVERY PATIENT NEEDS TO KNOW

by
Jonathan L. Halperin, M.D.,
and
Richard Levine

Times
BOOKS

"Sounding Board" by Benson B. Roe is excerpted by permission of *The New England Journal of Medicine*, vol. 305 (1981), p.41.

Copyright © 1985 by Jonathan L. Halperin, M.D., and Richard Levine

Library of Congress Cataloging in Publication Data

Halperin, Jonathan L.
    Bypass.   ✓ 2, Heart - Diseases.

    Includes index.
✓1. Aortocoronary bypass. I. Levine, Richard, 1949–   . ✓II. Title.
RD598.H28 1985   617'.412   84–40432
ISBN 0–8129–1157–1

Illustrations by Vantage Art Inc.

Designed by Doris Borowsky
Manufactured in the United States of America
9 8 7 6 5 4 3 2
First Edition

To Michelle Copeland and Janet Gold

Acknowledgments

WE ARE INDEBTED TO Kathleen Moloney; Ann Finlayson; Esther Newberg; Herbert LeVine; Paul Lieberman; John T. McDermott; Richard A. Knox; Jon Weeks; Dr. Valentin Fuster; Dr. Bruce P. Mindich; Dr. Richard Gorlin; Dr. Robert S. Litwak; Dr. W. Virgil Brown; Richard deAsla; Elizabeth B. Rothlauf; Ruby S. Gordon; and the attending physicians, surgical assistants, nurses, fellows, and residents of Annenberg 8 and Housman 3, and, of course, their patients.

Contents

Introduction

IN 1967, 622,114 AMERICANS died of coronary heart disease. One of them was my father. His heart attack came suddenly on a muggy August night, a few months after his forty-fifth birthday. He barely had time to clutch his chest.

In the months and years after his death, I often wondered about the disease that struck him down. How could it kill, without warning, an apparently healthy man in his prime? Why did it kill so many others? What was this disease that, over the course of a few decades, had grown from a rarity to an epidemic? Although I had only the most rudimentary knowledge of heart disease, I knew that it ran in families. That meant I had one strike against me. I also knew that cigarette smoking somehow made it worse. My father smoked Pall Malls; I preferred Camels, but like him I smoked more than a pack a day. Strike two. As for my other cardiac risk factors: I was male, and the disease primarily afflicts males, though to this day no one knows why; I was raised on the typical American diet, which was to say plenty of fatty foods like ice cream, eggs, and steak, and the evidence seems to indicate that the fattier the diet, the greater the likelihood of heart trouble. I was also out of shape and, like my father, was the sort of person who would complete the sentences of slower talking friends and grow exasperated even at the prospect of waiting on line—what we now call a Type A. Strike three, four, five, and six.

I didn't really start to worry, though, until my pre-employment physical at *The New York Times*, where I went to work in 1980 as an editor of *The Week in Review*. My blood pressure, which had been inching up over the years, stood at 159 over 110 —far too high for my thirty-two years. The doctor shook his head. It was time to do something.

So I went to see Jonathan Halperin, a college classmate who had gone into his father's business—cardiology, the science of the heart. After Columbia College, Jon attended medical school at Boston University and completed his internship and residency at the University Hospital and Boston City Hospital. Then he had conducted research in peripheral vascular disease at the Evans Memorial Foundation in Boston and was a fellow in cardiology at Boston University Medical Center. He moved to Mount Sinai Medical Center, a 1,212-bed hospital in New York City, in 1980 as assistant professor of medicine and liaison to the division of cardiothoracic surgery, supervising the medical care of open-heart surgery patients. In 1983, he became director of clinical cardiology services. Jon was always ready to help his friends with their medical problems, but he seemed to take a particular interest in my case. I was, after all, a member of the coronary prone population.

By that time, the scores of medical stories I had written and edited had rubbed off, for I had already stopped smoking and begun watching my diet and trying—without much success—to exercise regularly. Indeed, Jon was able to cut my blood pressure down to size with a single slip from his prescription pad. Needless to say, most of his cases are harder. Even for the most skilled physician, heart disease can be hard to diagnose and even harder to treat. It assumes a variety of forms and provokes a bewildering array of symptoms. Cases are like fingerprints: no two are alike.

Fortunately, the modern cardiologist has a medical arsenal with which to size up this fearsome opponent. Electrocardiographs developed at the turn of the century are now hooked up to computer-controlled treadmills to study the heart while it works. Radioactive tracers light up the heart muscle, revealing patches of disease. Catheters the width of cocktail straws can slide through the circulatory system and into the coronary arteries to photograph these tiny vessels as they transport nourishing blood to the heart.

Pharmaceutical companies, meanwhile, have been making good on the promise of better living through chemistry, developing several generations of cardiac drugs in the course of less than one. That age-old standby, nitroglycerin, is now augmented by beta blockers, calcium blockers, and enzyme inhibitors—and even miraculous properties of aspirin have been discovered.

And, if drugs fail, there is the most dramatic treatment of all —coronary artery bypass graft surgery, the rerouting of blood around the heart's blocked supply lines, using transplanted veins from the patient's own leg. As the surgical mortality rate plunged from 10 percent to about 1 percent, and the success rate in relieving the often paralyzing pain of coronary disease rose to 95 percent, it is little wonder that the number of Americans undergoing CABG (pronounced cabbage by those in the business) has soared—1,000 in 1968, 2,000 in 1970, 17,000 in 1972, 60,000 in 1975, 180,000 in 1982, and perhaps a quarter of a million this year. Some minor surgical procedures may be performed more frequently, but none consumes as many medical dollars—$5 billion a year—not to mention medical equipment, hospital space, or health care personnel.

Certainly no other operation can boast such a Who's Who of patients. The bypass parade includes two former secretaries of state, Henry Kissinger and Alexander Haig; Representatives

Henry Reuss and Ted Weiss, Governor William A. O'Neill of Connecticut, and former Governor John Y. Brown of Kentucky; Supreme Court Justice John Paul Stevens and Watergate Judge John J. Sirica; Rock Hudson, Jerry Lewis, Danny Kaye, Walter Matthau, Burt Lancaster, Bob Fosse (who turned his experience into a movie), drummer Buddy Rich and Barbara Bel Geddes (Miss Ellie of *Dallas*); former tennis champion Arthur Ashe, baseball manager George Bamberger, and Art Modell, owner of the Cleveland Browns; King Khalid of Saudi Arabia, President Joao Baptista Figueiredo of Brazil, Prime Minister Hussein Onn of Malaysia, and Benigno S. Aquino, Jr., the Philippine opposition leader who was assassinated in 1983. When Senator Barry Goldwater was informed that he might need bypass surgery, he told his surgeon, "Sharpen up your knife, Buster, we're gonna do it." Then there was Bernard Schuler, a retired insurance salesman whose bypass operation was televised, live and coast to coast, by the Public Broadcasting System in 1983, as more than 12 million looked on.

Surgeons, too, have become famous—cool, calm gunslingers in pastel masks and gowns. There were Denton Cooley and Michael DeBakey, one-time colleagues turned rivals who made Houston synonymous with heart surgery; Edward B. Diethrich, who founded the Arizona Heart Institute and officiated at Schuler's televised bypass, and René G. Favaloro, who developed the operation at the Cleveland Clinic, where 35,000 of the procedures have so far been performed, and where they sell T-shirts that read, "I was bypassed at Cleveland."

For most patients, bypass surgery is nothing less than a second chance at a pain-free life. Yet a series of studies have raised questions about the costly, complicated procedure and who should undergo it. Does bypass surgery prolong lives? Will it prevent a heart attack? Is it more effective than drugs? Are surgeons operating too often and charging too much? After all, there are 74 bypass operations performed per 100,000 people in the United States today, twice the rate in Australia and six times

that in the United Kingdom, and the average surgeon's fee here
—about $4,500—is four times what Canadian surgeons bill for
their labors. This debate culminated in a $24 million study spon-
sored by the National Institutes of Health at a dozen of the
nation's top medical centers. The verdict: Perhaps a third of all
bypass operations were premature. Bypass surgery, at least as
prescribed in the United States, would seem to be a case of too
much of a good thing.

Less investigated but no less worrisome are the subtle and
sometimes not-so-subtle side effects of surgery. Some researchers have found that for many making the trip to the operating
room, the ordeal of stopping, repairing, and restarting the heart
—maybe just the knowledge that their heart has literally been
in someone else's hands—leaves more than superficial scars. The
physical trauma is hardly surprising: Heart surgery affects the
lungs, the kidneys, the liver, the limbs, scores of muscles, the
immune system, the brain; in fact, it is hard to think of a major
system it doesn't affect. But few physicians were expecting the
psychological complications bypass patients are reporting: the
unsettling number who say their pain is gone but who nevertheless are having problems returning to their jobs and re-establish-
ing relationships with their families and friends.

Thus, the bypass dilemma: the decision of whether, and when,
to have bypass surgery, and what to do if problems develop after
it. In guiding his patients through an expensive and sometimes
dangerous diagnostic maze and interpreting the results, Jon
maintains a cautious, conservative attitude. He is one of those
special physicians who treats people, not diseases. This book,
born of his clinical experience, is organized along the path a
patient follows through the bypass experience. Much of it is set
on Annenberg 8, Mount Sinai's cardiothoracic center, where
you'll see the diagnostic tests used to unmask coronary disease,
get an over-the-surgeon's-shoulder view of an actual bypass operation, and tour an intensive care unit equipped with some of
the most sophisticated technology in medicine. Then it's on to

Housman 3, where a team of physicians, nurses, and social workers helps bypass patients get back on their feet.

  Bypass surgery is not a cure, only a treatment that will eventually be neutralized if the progression of the underlying disease—
atherosclerosis—isn't halted. In Lewis Thomas's memorable
phrase, it is a "halfway technology"—halfway to a genuine solution. No recovery is complete without a lesson in how to reduce
the likelihood of a repeat bypass. We provide the latest information from investigators around the world on how to reduce coronary risk factors. And, since no book on bypass surgery is
complete without a look at the underlying disease, we will also
take you to a laboratory where researchers are trying to untangle the destructive sequence by which atherosclerosis befouls
our arteries.

  Because so many bypass patients have trouble resuming
work, we have devoted an entire chapter to the physical, psychological, legal, and ethical obstacles to postoperative employment. We also review a typical bypass bill, page by page and line
by line, and discuss the larger economic impact of a procedure
that accounts for 1 percent of the nation's health care bill all by
itself.

  It is the hope of all physicians, even those who earn their living
by the blade, that procedures such as bypass surgery will become obsolete as less invasive treatments are developed. We end
the book with a look at what promises to be one such technique,
angioplasty, which can unclog some blocked vessels with less
trauma and, perhaps, less risk, forestalling or even eliminating
the bypass ordeal.

  About the time of my father's heart attack—and the time
Favaloro was perfecting coronary bypass—the heart disease
death rate began a decline that has continued to this day. It is
still our leading health menace, bigger even in its yearly toll than
the Black Death of the fourteenth and seventeenth centuries,
but it has lost 30 percent of its lethal power in two decades.

Medical advances, along with better diets and more healthy habits, have helped, but in large part the disease's fall is as much of a mystery as its rise. With that in mind, we have chosen to start *Bypass* at the turn of the century, with a famous series of lectures on the then obscure but fascinating subject of heart disease given at one of the nation's leading medical schools by one of medicine's leading figures.

One last word: This book is a collaboration of a cardiologist and a journalist, told in Dr. Halperin's voice. The names of the doctors, nurses, social workers, technicians, administrators, and other hospital personnel you will meet are real, although some have moved on to other jobs or institutions. The patients are real, too, although their names, occupations, and some personal details of their cases have been changed to protect their privacy. In this chronicle of bypass surgery at Mount Sinai, we do not mean to imply that the institution is the leader in cardiac surgery. The Cleveland Clinic, the Texas Heart Institute, the University of Alabama Medical Center, the Arizona Heart Institute, to name but a few, all were performing bypass surgery before Mount Sinai and are probably doing more of it now. But Mount Sinai, one of the oldest and most famous hospitals in the country, has a thorough, thoughtful program that, while it may not match the volume of some other institutions, ranks with the best in the quality of its care.

More than one million people have already had bypass surgery. About four million more suffer from coronary artery disease and may one day face the bypass dilemma. Through habit or heritage, virtually everyone has some coronary risk. All heart patients should have a physician with the knowledge, dedication, and sensitivity of Jonathan Halperin. Failing that, you have this book.

Richard Levine
New York City, 1985

BYPASS

1

The Cardiac Century, Part I
From Heartache to Epidemic

A FEW YEARS BEFORE the turn of the century, William Osler, the most respected physician of his day, delivered a series of lectures to medical students at the Johns Hopkins Hospital in Baltimore. His subject was angina pectoris, the paroxysmal chest pain that signals coronary heart disease and was then regarded as a prelude to death. It was a topic that stirred considerable professional interest, perhaps because physicians seemed to suffer from it more often than others. Angina could hardly have been described as a public health menace, however. "During the ten years in which I lived in Montreal," Osler told his audience, "I did not see a case of the disease either in private practice or at the Montreal General Hospital. At Blockley [Philadelphia Hospital], too, it was an exceedingly rare affection. I do not remember to have had a case under personal care. There were two cases in my service at the University Hospital. During the seven years in which the Johns Hopkins Hospital has been opened, with an unusually large 'material' in diseases of the heart and arteries, and with many

cases of heart pain of various sorts, there have been only four
instances of angina pectoris."

A formal man with a bushy walrus mustache, a balding pate,
and grave brown eyes, Osler had built a reputation as a relentless pursuer of diagnostic truth, tirelessly touring the wards,
exhaustively interviewing patients, and conducting some of the
most thorough bedside exams in the business. Few details es-
caped his notice, few clues failed to register, so it did not take
many cases of this strange malady for the great clinician to come
to a surprisingly comprehensive understanding of it. Unlike
many colleagues, Osler recognized that angina was not itself a
disease but rather a *symptom* of disease. It was often triggered
by exercise or emotion, when the heart is forced to pump harder,
but could also strike its victims in their sleep, when the heart is
in low gear. "It is an attendant rather of ease and luxury than
of temperance and labor," Osler told the students. "Though
occurring among the poor, it is more frequently met with among
the rich, or in persons of easy circumstances. . . . More wise men
than fools are its victims."

Angina was often heralded, he went on, by a consciousness of
the heart's action, an "indefinable uneasiness associated with
palpitation." And it could take a bewildering array of forms—
"darting, stabbing, tearing or boring, dull and heavy, or acute
and piercing." Even worse was the mental anguish it engen-
dered in its victims, as if they had been touched by "the very
hand of death."

Osler discussed the role of the coronary arteries, which supply
the heart with blood, and even passed around the hearts of some
autopsied victims, pointing out discolored patches where the
muscle had been compromised and damaged. He outlined a regimen of rest, relaxation, and dietary restraint that still is good
advice. He taught the young physicians when and how to break
it to their patients that the disease afflicting them was incurable.
Yet nothing in his seven elegantly constructed lectures could

have prepared his students for the vast increase in the number of cases they would confront in their own careers.

In 1981, the last year for which figures are available, heart disease and related vascular disorders accounted for 989,610 American deaths, far more than the deaths caused by all forms of cancer (422,720) and accidents (102,130) put together. As many as 1.5 million Americans suffer heart attacks annually, and more than a third will die. That's almost ten times the number of American casualties in the entire Vietnam War *every year*. As for the economic toll, the American Heart Association estimates that in 1984, cardiovascular disease cost the United States $64.4 billion in physician and nursing expenses, diagnostic tests, surgical and hospital bills, medications, and lost wages due to disability, a sum that is almost twice the annual budget of New York State and more than enough to buy Gulf Oil four times over.

We have made great strides in controlling high blood pressure and have virtually eliminated rheumatic fever, which damages the heart's valves and was in Osler's day the most common cause of heart disease. We have established special hospital units in communities across the country devoted solely to the care of coronary patients and trained cardiopulmonary resuscitation teams. We watch what we eat and we smoke less. We put on our Adidas and jam the parks. And still about one-sixth of us— 42,700,000 Americans—have some form of heart or blood vessel disease.

What has turned Osler's curiosity into an epidemic, as the famed cardiologist Paul Dudley White proclaimed it a mere two generations later? What has created the mushrooming market for coronary bypass surgery? What has made this the cardiac century?

Since the rise of heart disease coincided with the taming of many infectious diseases, it is tempting to assume that the containment of tuberculosis, smallpox, diphtheria, poliomyelitis, and pneumonia has enabled us to live longer and grow into coronary heart disease, which usually takes its toll late in life. And we are living longer on average—but only on average. Life expectancy has increased from forty-seven to seventy-four years during this century, not so much because the average American is living longer as because fewer are dying in childhood. "For persons 40 years of age or older, life expectancy has increased relatively little," wrote James F. Fries in *The New England Journal of Medicine.* "For those 75 years old the increase is barely perceptible."

Perhaps the holocaust of heart disease is a result of the pressures of our increasingly traffic-clogged, three-martini, absolutely, positively overnight life. White himself seemed to endorse this view. "Coincident with the beginning of cardiology as a specialty in the early 1920's," he wrote, "our ways of life began to change radically, especially with the rapid development of the automobile and the general enrichment of the diet, both of which I can well remember personally—they stand out strongly in my mind." The court of medical science demands more than anecdotes and observations, however, and so far, admissible evidence has been hard to come by.

It could be, of course, that heart disease has long been a leading killer—we just weren't very good at recognizing it. Even with an array of sophisticated tools that enable physicians to peer deeply into the heart, coronary disease can be difficult to diagnose. Their predecessors relied mostly on intuition, and often this was dulled by superstition.

If heart disease had been prevalent among the ancients, it seems likely they would have come up with a separate name for it. They didn't. In fact, in Egyptian, Hebrew, Greek, and Arabic the word for the heart could also be used to signify the stomach. Nor is it likely that many people could have suffered repeated bouts of angina given the Aristotelian view that the heart, the seat of thought and sensation, could not survive any injury, a belief that endured in some medical quarters until Osler's day.

Through the hindsight of paleopathology, however, we do know that at least some heart disease existed. One victim was the Egyptian pharaoh Merneptah. When scientists examined his mummy early in this century, they found the aorta dotted with calcified patches. In the 1920s, investigators in the pathology department of the University of Buffalo examined the egg-sized heart of one of the three-thousand-year-old specimens that had been entombed in the Metropolitan Museum of Art in New York City and discovered fibrous scar tissue and diseased coronary arteries.

There are also some intriguing hints of angina in the literature of the earliest civilizations. The Ebers papyrus, perhaps the best known of the Egyptian medical texts, contains this highly suggestive passage: "When you examine a man for illness in his cardia, he has pains in his arm, in his breast, on the side of his cardia. . . . Then you shall say thereof: . . . it is death which approaches him." And the Roman philosopher Seneca's description of his own ailment has an anginalike ring: "The attack is very short and like a storm. It usually ends within an hour. I have undergone all bodily infirmities and dangers, but none appears to me more grievous. Why not? Because to have any other malady is only to be sick. To have this is to be dying."

There are nearly a hundred references to the heart in the Old Testament, but most seem more metaphoric than medical. An exception, perhaps, is I Samuel 25:36–38. "And Abigail came to Nabal; and behold, he held a feast in his house, like the feast of a king; and Nabal's heart was merry within him, for he was very drunken: wherefore she told him nothing, less or more, until the morning light. But it came to pass in the morning, when the wine was gone out of Nabal, and his wife had told him these things, that his heart died within him, and it became as a stone. And it came to pass about ten days after, that the Lord smote Nabal, that he died."

The case notes of Hippocrates, the patriarch of medicine, also document anginal aches and pains. Not that his prescriptions were always on target. "If the pain points to the clavicle or if there be a heaviness in the arm, or about the breast, or above the diaphragm," he advised, "one should open the inner vein at the elbow." Although the Greek pioneer conducted no autopsies —they weren't permitted until the fourteenth century—and only cursory diagnostic exams, he was among the first to recognize that disease was something other than divine punishment. In fact, he correctly speculated that some sort of obstruction to blood flow was to blame for chest pain, though he failed to zero in on the heart. That connection was made in the second century A.D. by Galen, who was also the first to describe the blood vessels that circle the heart like a crown, popularizing the term *coronary*.

Thirteen hundred years later, in 1492, Leonardo da Vinci sketched these arteries in astonishing detail as they wound their way from their origin at the top of the heart and dived into the organ's interior. One drawing, "Anatomy of the Old Man," showed gnarled and narrowed vessels taking a particularly tortuous path that resulted, the artist-scientist explained, in the "debility through lack of blood" that often strikes the elderly. What makes Leonardo's drawings all the more impressive is that, since no human hearts were available as models, he had to base them on the hearts of oxen.

A collection of da Vinci's anatomical sketches, on loan from the Royal Library at Windsor Castle, drew long lines when it opened at the Metropolitan Museum of Art in New York City in 1983. The drawings had little impact in the fifteenth century, however, since they were quickly locked away in private collections. It would be another two hundred years before William Harvey would expand on the idea of coronary blood flow, setting out the concept of the body's three circulations in *"Exercitatio de Motu Cordis et Sanguinis"* ("Essay on the Motion of the Heart and of the Blood"): the flow of blood between the heart and the body; the flow between the heart and the lungs; and the "very short circulation . . . from the left ventricle of the heart to the right one, driving a portion of the blood round through the coronary arteries and veins, which are distributed with their small branches through the body, walls and septum of the heart."

From the Middle Ages through the Renaissance, clinicians relied on crude balms to soothe the aching hearts of their patients. "Take a handful of rue [an herb]," went one early recipe. "Seethe it in oil and add one ounce of aloes. Smear with that." Other remedies called for radishes with salt, vapor baths, broth of fennel, opium, abstinence, rest. Texts on heart disease began to appear, including *De Subitaneis Mortibus* ("On Sudden Deaths"), a report to Pope Clement XI on a curious epidemic of sudden deaths in Rome in 1707. For the most part, chest discomfort seemed associated with the well-off, perhaps because they could afford to have it attended to. One royal victim was England's King George II, who died of a ruptured heart in 1760.

A milestone in the investigation of heart disease, at least in retrospect, occurred twelve years later with William Heberden's "Some Account of a Disorder of the Breast." The lecture, delivered at England's Royal College of Physicians, provided the clearest description yet of cardiac chest pain and gave the malady the name *angina,* from both Latin and Greek for the sensation of strangling. "Those who are afflicted with it," he told his audience, "are seized while they are walking, and more particularly when they walk soon after eating, with a painful and most disagreeable sensation in the breast, which seems as if it would take their life away if it were to increase or to continue; the moment they stand still all of this uneasiness vanishes. In all other respects, the patients are at the beginning of this disorder perfectly well, and, in particular, have no shortness of breath from which it is totally different."

An Oxford-educated Latin and Greek scholar, Heberden was described by one of his patients, Samuel Johnson, as "the last of our learned physicians." In truth he was years ahead of his time. He lived in an age when physicians had to compete with astrologers and apothecaries, and surgeons with barbers. Still, his talk had an impact on his peers, and prompted one of them, known only as Dr. Anonymous (and only recently identified as a Dr. Haygarth of Chester), to contact the great Heberden about his own symptoms. "I have often felt, when sitting, standing, and at times in my bed, what I can best express by calling it an universal pause within me of the operations of nature, for perhaps three or four seconds," he wrote before proposing that his own body be examined after his death.

The letter had barely reached its destination when, three weeks later, the body of Dr. Anonymous lay on the autopsy table of John Hunter, London's leading pathologist. Unlike Heberden, Hunter was an Oxford dropout who taught himself surgery on the battlefields of France and Portugal. His first love, however, was anatomy, and his Leicester Square mansion contained a personal museum stocked with human and nonhuman specimens from around the world. Hunter found only "a few specks of a beginning ossification upon the aorta" of Dr. Anonymous, but it started him on the trail. By the end of the century, he had turned up victims whose "coronary arteries from their origin to many of their ramifications became a piece of bone." Thus was the Hippocratic concept of blocked flow linked with Harvey's third circulation.

Hunter may have made an equal contribution to our knowledge of heart disease as a patient. His first attack of angina in 1773 was recorded by a nephew: "While he was walking about the room he cast his eyes on the looking glass, and observed his countenance to be pale, his lips white, giving the appearance of a dead man. This alarmed him and led him to feel for his pulse, but he found none in either arm; the pain continued, and he found himself at times not breathing. Being afraid of death soon taking place if he did not breathe, he produced the voluntary act of breathing by working his lungs by the power of his will." Hunter soon came under the care of Edward Jenner, better known as the father of smallpox vaccination. In a letter to Heberden describing Hunter's case, Jenner suggested that there might be a causal connection between coronary artery disease and angina, the first time the possibility of such a link had been raised. "As the heart, I believe, in every subject that has died of the angina pectoris, has been found extremely loaded with fat, and these vessels lie quite concealed in that substance," he wrote, "is it possible this appearance may have been overlooked?"

Jenner urged Heberden to keep his letter secret for fear it would upset his patient. No matter. Hunter's attacks became frequent, and he complained that his life "was in the hands of any rascal who chose to annoy and tease" him. Sure enough, death came as he stormed out of a meeting of the governors of St. George's Hospital in a rage. An autopsy confirmed that his coronary arteries had become narrow and hard.

The connection between angina and coronary artery disease hardly took the European scientific community by storm. The Germans still suspected gout caused chest pain, while the Italians blamed the liver, and the French chalked it up to nerves. It fell to a young American surgeon, Allan Burns, to put the work of Heberden, Hunter, Jenner, and company in perspective. In 1809, he wrote:

The heart, like every other part, has particular vessels set apart for its nourishment. In health, when we excite the muscular system to more energetic actions than usual we increase the circulation in every part, so that to support this increased ac-

tion, the heart and every part has its power augmented. If,
however, we call into vigorous action a limb, around which we
have with a moderate degree of tightness applied a ligature, we
find then that the member can only support its action for a very
short time: for now its supply of energy and its expenditure do
not balance each other. A heart, the coronary vessels of which
are cartilaginous or ossified, is in nearly a similar condition.

And so the supply-demand theory of heart disease was born.
Simply stated, the more work the heart does, the more oxygen
the heart needs. And if, in the face of increased demand on the
part of the heart muscle, the narrowed coronary arteries are
able to provide only a limited amount of blood, the result is the
painful state of oxygen starvation Burns called ischemia.

Burns's promising career came to a premature end with his
death at the age of thirty-two. While the rest of the nineteenth
century proved fruitful for some branches of medicine—anes-
thesiology, bacteriology, and antiseptic surgery, to name a few
—research into the afflictions of the heart lagged. Even worse,
clinicians began to describe variations in symptoms that Burns's
supply-demand theory couldn't readily explain. Why, for example, did some people suffer pain without the stressful triggers of
exertion or emotion? And why did some recover from the attacks
while others died?

These questions were still lingering in 1912, when James Herrick, a Chicago physician and biographer of Burns, proposed a
swifter and more deadly form of coronary distress. If angina
was due to the gradual narrowing of a coronary vessel, this new
mechanism, infarction, represented a vessel's complete obstruction. And if angina was reversible, going away when the demand
on the heart eased, infarction resulted in the destruction of that
part of the heart supplied by the blocked artery—and sometimes
in the death of the patient. Herrick's theory, fortified though it
was by clinical observation and experiment, "fell like a dud," he

recalled some years later in his autobiography. "Recognizing the radical nature of the view I held . . . I doggedly kept at the subject, doing what I called missionary work . . . I hammered away at the topic. When in 1918 I showed lantern slides and electrocardiograms [of coronary obstruction], physicians in America and later Europe woke up [to the diagnosis which was] later to become a household word translated by the layman into 'heart attack.' "

2

The Cardiac Century, Part II
The Lessons of Framingham

In 1900, there were 165 deaths from heart disease for every 100,000 Americans. By 1920, it was up to 200. In 1930, it had nudged over 250 and showed no signs of letting up. Necessity is also the mother of medical specialties, and along about that time the field of cardiology was born. Not that there was much cardiology to practice beyond the Oslerian recipe of rest and relaxation. So some investigators turned from the physiological and pathological data to more circumstantial evidence. These epidemiologists studied societies rather than patients, looking for clues in common traits and activities, habits, and habitats. Sometimes the results were dramatic, as John Snow demonstrated when he cut off the supply of contaminated water in a London neighborhood in 1854 and reduced the incidence of cholera.

In his own way, Osler was a bit of an epidemiologist, for his Johns Hopkins lectures contained thorough discussions of several heart disease risk factors. To point out the importance of heredity, he recounted the history of England's famous Arnold family: William, customs collector of Cowes, died suddenly of a heart spasm in 1801; his son Thomas, the educator, died after an attack of heart pain in 1842; and grandson Matthew, the poet and essayist, suffered angina for several years before a fatal attack in 1888. Osler knew that the disease tended to strike males and was more common among older men than younger ones. The great clinician, who would be knighted before ending his career as regius professor of medicine at Oxford, also included "station in life" ("It is remarkable how many prominent individuals succumbed to the disease") and emotional stress ("mental worry, grief or sudden shock may precede directly the onset of an attack"), along with gout, diabetes, syphilis, and influenza.

The founding fathers of cardiology, Samuel Levine of Boston's Peter Bent Brigham Hospital and Charles K. Friedberg, chief of medicine at Mount Sinai, expanded Osler's list to include obesity, kidney disease, and hypertension. Since excessive amounts of thyroid hormone seem to kick the heart into high gear and aggravate angina, another pioneer, Herrman L. Blumgart of Beth Israel Hospital in Boston, proposed treating angina by wiping out the thyroid gland. Such a treatment, it was later realized, made the underlying disease worse. In the 1940s, Ancel Keys of the University of Minnesota examined the diets of cultures around the world and came away with persuasive evidence that the incidence of coronary disease was directly related to the amount of fat a culture consumed.

In order to weigh the relative importance of diet, heredity, and these other risk factors, Sir James MacKenzie, a Scottish physician (and, like John Hunter, a sufferer of coronary artery disease), began scheduling periodic checkups of his patients so he could track the progress of the disease. The effort soon proved too distracting from his regular practice, but Paul Dudley White, who had worked with MacKenzie in the 1920s, became convinced that only such a large, decades-long epidemiological study could reveal the pattern of heart disease and explain its exponential growth. By 1950, he and others had persuaded the National Institutes of Health to turn the town of Framingham, Massachusetts, a working-class community eighteen miles west of Boston, into a living laboratory and many of the 28,000 people who then lived there into guinea pigs in the most extensive examination of heart disease yet undertaken.

Framingham had several things going for it, not the least of which was its proximity to Harvard University, where White taught. Most residents worked in the area and were treated at two local hospitals or by a small number of highly cooperative and, for such a small town, relatively sophisticated physicians. And they had already been the guinea pigs in a study of tuberculosis by the Metropolitan Life Insurance Company.

The plan was to select residents who were free of coronary heart disease but who would vary in their exposure to the disease's risk factors. This cohort would be followed for twenty years. Working from the yearly census that Framingham, like all New England towns, compiled, researchers invited about 6,500 residents to join the study. An enthusiastic 70 percent accepted (740 volunteers were also included in the study). Of that group, 2,282 men and 2,845 women had no symptoms of coronary disease. They returned every two years to undergo thirty-five blood tests, have their breath analyzed for carbon monoxide, their lung capacity measured, their bodies inspected for flab, and their heart rhythms recorded. When any of the participants died, the Framingham researchers ignored the death certificates, which are notoriously inaccurate, examined the records themselves, and came to their own conclusion.

It is no easy task to assess the progress of a disease in which the symptoms are latent in the early stages and extremely variable in the latter ones. Sometimes there are no symptoms at all. One of the first Framingham findings was that there are such things as "silent" heart attacks. (A recent report from the town indicated that 12 percent of heart attacks are completely painless.) There were also considerable bureaucratic tangles, especially when the NIH insisted on keeping the Framingham data in its Maryland computers. At another point, federal officials ignored the advice of many researchers and decided to halt the study when the original twenty years had elapsed. Fortunately, Boston University was able to raise enough money for four more years, until the NIH saw the light and returned to Framingham.

There are those who still question the merits of spending so much time, not to mention millions of dollars, studying a group of factors already implicated in heart disease. But Framingham did more than round up the usual suspects. It got enough evidence to convict some of them. And in so doing it provided us with a precise outline of the clinical course of heart disease. Hippocrates knew that it was a predominately male disorder that affected more older men than younger ones, but not until Framingham did we get reliable numbers. The study found that the incidence of heart disease in males age thirty to thirty-four was 163 per 1,000. In males age fifty-five to fifty-nine, it was 604. The corresponding rates for females were 61 and 386.

As expected, the Framingham Heart Study showed a strong relationship between blood pressure and coronary artery disease, although it failed to pinpoint the mechanisms of hypertension. Males with high blood pressure—160/95 or greater—had twice the risk of coronary disease of those with normal blood pressure—below 140/90. In females, the ratio was almost three to one.

Framingham also got the goods on cholesterol, a major ingredient of the blockages that clog coronary arteries that is also found in red meats, eggs, and dairy products. Men between thirty and forty with blood cholesterol levels of 260 mg per deciliter or more had more than four times the heart disease risk of men with cholesterol levels below 200; for females between forty and fifty years of age, high cholesterol levels tripled the risk (though it did not do so for younger or older women). Framingham also showed us that some fat compounds, or lipids, are linked to substances that are actually beneficial. One of them, high density lipoprotein (HDL), is in fact a marker of cardiovascular health: Fifty-five-year-old men with HDL-cholesterol levels of 65 mg per deciliter had half as many heart attacks as those with HDL-cholesterol levels of 45.

As for physical activity, the Framingham study found that there was probably a benefit from avoiding a sedentary life, but only modest additional gains from strenuous exercise. The coronary disease rate for inactive males was three times that of the most active males; among females, the rate was 2.5 times higher. For both sexes, the disease showed up earlier in the unfit.

Although Framingham found no indication that pipe or cigar smoking was harmful to the heart (subsequent studies disagree), quite the opposite was true for cigarettes. Male smokers between thirty and forty-nine had three times the rate of coronary disease of nonsmokers, while males fifty to fifty-nine had twice the rate. These findings were recently buttressed by the United States Surgeon General, C. Everett Koop, who reported that cigarettes cause up to 170,000 coronary deaths each year, three times the number of lung cancer deaths attributed to them.

For a while, the Framingham researchers believed that, contrary to the old saying, you could be too thin. It turned out that they had failed to take into account the weight loss many experience shortly before death. Recalculating their figures, they found that the thin indeed outlived the fat, confirming numerous actuarial studies conducted by insurance companies. Men and woman who were 20 percent or more above the median weight for their age and sex had twice the risk of developing coronary artery disease of those below the median weight. Subjects regarded as thin—80 percent or more below the median—had an even lower risk.

Framingham also exonerated several suspected risk factors,

including alcohol. A jigger of scotch or a stein of beer once a day seems to raise HDL levels and might decrease risk. On the other hand, the study provided a surprising insight into estradiol, a female sex hormone also found in small quantities in males. Although the estrogen-related substance is assumed to be a major reason why premenopausal women have a low incidence of heart disease, it appears to have just the opposite effect in males. When researchers looked at the fifteen Framingham males with the highest levels of estradiol, thirteen turned out to have coronary artery disease. Even more perplexing, they also found that when estrogens were given to women *after* menopause, their risk of heart disease increased by 50 percent.

The willingly captive community has also provided researchers with the chance to gauge the physiological impact of social changes not on the horizon in 1949. In the mid-1960s, for example, questionnaires were designed to uncover the cardiovascular significance of the changing role of women. The results: Men married to women with thirteen or more years of education were 2.6 times more likely to develop coronary artery disease than men married to women with only a grammar school education. While the incidence of disease was similar for men married to working and nonworking women, men married to women with white-collar jobs had a risk three times higher than normal. The combined risk of men married to working women with more than a high school education was 7.6 times that of men married to women with just a grammar school education. The researchers did not attempt to explain these provocative findings, but did note that they were hardly justification for a man to avoid marriage to a well-educated woman who wants to work. Married men have a lower mortality rate than single, widowed, or divorced men.

Three and a half decades after researchers arrived in Framingham, faithful participants still troop to the white four-story frame house across from Union Hospital to have their vital statistics entered on clacking IBM desktop computers. The original group is getting on in years, of course, but a study of their children, a "Son of Framingham," was begun in 1974 and should add details on the genetics of coronary disease to the epidemiological bounty. Can "Grandson of Framingham" be far behind?

As the longest-running epidemiological study in medical history, Framingham has had an impact far beyond its borders. It is credited with helping to persuade a generation to change diets, stop smoking, and start exercising (although, truth be told, the town is surrounded by a better-than-average assortment of McDonald's and Burger Kings that seem well-patronized). Then again, Framingham has provided some powerful incentives to change the way we live.

"If you start with a group of healthy Americans, as we did, and follow them, it's very frightening," said William P. Castelli, the white-haired director of the study and spreader of the Framingham gospel of prevention. "In the first fourteen years, every eighth man age forty to forty-four, every sixth man forty-five to forty-nine, every fifth man fifty to fifty-four, and every fourth man age fifty-five or older had a heart attack. It was every seventeenth woman. Women don't get heart attacks prior to menopause. Once they go through it, though, they catch up to the men. They have the same rates, ten to fifteen years later.

"You could say, 'Well, that's Framingham. Get out of Framingham and go someplace else.' But we know now that while Framingham may have been the first of these studies, efforts in Chicago, in Minneapolis, New York City, and elsewhere have found the same thing. Every place in America where someone kept track, the rates were the same."

Indeed, a slew of other epidemiological efforts in the United States and overseas—the National Cooperative Pooling Project, the Tecumseh Study, the Western Collaborative Group Study, the Puerto Rico Study, the Seven Countries Study, the Ni-Hon-San Study, and the Göteborg (Sweden) Study, to name just a few

—have helped confirm Framingham's findings and make up for its blind spots. For example, Framingham was and is a largely white community, but from other studies we can chart the racial patterns of heart disease. In 1950, the death rate for white males was 260 per 100,000; for black males, it was 164 per 100,000. By 1977, the rates were almost even, 265 to 245, respectively. The death rate for black females, which in 1950 trailed the rate for white females, 113 to 121, shot ahead to 152 to 119 by 1977. Why? We don't know.

Nor can we readily explain studies that show the highest death rates for heart disease on the southeastern Atlantic coast, along a belt through Georgia and Alabama, and in the industrialized states of the Midwest and the Northeast. The lowest rates are in the Great Plains and Mountain states. A map drawn in 1950 would have shown the East and West coasts to be the prime areas of cardiovascular jeopardy, with California the most dangerous place of all. For some reason, though, the states with the highest rates had the smallest increases during the following years, shifting more of the risk toward the east and south. West Virginia had one of the greatest increases, while Connecticut, which once had one of the highest rates, now has one of the lowest.

Recent research has also turned up a varied list of additional risk-factor candidates, including such things as a lack of vitamin C and exposure to noise, X rays, and nonionizing radiation. British and American studies indicate that occupation is a reliable predictor of disease, with those at the lower end of the employment spectrum, holding jobs offering little control over the pace or conditions of their work, suffering two or three times the risk of their bosses. (Osler's theory that heart disease primarily afflicted the rich seems to have been outdated by the assembly line.)

Others are convinced that the biggest dangers lie within, in the interplay of mind and environment that molds our personalities. This school was founded in the mid-1950s by Meyer Friedman and Ray H. Rosenman, two cardiologists who had set out to study cholesterol and who ignored for years hints from patients and their spouses about the toll of stress and anxiety. Nor did they place much significance in their upholsterer's observation that the front edges of the chairs in their San Francisco waiting room were worn out. Gradually, though, they became convinced that this edge-of-the-seat behavior leads to heart disease almost as surely as a compass points north.

The Type A personality, as they would come to define it, "can be observed in any person who is aggressively involved in a chronic, incessant struggle to achieve more and more in less and less time and, if required to do so, against the opposing efforts of other things or persons." Type As, unlike others feeling fear or anxiety, rarely despair of losing. They are often preoccupied with deadlines and are work-oriented and impatient. Type Bs are generally free of such traits and generally feel no pressing conflict about time or competitiveness with other people. Between 50 and 60 percent of the population are said to be Type As, of which 10 percent are extreme cases.

When Friedman and Rosenman compared eighty middle-aged males with Type A personalities with eighty middle-aged Type Bs, they found the Type As had seven times as much heart disease, even though the diets and exercise patterns of the two groups were nearly identical. After a five-year study of more than 3,000 Type A and Type B men, the Western Collaborative Group Study found that the Type As had twice the risk of coronary artery disease of the Type Bs. Similar ratios have been found for Type A women. (However, most data about Type A personality have been collected from men; a distinct "female stress syndrome" that also embodies coronary-prone behavior has only recently been recognized.)

The verdict on all this is far from unanimous. Indeed, a major study based on data from participants in California's Kaiser-

Permanente Health Plan failed to show a correspondence between Type A behavior and heart disease. Other studies indicate that an individual's response to stress may be more important than his overall personality, with so-called hot reactors, people who explode under pressure, at the most peril. That could explain why some Type As don't have heart attacks and some Type Bs do. Nevertheless, a blue-ribbon panel of the National Heart, Lung, and Blood Institute declared in 1980 that Type A personality was "solidly established" as a risk factor.

The notion of Type A behavior would hardly have surprised Alexis de Tocqueville. Consider this passage written in 1835, when coronary artery disease was still almost unheard of: "In the United States a man builds a house to spend his latter years in it and he sells it before the roof is on. He plants a garden and lets it just as the trees are coming into bearing. If his private affairs leave him any leisure, he instantly plunges into the vortex of politics; if at the end of a year of unremitting labor he finds he has a few days' vacation, his eager curiosity whirls him over the vast extent of the United States and he will travel fifteen hundred miles in a few days to shake off his happiness. . . . He who has set his heart exclusively upon the pursuit of worldly welfare is always in a hurry for he has but a limited time at his disposal to reach it, to grasp it, and to enjoy it." More than 100 years later, another chronicler of America, Bob Dylan, would sing of "heart attack machines."

As land of the Type A and home of the hot reactor, the United States has one of the world's highest rates of coronary artery disease. By and large, though, international comparisons of heart-disease mortality raise far more questions than they answer. Although data from much of Asia, Africa, and Latin America aren't always reliable, it is believed that coronary disease is uncommon in most nonindustrialized countries. Then again, there is a tenfold variation between Finland, which according to 1977 statistics had the highest coronary death rate in the world,

997 per 100,000, and Japan, which had a rate of 94 per 100,000. After Finland, the next seven countries on the list, oddly, are the major English-speaking nations: Northern Ireland (925), Scotland (900), Australia (731), New Zealand (767), the United States (715), England and Wales (711), and Canada (697). Israel, Norway, Denmark, and the Netherlands all have rates in the 500s; West Germany, Hungary, and Austria in the 400s; and Italy and Switzerland in the 300s.

Within this puzzling pecking order, statistical paradoxes abound. The Finns have essentially the same diet as the Dutch, yet they have two and a half times the rate of coronary artery disease. (Then again, Finns living in the eastern half of the country have the same diets as those in the west but suffer twice as much coronary heart disease.) A comparison of Boston Irishmen with brothers who remained in Ireland found that, despite a fattier diet, those in the ould sod suffered half the number of heart attacks. The average Japanese adult smokes nearly as many cigarettes as the typical Finn (1,667 cigarettes a year to 1,925) yet has one tenth the risk of dying from heart disease. If Japan's low rate indicates that genetics, rather than such environmental factors as industrialization or a leaner diet, explains the low incidence of coronary artery disease, then why do Japanese who emigrate to the United States and assimilate into the American culture quickly assume the much higher risk of Americans? And what could account for the seemingly arbitrary changes in heart disease rates from 1969 to 1977, the dramatic upsurges in Northern Ireland, Sweden, and Hungary, and the dramatic plunges in Australia, Israel, and Japan? Or the changes after that, which have seen Scotland and the white population of South Africa rise to the top of the list in risk?

No country has experienced a bigger drop than the United States. After a thirty-year rise that began suddenly in 1920, the mortality rate peaked in the mid-1950s and began a decline that accelerated sharply after 1973. Cardiovascular disease is still a long way from losing its title as Public Health Enemy Number 1, but the mortality rate is 25 percent lower today than it was a decade ago and 36 percent lower than in 1963. This translates into half a million fewer deaths a year than would have been projected two decades earlier. It is also the reason why the average life expectancy at age thirty-five increased 2.6 years between 1972 and 1982—a greater increase than during any decade since vital statistics were first recorded in 1900. The data for coronary heart disease are even more impressive: The mortality rate has decreased nearly 40 percent since 1963.

Though the drop is significant, it's hard to take too much credit for it since, like the rise, we aren't at all sure why it occurred. There is ample evidence that Americans have reduced their intake of cholesterol in recent years, but if low-fat diets brought about the current decline, asked Revel A. Stallones in *Scientific American*, why didn't the deprivations of the Depression years have an impact on heart disease in the 1930s? After all, the death rates went down in many European countries during World War II, when supplies of cholesterol-rich beef, eggs, and dairy products were interrupted and vegetable consumption rose. And why did the heart disease death rate in Switzerland decline 13 percent for men and 40 percent for women between 1951 and 1976, while the average animal fat intake rose by 20 percent?

Cigarette smoking increased in the United States after World War I, as the heart disease death rate was rising, and decreased during the last two decades, again paralleling the death rate. But many more men than women have kicked the habit, while the decline in mortality actually occurred first in females. The invention of the automobile and the proliferation of the modern factory have made our lives less active. This coincides with the rise in heart disease, but most researchers agree that there aren't nearly enough joggers to account for the decline. And the exercise hypothesis hardly explains the equal drop in heart disease mortality that has occurred among the elderly.

Part of the problem is that we are forced to rely on mortality figures that depend on both the incidence of disease and the rate at which people die from it. A drop in mortality could mean either a diminished incidence and a steady fatality rate, or a steady incidence and a diminished fatality rate. The statistics are not entirely reliable, but there is some reason to believe the latter is true.

What's more, an epidemiological study from the other side of the grave has uncovered more severe disease in autopsy victims than might have been expected, considering the plunge in mortality. Researchers from the Mayo Clinic, surveying records of people over thirty in Olmsted County, Minnesota, found that the prevalence of significant coronary artery disease increased from 25 percent in the 1950s to nearly 50 percent in the 1970s. This suggests that rather than a drop in the underlying rate of heart disease there has been an increase in our ability to deal with it. It would be tempting to credit the strides we have made in treating heart disease, especially since parts of the country that may still lag in health care resources, such as Appalachia, have yet to see the full reduction in coronary mortality. Then again, the drop in mortality preceded by a decade the development of coronary care units and coronary bypass surgery, not to mention the pacemakers and valves installed by the hundreds of thousands annually and the cardiac drugs that have come on the market in the last half dozen years. Scientists have encountered such a puzzle before, when the death rate of tuberculosis began to drop even before an effective treatment was developed. Despite the fifty or so years that have intervened, it remains unexplained. It seems to be one of the mysteries of medicine that the disappearance of disease does not always correspond to the appearance of a cure.

So perhaps it's not really surprising that there doesn't seem to be an explanation for the epidemiological ups and downs of heart disease, no smoking gun or magic bullet. In medicine, as in law, there are limits to guilt by association. Risk factors only tell part of the story. After all, most of us have at least one of the major ones—being a male or a postmenopausal female, being more than fifty years old, having a family history of coronary disease, smoking cigarettes, being overweight or sedentary, having hypertension or diabetes, or possessing the hard-driving personality that seems so endemic in our society. Nor does an individual's risk profile help predict when, and in what manner, a coronary event will strike.

Is the drop in mortality a brief fluctuation in a still rising curve or the first dividend of our fight against heart disease? As of now, we don't know. If there is an explanation for the cardiac century, it will probably come from laboratories around the world where investigators are trying to untangle the biochemical knot of cardiovascular decay. For now, we can say only that coronary heart disease, as Osler intuitively grasped, involves a complex series of mechanisms that vary from time to time, from culture to culture, and from individual to individual.

3

Circulation and Its Discontents
The Process of Coronary Disease

AT THE TEXTBOOK SPEED of 80 beats a minute, the heart pounds out the rhythm of life 115,200 times a day, 42,048,000 times a year, and 2,943,360,000 times during the Biblical lifetime of three score and ten. In this time, it pumps enough blood to fill the Yale Bowl and works hard enough to lift the battleship *New Jersey* fifteen feet out of the sea. But to concentrate on its prodigious labors is to risk ignoring what perhaps is the heart's singular characteristic—its indomitable will to beat. Excised from the chest and laid on a laboratory table, the heart will keep up its pace, at least for a while. Separate its four chambers, and each quarter will continue to beat. In fact, were it possible to isolate a single heart cell from its innumerable colleagues, it too would follow the complicated choreography of contraction. In short, the heartbeat is vested in every cardiac cell.

The beat begins when a microscopic waterwheel built into each cell pushes electrically charged sodium atoms out into a no-man's-land, allowing charged potassium to dominate the cell's interior. This upsets the natural electrical balance and causes calcium atoms to be released from tiny cellular storage depots. Calcium, in turn, causes two other substances, actin and myosin, to fuse into actomyosin, which makes the muscular fibers of the heart cell draw together. Once the switch is flipped, sodium is allowed back into the cell, and the cycle begins again.

If the millions and millions of heart cells were to fire whenever they felt like it, the result would be chaos, not contraction. So in addition to the ability to generate a beat, the master mechanic of evolution has programmed each heart cell to pass the impulse to beat along to the next. The first cell to fire thus triggers its neighbors to fire, and they trigger their neighbors, and so on until the entire organ is convulsed in a single, coordinated contraction. Because of the way the cells are wired together, virtually any cell in the heart can set off a heartwide contraction. Usually, though, a beat originates in a small area on the upper part of the heart called the sinoatrial node, which has direct lines to the brain and a myriad of other organs.

Constantly aware of the body's changing needs—Are we running for the 5:25 to Rye? Have we just finished a long lunch at the Four Seasons? Are we holding a full house?—the cells in the sinoatrial node take it upon themselves to speed up or slow down the heart accordingly. From there, the electrical wave radiates across the upper part of the heart like the ripple when a penny is dropped into a pond, leading the two upper chambers, the atria, to contract. An instant or so later, the wave arrives at a substation between the atria and the two lower cavities, the ventricles, appropriately called the atrioventricular node. Here the wave is delayed by one or two tenths of a second; without this pause, the ventricles would contract at virtually the same instant as the atria, before they have had a chance to fill with blood. When the electrical signal resumes, it travels along a special wiring network, the His-Purkinje system, running between the ventricles to the tips of the chambers. Then the wave proceeds up toward the atria, this time along the outer walls of the ventricles. Like a tube of toothpaste, they wring themselves from the bottom up, squeezing the blood to the top of the chambers where the exits are located.

And what of this marvelous fluid that the heart whisks around the body in fifteen seconds flat? Mephistopheles may have been engaging in understatement when he told Faust that blood was "a truly remarkable juice." Half of it is a straw-colored liquid called plasma. The rest is cellular material, mostly saucer-shaped red cells. These bags contain hemoglobin, an iron-bearing compound that soaks up and delivers to the tissues of the body the oxygen they need to burn fuel, then carts away carbon dioxide and other waste products, the ashes from the furnace of cellular metabolism. The spent, used-up blood then travels back to the heart, arriving at the right atrium, the body's drain. As that chamber contracts, the oxygen-poor, indigo blood is transported through the one-way gates of the tricuspid valve into the right ventricle. The ventricular contraction forces the blood through the pulmonic valve into the lungs, where it flows through 600 million capillaries around 300 million air sacs. Here, the hemoglobin shifts into reverse and trades its carbon dioxide —the lungs will exhale it—for a new supply of life-sustaining oxygen. The now vermillion blood flows into the left atrium, through the mitral valve and into the left ventricle, the heart's main pumping chamber. When its powerful walls contract, the blood is propelled through the heart's main exit, the aortic valve, and out into the body. All this opening and closing is executed "so harmoniously and rhythmically," William Harvey observed, that "only one movement can be seen."

Once it leaves the heart, the blood is confronted with a choice of numerous paths through the body. As an interstate highway has exits, the aorta is lined with turnoffs to the arms and to the head, to the chest and to the spine, to the kidneys, liver, and intestines, to the genitals and to the legs. Fittingly, the very first of these "regional circulations" serves the heart itself. Built into

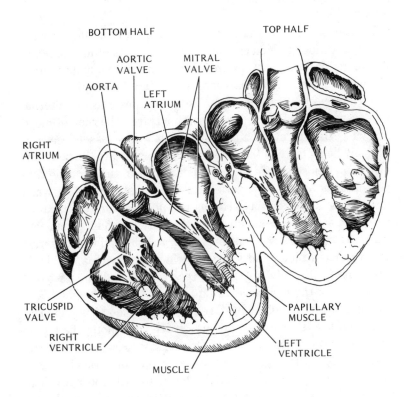

BOTTOM HALF   TOP HALF

AORTIC VALVE   MITRAL VALVE

AORTA   LEFT ATRIUM

RIGHT ATRIUM

TRICUSPID VALVE   PAPILLARY MUSCLE

RIGHT VENTRICLE   LEFT VENTRICLE

MUSCLE

CROSS-SECTION OF THE HEART: The four chambers, sliced in half and opened for inspection. Note the relatively thin walls of the atria, the thicker walls of the right ventricle, and the massive muscle of the left ventricle, the heart's main pumping chamber. The gateway into the left ventricle, the mitral valve, has cordlike supports that can withstand great pressures.

the aortic valve is a triad of parachute-shaped funnels designed to draw blood into the coronary circulation, three main arteries and innumerable branches and tributaries Osler called "the citadels of life."

It is the supreme cardiac irony that an organ that pumps such vast quantities of blood cannot use the contents of its chambers to satisfy its own not inconsiderable needs. Only the inner 100,000th of an inch of heart muscle can tap the supply of blood that courses through the organ. So nature designed an alternative system. When the left ventricle contracts, the rush of blood stretches the aorta like a balloon; as the great vessel recoils, it not only helps to keep the blood flowing forward to the body but also squeezes some of the precious fluid down through the funnels into the coronary arteries. All this must happen between heartbeats, since the tiny arteries running through the meat of the heart are squeezed shut when the muscle around them contracts. If the lungs have the only artery in the body that carries deoxygenated blood and the only vein with oxygenated blood, the heart is the only organ that receives the bulk of its blood supply when the ventricles are at rest.

The heart is supplied by three principle blood vessels. The largest is the left coronary artery, which runs along the top of the heart before dividing in two. One fork, the circumflex artery, travels along the organ's left edge, giving off branches that circle around the left side of the heart toward the back. The other fork, the left anterior descending artery, supplies the entire front wall of the left ventricle, where the chamber gets most of its power, giving off branches that spread across the ventricular surface and dive into the muscle's interior. The right coronary artery serves the right side of the heart. It travels from the atrium to the ventricle, supplying both the sinoatrial and atrioventricular nodes and, through a branch called the distal right coronary artery, the bottom of the heart bordering the diaphragm. Nine times out of ten, the right coronary artery also gives rise to another branch called the posterior descending artery, which supplies the back wall of the heart. (The rest of the time, this branch grows out of the circumflex artery on the left side. People in the first category are called right dominant, the others left dominant.)

In the 0.15 to 0.3 seconds it takes to beat—60 percent of the cardiac cycle is normally spent at rest—the heart sends about eighty milliliters of blood, give or take a drop or two, to the aorta. That's about half the contents of the left ventricle. (A 50 percent ejection fraction, as it is known, is considered normal; metabolically, it is just too costly for the heart to empty the entire contents of the chamber with one contraction.) At cruising speed, roughly 5 percent of the cardiac output goes through the coronary arteries back to the heart, about a cup each minute. In contrast, the kidneys normally get 20 percent of the heart's output, the skeletal muscles between 10 and 25 percent (depending on the amount of work they happen to be doing), the brain 10 percent, the skin from 1 to 9 percent (skin doesn't require much blood to live, but the body uses its surface to regulate temperature like the radiator in an automobile), and the liver and intestines 20 to 25 percent (depending on whether they are at work digesting a meal).

With a myriad of organs constantly signaling their needs to the cells in the sinoatrial node, the activity of the heart is infinitely adjustable, at least theoretically. When researchers at Boston City Hospital studied thousands of electrocardiograms, they found that the heart seems to like some speeds more than others, such as seventy-two beats per minute, or eighty-eight. Though hardly ever called upon to shift into top gear, under great physical or emotional stress the heart can almost instantly raise its output from four liters per minute to twenty. This fivefold increase requires that the heart work as much as eight times harder, however, since the pressure throughout the circulatory system rises with the output. The more pressure, the

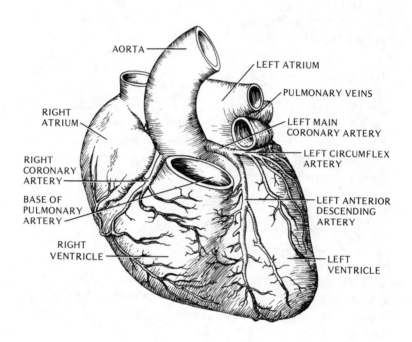

THE CORONARY ARTERIES: The heart is supplied with blood through slender arteries and their branches that run along the surface before diving into the muscle's interior. By far the most important of these vessels is the left main coronary artery, which keeps the left ventricle running.

more work the heart must do to overcome it. And the more work the heart does, the more oxygen *it* needs. The heart is already highly efficient at removing oxygen from the hemoglobin in the blood. Most of the tissues in the body take out less than half the available oxygen; the heart extracts virtually all it can get, turning the blood blue-black. So, to keep up with the body's increasing needs—and its own—the heart must get more blood. Under great stress, microscopic branches of the coronary arteries automatically open wider, allowing four or five times more blood to reach the starving muscle. This sounds like a lot, but don't forget that the heart may be working eight times harder. Thus, there is a tenuous balance between the supply of life-sustaining oxygen and the demands of a highly stressed organ. Unfortunately, there is a disease that can throw this balance entirely out of kilter—atherosclerosis. Slowly and silently, atherosclerosis clogs up these precious coronary pipelines with a fibrous, fatty glop, inviting blood clots, hemorrhage, and vascular spasm. This can choke off the flow of blood, causing angina or a heart attack.

Baboons suffer from it. So do dogs. Rabbits develop it with astonishing speed when fed a typically fatty human diet. But it may be social as well as scientific commentary that no species so resembles man in cardiovascular deterioration as the pig. The leading cause of death among pigs is no doubt the butcher, but left to their own devices, more than a few will end up with coronaries, just like people. "No one likes to work with the pig because they are much more expensive than other laboratory animals, and they grow so large," says Valentin Fuster, chief of Mount Sinai's division of cardiology and professor of medicine in its medical school, "but I made a commitment to myself that, if I was going to study this disease, I was going to study it in the animal that is closest to human. And we are really dealing with the same biochemistry as in humans."

High in the rust-red tower of Mount Sinai Medical Center's Annenberg Building, in laboratories equipped with an assortment of expensive, gleaming, high-tech devices, Fuster's group of immunologists, hematologists, cardiothoracic surgeons, and vascular physiologists is exploring the modus operandi of the nation's leading killer. They are concentrating on three suspects: platelets, the smallest cellular component of the blood and a main element in the blood-clotting system; prostaglandins, a group of chemicals summoned by the platelets that alter the arteries and seem to set the stage for trouble; and lipids, fats that are invariably found at the scene of the arterial crime.

That is where the pigs come in. Fuster orders them by the pen from an upstate New York farm for his veritable pig penthouse on the twenty-sixth floor. The animals have a view that stretches from Central Park to the East River (and is envied by some Mount Sinai physicians unlucky enough to have windowless basement offices), but it pleases few of them. Solitary in their steel and concrete pens, the pigs snort their loneliness. For many, the travail will be brief before their sacrifice in the name of science. Fuster's investigators will assault the aortas with blasts of air calculated to be equivalent to the pounding of half a lifetime of natural circulation. Then they will remove the arteries from the pigs and place them in a device that pumps blood through the vessels, enabling the team to study how platelets and injured vessels interact.

Some of Fuster's pigs will live longer, growing to two hundred pounds or more. Half of this group are being fed a diet laden with saturated fat, half a cod-liver-oil diet based on that of the Eskimos, among whom atherosclerosis is as rare as a sunburn and bypass surgery as necessary as Solarcaine. Still another group of animals has von Willebrand's disease, an ailment that causes their platelets to malfunction. Will these pigs be protected from atherosclerotic decay? If so, they may help Fuster define the critical role platelets are suspected of playing in the disease.

Such questions have baffled researchers for a long time. Rival theories of atherosclerosis began to emerge in the nineteenth century, propagated by the leading pathologists of Eastern Europe: Karl von Rokitansky, who is said to have performed three thousand autopsies, and his prize student, Rudolf Virchow, whose curriculum vitae contains more than a thousand scientific papers. Rokitansky believed that a vessel became blocked first as blood coagulated on the arterial wall and secondarily as fatty deposits accumulated there. This process, perhaps a result of some abnormality of the vessel lining, came to be known as encrustation. Virchow, on the other hand, theorized that fats from the bloodstream were absorbed through the smooth muscle cells of the vessel lining, causing it to bulge like blistering wallpaper. When this process, called insudation, blocked enough of an artery, the blood flow would slow to a stop. The stagnant fluid would clot, a process known as thrombosis, which derives from the Greek for "lump."

A hundred years later, Fuster and other researchers are finding that, as so often happens when rival scientific theories clash, Rokitansky and Virchow were both partly right. Both would have been astonished to learn, however, that the process they were investigating on their autopsy tables actually starts quite early in life. Autopsies during the Korean War showed atherosclerotic deposits in half the American soldiers, whose average age was about twenty-two. Fatty streaks, the flat yellow marks on the arterial wall that are the first signs of atherosclerosis, develop far earlier. They are almost always present in children over the age of three and sometimes can be found even earlier.

From the sorrowfully ample supply of young corpses at the New York City morgue, we know that fatty streaks tend to appear wherever major arteries branch or turn, places where the flow is most turbulent as the blood courses by 100,000 times a day. But the wear-and-tear theory doesn't explain how so much damage can be done over a few short years of childhood. Nor is it the only way an artery can be injured. Chemical derivatives from tobacco smoke can also wreak havoc.

Although autopsies of 23,000 patients from fourteen countries and nineteen racial groups have shown fatty streaks to be a universal birthright, their progression into atheromas—fibrous pale-gray plaques that protrude into arteries, usually in the third decade—appears limited to people in industrialized nations. Though we can't say what has put them at special peril, at least we are beginning to understand the further development of the disease. In a sense, atherosclerosis is an unfortunate consequence of the natural activities of the body's defense system. As the fatty streak comes to infringe on the interior of the vessel, it increases the already turbulent blood flow, which leads to more severe arterial injury. The body responds the same way it responds to any injury. The sticky little platelets race to the scene and plug up the wound, stopping the oozing and entrapping strands of fibrin that form a natural Band-Aid.

Platelets play a more complicated role than simply gumming up the works. They also release a variety of substances, including prostaglandins, a ubiquitous but little understood group of bodily chemicals. Some prostaglandins are Good Samaritans; prostacyclin, for example, dilates blood vessels. Other prostaglandins have been implicated in ailments ranging from arthritis to headaches to birth defects to cancer. One particularly felonious prostaglandin is thromboxane A_2, which causes blood vessels to squeeze shut and perhaps is a factor in the coronary spasm that often occurs near atherosclerotic deposits. It may also strip the arterial wall of its impermeability.

A key element in the atherosclerotic saga is the smooth muscle cell, housed in the media of the blood vessel, sandwiched between a thin inner lining—the endothelium—which faces the moving stream of blood, and the outer coat—the adventitia—which buttresses the vascular pipe. Cells in the medial layer are

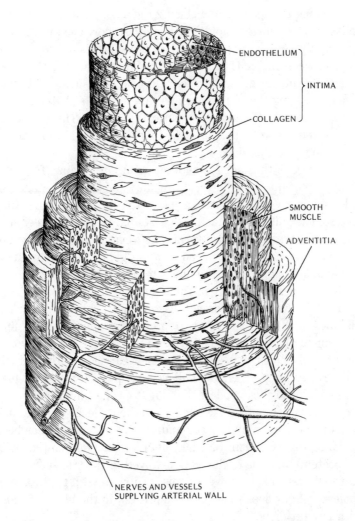

ENDOTHELIUM

INTIMA

COLLAGEN

SMOOTH
MUSCLE

ADVENTITIA

NERVES AND VESSELS
SUPPLYING ARTERIAL WALL

INSIDE A CORONARY ARTERY: A quarter inch at its widest, a coronary artery has four main layers: The thin endothelium is the innermost lining; collagen provides support; the smooth muscle regulates the diameter of the pipeline; and the adventitia buttresses the entire vessel.

responsible for opening and closing the artery and also produce collagen, the glue that holds the body together. The fatty streak apparently begins the process of atherosclerosis by working its way between the cells of the endothelium, loosening them like flagstones on an aging terrace. Occasionally, a stone breaks away, exposing the collagen cement underneath. Platelets flock to the denuded area and release prostaglandins. These, in turn, induce the smooth muscle cells to proliferate like a cancer, spreading into the blood's path.

The stage is thus set for another group of villains: fats. The most important is cholesterol, an alcohol-based substance of pale-yellow crystals that feel greasy at room temperature. Cholesterol isn't all bad. In fact, it is essential to life. We need it to make sex hormones, and it forms the I-beams and insulation of our cells. We consume it in red meat, eggs, and dairy products, but about 70 percent of the cholesterol in our bodies is home-made, synthesized chiefly in the liver.

Like oil in water, fats do not dissolve in the bloodstream. The globules must be packaged in protein wrappers called lipoproteins to allow them to circulate to the areas of the body that need them. Cholesterol, as it happens, is carried mostly by LDL, low density lipoprotein. We believe that particles of LDL may help kick loose those endothelial flagstones, stimulating the reproduction of smooth muscle cells, and then release their fat into areas made porous by prostaglandins. Recently, there has been evidence that a cousin of LDL, beta-VLDL (very low density lipoprotein), may be exclusively involved in the transport of dietary cholesterol. The level of this lipid rises with the intake of cholesterol but doesn't seem to be present in the blood of those with low-fat diets.

Fortunately, the body has a natural fat-removal system that runs on HDL, high density lipoprotein. As it travels through the bloodstream, HDL scoops up loose cholesterol and returns it to the liver, which expels it from the body. The Framingham study was among the first to tell us that the more HDL we have, the better.

After the fat comes more fibrin, which builds up in the form of scar tissue. Sometimes the scars, in turn, attract blood clots. In a particularly rapid version of the disease, thrombosis comes first, and then scar tissue forms over it. In the late innings of atherosclerosis, usually the sixth decade of life, the plaque becomes ulcerated and spotted with hardened calcified patches. The artery loses its elasticity, and superficial tears, pits, and valleys appear. As the vessel gets sicker, more blood clots form, more holes appear, and more platelets gather, accelerating the vicious cycle of arterial degradation. The accumulation of fats sometimes prevents the vasa vasorum, the tiny blood vessels that supply the arteries, from doing their job, further multiplying the damage.

Above all, atherosclerosis is dynamic. An obstruction can have a life of its own. It can shed clots and other debris downstream, narrowing or blocking a smaller branch artery. It can be stable or in a state of flux, constantly growing and shrinking due to actions and interactions of the blood-clotting system. It can be covered by hard, impermeable caps or mounds of clotted blood. Because of the role of the smooth muscle cells, spasm can occur at any point in the process, squeezing off an artery that had been only partially blocked by a deposit. Perhaps the most common coronary accident is when the plaque suddenly tears loose from the weakened vessel wall and juts into the bloodstream, often with devastating results.

This grim scenario is influenced by acquired and genetic factors, some for the worse and some for the better. One out of every five hundred Americans, for example, suffers from hypercholesterolemia, a genetic disposition to high lipid levels in the blood. One of the most severe, and heartbreaking, cases of hypercholesterolemia on record was that of Stormie Jones. When she was three months old, her mother first noticed tiny

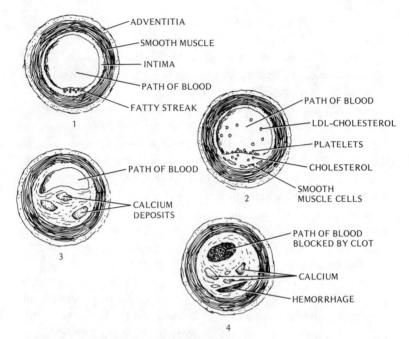

STAGES OF ATHEROSCLEROSIS

1 Cross section of a coronary artery at age ten. A fatty streak—a flat, yellow patch where cholesterol has been deposited within the vessel lining—has already formed. These streaks are usually found at stress points in the circulatory system.

2 By age thirty-five, platelets adhere to the growing fatty deposit, stimulating the proliferation of smooth muscle cells, which make the blockage bulge even more. Cholesterol carried in the blood by low density lipoprotein (LDL) continues to accumulate. This is the point at which risk factors can accelerate the progression of disease.

3 Fifteen years later, the artery's collagen layer has become scarred with fibrous tissue, and calcium deposits have formed, adding to the size of the blockage. As the deposit comes to impinge on 70 percent of the artery, symptoms such as angina are produced.

In its final stages, atherosclerosis often strikes suddenly.

4 Hemorrhage, spasm, or, most commonly, blood clots can completely clog an artery, halting the flow of blood and causing heart attack and, perhaps, death.

bumps on her buttocks. In a few years, wartlike deposits of cholesterol covered her elbows, knuckles, knees, and toes, and doctors found that her blood cholesterol level was nine times higher than normal. She suffered a heart attack, then gripping angina. When two bypass operations failed, she became the first person to undergo simultaneous heart and liver transplantation —all before her seventh birthday.

Others are born with hyperactive blood-vessel walls or mutations of the arterial lining. High blood pressure creates more stress in the circulatory system, more endothelial damage, and thus greater potential for atherosclerosis. Cigarette smoke might enhance platelet activity, alter prostaglandins, lower HDL levels, damage arterial walls, or all four. Diabetes affects mechanisms related to lipid levels, seems to activate platelets, and may increase the rate of smooth muscle cell proliferation. There is also evidence that Type A behavior goes hand in hand with high LDL levels.

Bad enough in their own right, risk factors can be devastating when they gang up. And they usually do: Heavy smokers don't exercise; people with cholesterol-rich diets are frequently overweight; diabetics often develop high blood pressure and high serum lipid levels. A study of 129 men age forty-five or younger, who had had heart attacks, showed that 89 percent smoked, 48 percent had coronary disease in their family, 21 percent had hypertension, and 21 percent had cholesterol abnormalities. A healthy forty-year-old male with normal blood pressure and blood cholesterol readings has a 1 percent chance of developing coronary disease over the next eight years. Add hypertension, and the risk quadruples. Load the blood with cholesterol until it reaches a level a third higher than normal, and the risk more than quadruples again, to 17 percent. Mix in diabetes, and it nearly doubles, to about 30 percent. Add cigarette smoking, and the chance of developing coronary disease is 46 percent. With a sedentary life, a family history of heart trouble, and a little bad luck, the danger can exceed 50 percent.

Some risk factors are riskier than others. For a young man, a history of coronary disease in the family is a—perhaps *the*—key factor. As men get older, age comes to dominate their risk profile. A man who has made it to a ripe old age, in fact, can smoke and eat pretty much as he pleases, and it will make very little statistical difference. If cigarettes and cholesterol haven't affected his coronary arteries by then, they probably never will. For women under forty-five, on the other hand, cigarette smoking and cholesterol levels have great importance. A young woman who doesn't smoke or have a high cholesterol level is unlikely to get coronary artery disease at all. Indeed, a young, thin, nonsmoking woman, with no trace of diabetes or high blood pressure, and no relatives who have had heart attacks at an early age, who exercises regularly, eats a diet low in saturated fat and cholesterol, and is cool, calm, and collected is the cardiological ideal. The rest of us—most of us—have one or more of the risk factors for coronary heart disease and are thus potential victims of atherosclerosis, and, perhaps, candidates for coronary bypass surgery. That's hardly surprising, since we're talking about an epidemic that kills more than a million people a year and disables millions more in the United States alone. Indeed, nearly all of us already have at least the beginning of a coronary blockage. However, Framingham taught us that the coronary risk can be reduced. We can't do anything about our age, our sex, or our genes, of course. But other risk factors, such as hypertension, diabetes, and high levels of fats in the blood, can be altered with drugs or diet, while smoking, physical inactivity, obesity, and coronary prone behavior can be changed by dint of will. (For more on risk factors and how to change them, see Chapter 10.)

Can atherosclerosis be reversed? After feeding rhesus monkeys a plaque-inducing high-cholesterol diet, scientists found that they could shrink the resulting blockages with a switch to a low-cholesterol diet. Exercise has been shown to have similar effects in apes. Most cardiologists have seen what seems like regression in their patients, too, deposits that were here one month and gone the next. No one has yet found a way to make them disappear on command, but Fuster has come up with some fascinating evidence that a drug practically no household is without—aspirin—might be effective in at least slowing the disease's progress. Perhaps as little as half a tablet of baby aspirin every other day may be enough to disarm the platelets and prostaglandins, hindering the blockages' development. That doesn't mean we should rush to the medicine cabinet, however. Platelets are the body's main defense against bleeding to death, and even prostaglandins have their virtues.

4

Worst Case Scenarios
Heart Attack and Sudden Death

ATHEROSCLEROSIS CAN OCCUR ANYWHERE the pounding of circulating blood takes its toll on our plumbing. Blockages in the thigh, where tendons cross the femoral artery, deprive the calf muscles of oxygen, causing a painful limp. Deposits in the carotid arteries of the neck cause strokes. The aorta, which is directly downstream from the heart, is the most common site for atherosclerosis. Situated on a constantly moving muscle, the coronary arteries are also subject to stress and strain. And since they are just a quarter-inch wide, a relatively small deposit that would be insignificant in the aorta can have devastating consequences in the coronaries.

Even so, it takes decades for atherosclerosis to overcome the natural fail-safe mechanism by which the coronary arteries open wider and increase the flow of blood. An atherosclerotic deposit can progress to the point at which it reduces the diameter of an artery by as much as 70 percent or more without affecting an unstressed heart. If that heart begins to work harder, however, it will soon run short of oxygen. Once the blockage reaches about 75 or 80 percent, very slight changes in the heart's work load can dramatically worsen symptoms. And as the vessel comes to be more than 90 percent obstructed, pain can occur even at rest, when the heart's demand for oxygen is minimal.

Blockages come in a variety of shapes, sizes, and locations, which explains why some people can run a marathon with an 85 percent blockage while others are immobilized by a lesser one. A three-inch-long deposit that cuts a vessel's diameter in half might be worse than one that fills 70 percent of an artery but is only half an inch long. Like rocks in a stream, a series of small deposits can cause hemodynamic white water, disrupting the flow of blood much more than a single, larger clog. An upstream, or proximal, blockage affects more arterial derivatives—and thus a greater area of the heart—than a downstream, or distal, occlusion.

Another reason atherosclerosis is so variable is that some patients actually develop an accessory system of circulation, which funnels blood from unaffected parts of the heart into areas that aren't receiving enough of the precious fluid. Physicians had long suspected that such vessels existed; in the late 1930s, Herrman Blumgart injected a plastic substance into the coronary trees of hearts from dead victims of atherosclerosis, then "melted" away the muscle, leaving the proof behind. Do these "collateral" vessels sprout like buds on a newly pruned tree? Or are they always there and simply open up at the first pangs of oxygen deprivation? That's still a matter of debate. Either way, collaterals can be effective in compensating for clogged arteries, sometimes even routing blood around blockages like natural coronary bypasses.

Sometimes the blood itself contributes to the problem. Some patients have fluid so thickened by extra red cells that it is too viscous to pass through narrowed vessels. Victims of sickle-cell anemia have red cells that, because of their spiny shape, are hard to push around. And sometimes blood vessels are prone to vascular spasm, which can occur with or without an atherosclerotic blockage.

When the heart is deprived of the oxygen needed to burn its fuel, it switches from the usual aerobic metabolism to an anaerobic, or oxygenless, state based on a backup enzyme system. It can keep the cells alive, but only temporarily. Soon, poisonous waste products like lactic acid build up in the heart muscle. As they accumulate, these substances can cause pain—angina. Meanwhile, the motion of the affected part of the heart becomes sluggish as cells lose their ability to beat.

The organs of the body can survive varying lengths of time without oxygen. The cortex of the brain has an anaerobic life span of about four minutes. The spinal column can live for nearly an hour and the kidneys even longer. About twenty minutes is all the heart can take before its cells are destroyed, a state cardiologists call infarction and patients know as a heart attack. It is usually heralded by crushing, oppressive pain behind the breastbone that often radiates toward the arm (more often the left than the right), neck, or jaw and can be accompanied by nausea, vomiting, dizziness, shortness of breath, and a special sort of facial perspiration that can occur even under the most chilly conditions. And yet some heart attacks are accompanied by symptoms as subtle as a toothache, while others have no symptoms at all.

Whatever happens on the outside, an invariably sad story is played out internally. The mortally wounded heart cells, their thirst critical, drink up the last remaining molecules of oxygen, causing the blood to turn very dark blue, a hue that comes to shade the muscle. Eventually, the blood vessels in the afflicted area become leaky and ooze fluid into the surrounding tissue. The cells begin to swell as they die, leaking enzymes into the bloodstream.

From autopsies of victims who have died days, weeks, or months after they were first stricken, researchers have learned that a heart attack can take time to run its course. After three days, the wall of the injured but still living heart has a pale, dry appearance, with red or purple mottled areas of hemorrhage. By the next day, a fine yellow line circles the edge of the devastated zone like a water stain, as blood cells leak into the tissues and release lipids. Gradually, the wounded area takes on a yellow tinge. After eight days, it turns soft with oozing hemorrhagic lesions. At ten days, the body has begun to liquefy the dead myocardial fibers and replace them with fibrous scar tissue. This process continues over the next three or four weeks, by which time red to purple scars cover the whole area. Two or three months after the attack, the infarct zone has taken on a gelatinous gray appearance. It will gradually shrink to a firm pearly scar as the body coats the wound with collagen.

Although people with coronary problems are commonly warned to avoid strenuous work such as shoveling snow, most heart attack victims are struck while they are at rest. This implies that the process begins with a change in the coronary vessels—in the supply—rather than with a sudden increase in the heart's need for oxygen—the demand. But even as our knowledge of the consequences of infarction has grown, we have become less and less certain of the mechanisms that bring it about. Since Herrick's day it has been cardiologic gospel that a heart attack occurs when a blood clot completely occludes a partially blocked artery. However, recent studies have shown that evidence of thrombosis, as the clotting process is called, is present anywhere from 21 percent to 90 percent of the time, depending on the kind of heart attack and who was studying it. Speculation is hazardous, but it is possible to conceive of a case in which Herrick's clots are an effect rather than a cause. Say spasm squeezes a coronary artery completely shut, causing a heart attack. Then the stagnant blood in the closed artery begins to clot, as Virchow theorized it would. Eventually the spasm loosens its grip and the artery expands to its normal diameter, leaving behind a freshly formed blood clot, a false clue at the scene of the crime.

A heart attack can strike anywhere in the organ, but the most common target is the left ventricle. That is because of its tremendous work load, which makes the need for oxygen more critical, and its high pressure, which tends to strangle coronary arteries. As more of the left ventricle is destroyed, less muscle is available to pump blood through the body. If the heart loses too much power, blood backs up in the lungs, flooding the microscopic air sacs. Meanwhile, the lack of forward flow causes low blood pressure and poor circulation to the brain, kidneys, liver, and other organs. This state, known as cardiogenic shock, leaves few survivors. After a less serious attack, drugs can sometimes buy enough time for the heart muscle to regain some of its strength, but often the patient is left in a state of chronic heart failure.

A heart attack can also blow out the ventricular wall like a tire, which is almost always fatal, or cause it to balloon into an aneurysm, which can cause angina, heart failure, or abnormal heart rhythms. Or a blood clot can form on the inner surface of the ventricle, break off, and travel to the brain or the limbs. Or inflammation can spread from the surface of the heart to the pericardium, the sac that surrounds it, causing chest pain, difficulty in breathing, and a racing heartbeat. Or any combination of the above.

The death of heart muscle can also incite an electrical riot. Infarction has a way of confusing the cells so that charged atoms of sodium, potassium, and calcium no longer know where to go. After a healthy heart cell discharges, there is a short rewinding period when it is immune to electrical disruption. This keeps the cells from firing more than once in a given beat. But in an oxygen-starved heart, cells can gallop out of control, setting off a writhing, wriggling, disorganized parody of a heartbeat called fibrillation. If this happens in the atria, it isn't much of a problem, since those chambers don't contribute much to the pumping; ventricular fibrillation, on the other hand, is invariably fatal if not attended to immediately. Hence its other name: sudden death.

Not all victims of sudden death stay dead, but about 85 percent of them do. It is not only the most common cause of death in heart attack victims, it is also a major coronary hazard in its own right. A sudden-death victim, unlike an infarction victim, can be walking down the street feeling fine one moment, then collapse, clutching his chest, the next. There are more than half a million coronary deaths per year in the United States, about one every minute, and two thirds of those are sudden. Remarkably, studies show up to one third of these victims had seen a doctor within a month of their demise. Although coronary atherosclerosis is found in 80 percent of sudden-death victims, the Framingham study indicates that 50 percent of the survivors of sudden death had had no symptoms before their attack. It also identified some sudden-death risk factors: smoking, high blood pressure, high cholesterol levels, diabetes, evidence of prior infarction, abnormal heart rhythms, a tendency to become dizzy with exercise, and psychological stress—the same risk factors linked to coronary heart disease.

But there are causes of sudden death that are completely unrelated to atherosclerosis, like coronary spasm, and about 20 percent of the time sudden death may have nothing to do with the coronary arteries at all. Metabolic abnormalities such as low blood potassium levels or overdoses of drugs such as digitalis can trigger short circuits, as can very severely damaged heart muscle caused by valve problems and infections. Some people may simply be born with electrical irregularities or develop "muscle-bound" hearts. We read about them all the time: the salesman whose car swerves off the highway for no apparent reason or the high school football player who collapses on the practice field.

In yet another example of the mind-heart connection, sudden death has been associated with emotional stress. It occurs frequently in the recently widowed and the overtly depressed. In a striking case, reported by Bernard Lown of the Harvard Medical School, a patient suffered salvos of premature beats, the harbinger of fibrillation, whenever a psychiatrist entered his room. On the other hand, the incidence of sudden death is much higher on weekends than during stress-filled weekdays.

Since most people don't survive their first encounter with sudden death, physicians are making great efforts to identify those vulnerable to it. Holter monitors, Walkman-sized devices that record the electrocardiogram, or EKG, as a patient goes about his daily activities, can pick up the patterns of premature beats that may be a warning of electrical trouble. There are also devices that record strange heart rhythms and transmit them over the telephone. Several companies are readying sophisticated units that are programmed to recognize abnormal rhythms that herald sudden death, then shock the muscle back into a normal rhythm or trigger the injection of an antiarrhythmic drug from an implantable pump. A more controversial approach entails the surgical removal of the area of the heart suspected of originating the electrical disturbances—in effect, a cardiac lobotomy.

Just before the turn of the twentieth century, two French scientists reported that they had managed to reverse sudden death in dogs by giving them a strong jolt of direct current. But that potentially life-saving research was apparently ignored for three decades, until the Consolidated Edison Company of New York, alarmed at the number of utility linemen who had been electrocuted (that is, thrown into fibrillation by faulty wiring), enlisted the aid of several teams of researchers, one of which found a translation of the French report. By 1940, scientists at Case Western Reserve University in Cleveland had shown that an electrical shock delivered to a ventricle during its vulnerable period—when cellular electrical charges are in a state of flux—

leads to fibrillation. At another time, a shock defibrillates the ventricle by bringing about a powerful, coordinated contraction that clears the electrical slate, after which the heart's natural pacemakers reassert themselves. (Actually, you can sometimes accomplish the same thing with a simple bang on the chest, which generates a tiny electrical charge, erases the abnormal pattern, and allows the cells in the sinoatrial node to assume command.)

A defibrillator soon found its way into the Cleveland operating room of Claude Beck, whose pioneering work would lay the foundations for the coronary bypass operation. After a handful of failures, Beck managed in 1947 to defibrillate a teenaged boy with a congenital heart deformity, using 110 volts of alternating current. Within a few years, defibrillators were developed that did not require the chest to be open, and in 1957 Beck used such a model outside the operating room to revive a sixty-five-year-old physician.

The next step was the coronary care unit, a special ward where patients at risk could be watched around the clock by a staff trained to deal with heart attacks and their consequences. The first units were built in 1962 in Kansas City, Toronto, and Philadelphia, and by the late 1960s almost every major hospital had one. Designs vary from institution to institution, but many believe that the ideal unit is a wheel-shaped room with the nurse's station and computer monitors in the hub and patient cubicles radiating like spokes, at a slight incline to make it easier to roll equipment to the bedside. Today, no community feels safe without a CCU, and whole industries have flourished by manufacturing the expensive technology the units require.

Even with the advent of CCUs, doctors still had to get the heart restarted within four or five minutes or oxygen-starved brain cells would begin to die, and too often they were beaten by the clock. So emergency care was placed in the hands of paramedics, working under the supervision of hospital-based physicians. We have turned ambulances and even helicopters into mobile intensive care units, equipped with devices that can broadcast an EKG to the hospital, where physicians tell the paramedics what to do and how to do it. But there still is that five-minute limit, after which help is usually too late. And in how many places can an ambulance be expected to arrive in five minutes? After an ambitious program involving tens of millions of dollars, New York City's Emergency Medical Service was able to cut the ambulance response time in half, but the current average of about nine minutes, while generally swift enough for someone injured in a car accident or slashed by a mugger, is still much too late to restore life to a victim of sudden death. In spite of all the strides we have made in understanding heart attacks and all the money we have invested in coronary care units, ambulances, and communications links, the coronary death rate is still fearsome.

A solution to this problem is cardiopulmonary resuscitation, a combination of heart massage and mouth-to-mouth respiration that can keep the supply of oxygenated blood circulating in a victim's body until help arrives. CPR came into vogue in the 1960s, but it was hardly a new idea. Researchers a hundred years before had shown that the vigorous manipulation of a chest could maintain adequate blood flow in laboratory animals, but they had apparently assumed that the technique wouldn't work on the much broader chests of humans. (There seems to be a Biblical precedent, however. In II Kings 4:34–35, Elisha revives his stricken son by putting "his mouth upon his mouth, and his eyes upon his eyes, and his hands upon his hands: and he stretched himself upon the child, and the flesh of the child waxed warm . . . and the child opened his eyes.") Even today, a survey showed that although 86 percent of physicians polled backed CPR, 92 percent of them didn't advise their patients' families to learn it. They were afraid of alarming them—the Catch-22 of cardiology.

Nowhere is the value of CPR more apparent than in Seattle, Washington, one of the first cities to embark on an organized effort to train the citizenry, where nearly 200,000 people were taught the technique. A ten-year study of 1,567 sudden-death victims treated by paramedics found that 30 percent lived long enough to be admitted to a hospital—about twice the national average—and 19 percent lived long enough to be discharged. Of that small but lucky group, incidentally, 81 percent were alive after six months, 76 percent after one year, 66 percent after two years, 55 percent after three years, and 49 percent after four years. In contrast, half of all infarction victims in the United States make it to a hospital and, of that group, about 73 percent are alive after four years. The prognosis for sudden-death victims improves, in fact, if they have also suffered an infarction, suggesting that there is something extremely sinister about fibrillation triggered by noncoronary causes.

Cardiologists have had to look mighty hard to see a bright side in all this. Addressing a conference on sudden death, Henry Greenberg of the St. Luke's–Roosevelt Hospital Center in New York City seemed to find one:

In a short, uncontrolled series, I sampled the opinions of a variety of physicians, their friends and spouses, and not one wished anything but a sudden, unexpected exit while in the pink of health. There were not even any votes for a classic deathbed scene, with the family gathered at the last great congress before death, sadly but resignedly helping to prepare for the final journey. . . . There was another characteristic of the vote that should be mentioned: The minimum age suggested for shuffling off this mortal coil was at least fourscore and some years. Obviously, sudden death at 85 years of age is far preferable to a grizzly carcinoma at age 40. I asked some respondents about the reciprocal, namely, a grizzly carcinoma at 85 years of age versus sudden death at 40. This produced a pause, often followed by more silence and finally by a nonverbal indication that the age of 40 was simply unacceptable. Death at such a childlike age had little appeal, confirming that the desire for sudden death is not a death wish, but in fact a life wish blended with a comprehension of one's own mortality and an understanding of the real world. . . . We all want to live to the fullest extent of our capacity as a sapient being capable of joy and delight, but at the proper time life can be quickly and gently rounded with a sleep.

5

Anginal Syndromes
Four Case Histories

THE ATHEROSCLEROTIC SPECTRUM RANGES from inconsequential specks on the artery wall all the way to heart-attack-sized occlusions. Most patients fall somewhere in between, in a territory marked by fear and uncertainty. The telltale anginal pain that William Heberden described so carefully two hundred years ago can be felt almost anywhere from the waist up, and it can be triggered by agents as varied as life. Some people feel discomfort beneath the breastbone, others in the neck, arms, teeth, jaw, throat, back, or upper abdomen. Just about the only place from which angina seldom seems to emanate is directly over the heart; pain there is more likely to be the result of arthritis, muscle strain, or other noncoronary problems such as indigestion.

Even to call angina a pain is pushing it—patients use the words pressure, tightness, squeezing, smothering, choking (but rarely sharp or stabbing). When describing the sensation, many simply clench a hand to their chest, a gesture encountered so often that Samuel Levine used it to make the diagnosis. Today it is known as the Levine sign, and cardiologists swear by it.

57

The array of aches is partly due to what physicians call referred pain. The heart is wired into the central nervous system
in such a way that it's easy for the brain to be fooled into
thinking that cardiac pain is coming from somewhere else. A
shortage of oxygen in the heart can also set off reflexes that
affect nerves throughout the body, especially in the extremities,
producing sensations that add to the anginal experience. Then
there is denial, the psychological defense mechanism by which
intolerable thoughts (what could be more intolerable than the
thought of a heart in jeopardy?) are avoided. There is a paradox
about angina that plays itself out in case after case: Patients
frequently don't recognize their first episode, but after it has
been interpreted, angina often acquires a frightening meaning.
It doesn't hurt as much as a broken leg or a sprained ankle, but
there is something about it that leads to feelings of mortality.
As Heberden observed in his patients, it "seems as if it would
take their life away if it were to increase or to continue."

The Canadian Cardiovascular Society officially classifies angina according to the degree of exertion that brings on the pain:
Class I angina occurs only with extreme stress; Class II with
normal activities such as walking to work; Class III with minimal effort, such as brushing teeth; and Class IV while the patient
is at rest. Class IV angina is, of course, the most serious form.
The problem with this system is that it does not take into account
emotion, which also can bring on the pain, since, like exertion,
it increases the heart's need for oxygen, the demand side of
Burns's supply-demand equation. If you are just watching television when the feeling comes on, you may be in Class IV; if you
are watching the seventh game of the World Series, it's only
Class I.

A diagnosis isn't always that easy, however. A person might
stay in Class I for years, or rapidly work his way up to Class IV,
indicating a deteriorating condition. And while patients understandably focus on symptoms, physicians know the amount of

pain does not always correlate with the degree of disease, the number of vessels blocked, and the portion of the heart at risk. Severe pain doesn't necessarily mean severe disease. Mild pain —or even its absence—doesn't necessarily guarantee a clean bill of health.

In deciding whether, or when, to recommend bypass surgery or an alternative treatment, I like to think in terms of anginal syndromes—not just the symptoms but the circumstances of disease. What follows are the case histories of four patients whose syndromes fall within the center of the atherosclerotic spectrum. They represent the hundreds of thousands of patients who are the potential candidates for bypass surgery. The onset of angina can be a particularly difficult and dangerous state. Assessing it, then deciding on the therapy to bring it under control, is the essence of the first case. The next case involves a patient with severe coronary disease but no angina. Sometimes the cardiac nerves of such asymptomatic patients have been damaged or destroyed by prior heart attacks or other disease; sometimes there's no apparent reason why the anginal warning system is defective. Either way, patients like these remind us that pain can be a blessing. The third syndrome, stable angina, involves a long-standing pattern of atherosclerotic difficulties in many areas of the body. Here, the new cardiac drugs can indeed make for better living through chemistry. If the essence of stable angina is an unchanging coronary blockage, the fourth syndrome—unstable angina—indicates that a plaque is active and even more treacherous than a fixed occlusion. Patients whose symptoms are becoming more severe or more frequent, or both, need to be hospitalized immediately. Studies show that, if not treated, they have nearly an even-money chance of having a heart attack within six weeks.

Cardiologists have an impressive array of diagnostic devices —treadmills, radioactive tracers, computers that can scan the heart and chart its movements, spaghetti-thin catheters that can

slide into its chambers and even into the coronary arteries themselves—but the wise clinician knows the patient is just as important as the anatomy. How old is he? How healthy? What is his
state of mind? Does he have a family to lean on? What kind of
work does he do? What impact has the disease made on his life?
These factors play a large role in determining the course of any
ailment, and a physician has to bear them in mind before recommending treatment.

CASE ONE: THE DISCOVERY

"It's not a pain, doctor. It's hardly anything, really. I just get
this feeling in my chest—not over my heart, more under the
breastbone in the middle. At first I thought it was indigestion or
the start of a chest cold."

Sitting across my desk, Edward Thayler, a fifty-five-year-old
tax attorney, made a vague rubbing motion across the front of
his worsted suit. He appeared prosperous and pin-striped, with
a bit of gray at the temples, a bulging Daytimer in his pocket,
and an unmistakably anxious countenance.

"Why don't you tell me how it started?"

"I guess I really noticed it a few weeks ago."

"What were you doing?"

"Playing golf. It wasn't going very well. I was slicing everything. I guess I got a little annoyed. Anyway, I was walking up
the sixteenth hole—it's pretty steep—and I felt this squeezing.
It went right away when I stopped walking, so I didn't think
much of it."

Mr. Thayler said he felt fine for two days, but on the third,
while rushing to make his train, he felt that same tightness.
Though it stopped when he reached his seat, he began to worry.
During the next three or four weeks, he suffered two more
episodes, but despite his increasing concern, he was reluctant to
see a doctor. Then, one night, while making love to his wife, the
discomfort came again, and he had to stop. That prompted his
call.

"Is this sensation sharp or dull?" I asked.

"Dull, like a heaviness, a weight. I thought it was gas at first." Mr. Thayler was fairly certain the pain did not come from his heart, but he had a hard time pinpointing its origin. He felt slightly winded during the attacks but had no cough and was not nauseated. When pressed, he remembered a half dozen other episodes of chest discomfort during the past few months. Each time the sensation seemed to come on with physical effort and go away with rest, usually after a few minutes. Such reluctant recollections are characteristic of patients with coronary disease.

It was evident from Mr. Thayler's hectic schedule and competitiveness on the sixteenth fairway that he had at least some aspects of the hard-driving, Type A personality linked with heart disease. As for other risk factors, the 187 pounds on his 5-foot 10-inch frame told me his appetite for food was greater than his appetite for exercise. He smoked a pack and a half of Chesterfields a day and had done so since he was eighteen. His father had suffered a heart attack at the age of fifty-eight and died some years later of a heart ailment. Mr. Thayler had been mildly hypertensive for a number of years but had taken no medicine for it. In short, he was batting five for five.

A physical examination showed that his heart was beating regularly at 76 beats per minute, and his blood pressure was a high 158/96 in both arms, lying down and standing. With an ophthalmoscope, I saw a mild narrowing of the eye arteries, a sign his hypertension predated the worrisome events of the past few weeks, not to mention the anxiety-provoking visit to my office. Mr. Thayler also had xanthelasma, raised yellowish marks where the eyelids meet the nose that indicate a high blood-lipid level, and arcus senilis, a fine white rim on the cornea—signs thought by some to be markers of coronary disease.

When facing such a bewilderingly varied ailment, physicians have to turn detective and proceed along negative lines, eliminating other sources of chest discomfort. In Mr. Thayler's case, the heart's well-focused tapping against his chest wall and the brisk rise and fall of the main artery in his neck ruled out the valve problems that are an occasional source of cardiac pain. With a stethoscope, I heard the normal "lub" as his mitral and tricuspid valves closed and the "dub" as the aortic and pulmonic valves shut. There was an extra sound as the atria contracted and flushed their blood into the ventricles, a sign that his heart muscle might be slightly stiff from hypertension or ischemia.

By this time, I was convinced that the sensation Mr. Thayler was suffering was angina. An electrocardiogram, which would record his heart's electrical activity from various points on his body, would tell me if the cardiac muscle had already been damaged. Antennalike electrodes attached to the arms and legs and placed across the chest sense the currents from their respective vantage points. The mountain and valley tracing of the pen, so perplexing to patients, corresponds to the direction the current takes through the heart muscle: Electricity flowing toward an electrode causes the pen to rise, while current moving in the opposite direction causes it to fall. Using combinations of electrodes, it is possible to get a three-dimensional view of the heart and spot any areas of damaged muscle where the current can't get through.

Electrocardiography, like bird watching, is all in the recognition. In the normal EKG, the heartbeat begins with the P-wave —when Willem Einthoven, the Dutch physiologist, was developing the machine at the start of the century, he selected the letter from the middle of the alphabet to allow room in both directions for the discoveries of his successors—a small curving deflection of the pen upward representing the electrical activation of the atria. The line then remains horizontal for an instant as the signal passes through the atrioventricular node in the center of the organ. Next, the ventricles are switched on—a downward glitch of the pen followed by a steep rise and fall. This is called the QRS-complex. Then comes the recharging phase, during which the EKG gradually slopes up into the T-wave. Should this part of the EKG, called the ST-segment, be depressed instead, it might mean the heart is not getting enough oxygen. The more it droops, the more severe the ischemia. A sharp rise in the ST-segment, on the other hand, is evidence of cardiac irritation or injury, and a patient whose T-waves become peaked or inverted may have suffered a major infarction. With time, however, even signs of a heart attack can disappear without an electrocardiographic trace.

Mr. Thayler's EKG was normal—hardly surprising, considering that he wasn't having angina when it was taken—so there was no reason to believe his heart was starving for oxygen. Results like this can lead to a false sense of security, however, and I was still fairly sure that Mr. Thayler had a blockage of at least one coronary vessel. Although nothing in the EKG indicated any permanent damage to to the muscle, I was concerned that, the way things were going, it could happen at any time. Something in his arteries was changing, and I wanted him to check into the hospital where he could be monitored around the clock.

"No way," he said tersely. "I just don't feel that bad."

We both shifted in our seats. Mr. Thayler and I had come to a difficult point in our relationship, one that many patients and cardiologists reach sooner or later. Perhaps as a defense mechanism, he was treating his problem as if it were a corporate tax issue, putting it into a compact bundle and trying to tie up all the loose ends. Disease isn't like that, especially heart disease. Still, he was not going to sign his life over to a physician he had just met, and I didn't want to push so hard I would end up pushing him away. So we compromised. Mr. Thayler went home, but with orders to call me if he had another attack, and with a tiny brown vial of nitroglycerin containing thirty tablets, each with $\frac{1}{150}$th of a grain. Although nitroglycerin has been around for nearly 150 years, only recently has there been agreement on how it works. Basically, it dilates vessels in many parts of the body, and this opening of the circulatory floodgates lessens the force the heart must expend to pump blood through the vascular network. Nitroglycerin also minimizes the effects of arterial spasm, perhaps by interfering with prostaglandins.

"If you feel that chest sensation again," I told him, "stop what you're doing and sit or lie down. Nitroglycerin can lower your blood pressure, so you don't want to take it standing up, like in a phone booth. Nature has provided falling over as a safety mechanism (assuming, of course, you don't smack your head); you can't keep the blood flowing to your brain if it's uphill from your heart. When you place the tablet under your tongue, you'll feel a mild burning sensation, then a feeling of fullness and perhaps a brief headache. The chest pressure should go away within minutes."

Nitroglycerin would be even more wonderful if its effects lasted longer. Unfortunately, it does its job and is gone in about ten minutes.

As a preventive measure, I also prescribed a daily 50 mg dose of atenolol, a member of a group of drugs called beta blockers. Since their introduction in 1966, they have become mainstays in the battle against heart disease. In 1981, propranolol, the first of the beta blockers, was the third most prescribed drug in the United States, behind the tranquilizer Valium and the ulcer-inhibiting Tagamet. If those two pharmacological standbys are downers for the mind and stomach, atenolol, propranolol, and the other beta blockers are downers for the heart. Under physical or emotional stress, the body releases adrenalin, a hormone that plugs into little outlets on the surface of cardiovascular cells and activates them, making the heart beat faster and more forcefully. That increases the organ's need for oxygen—bad news for patients with coronary artery disease, whose hearts already have difficulty getting enough. Beta blockers block these beta-adrenergic hormones by plugging into the cellular outlets before the hormones can, but unlike the hormones they don't switch the cells on. This has the effect of lowering the heart rate, the blood pressure, and the need for oxygen, making the crescendos of activity that culminate in attacks of angina far less frequent.

Beta blockers also lower blood pressure by decreasing the activity of renin, a hormone produced by the kidneys, which leads to the formation of angiotensin, one of the most potent blood vessel constrictors known. They are used to treat the racing heart of tachycardia and to lessen the adrenalin-related jitters of stage fright. Recent studies have shown that the drugs protect heart-attack victims from future coronary events, improving their chances for survival when given during the late stages of recovery. Even wonder drugs like beta blockers can occasionally produce side effects, however. They tend to constrict blood vessels, leading to speculation that they might provoke coronary spasm. They can weaken the contractions of the heart enough to worsen congestive heart failure, lessen the benefits of physical exercise, and raise the fat content of the blood. They can also cause impotence, confusion, fatigue, wheezing in asthmatics, and even strange dreams. Most patients, though, don't experience any of these problems, and neither did Mr. Thayler. When he called a few weeks later, he told me that he had followed my advice and taken a few weeks off. There had been no additional attacks, and he hadn't needed any of the nitroglycerins.

About four weeks later Mr. Thayler called again with less encouraging news. Since returning to work, he had found that he regularly experienced pain walking up hills or against the wind on cold days. That was all I had to hear. I told him in no uncertain terms that the time had come for a stress test, which would give both of us a more precise idea of his functional limits and tell me if he had a form of coronary disease that might require prompt surgery. Such a test would have been too risky on his first visit, when his disease was unstable. Now, even though he was still having attacks, they were occurring regularly, in response to similar kinds of physical effort. That meant his condition had stabilized, and it had become safe for him to exercise under supervision.

On a rainy afternoon the next week, Mr. Thayler reported to a cubbyhole on the eighth floor of Mount Sinai's Annenberg Building. In a corner of the examination room was what looked like the platform on which Olympic medal winners stand. In the first stress tests, developed at this very institution by Arthur Master more than a generation ago, patients had to climb up and down the steps, over and over, until their hearts revealed their inner secrets. Today, in the electronic age, we use a computer-controlled treadmill that insidiously increases its speed and tilts to steeper angles at predetermined intervals, all the while tracking the EKG. Even a marathon runner would have trouble staying on one of these machines for more than about fifteen minutes. That the machine is in complete control adds an element of psychological stress—too much, some patients say. But people who are afraid of a stress test often are really afraid of diagnostic truth. After all, the idea is to find out before any irreversible damage is done just how the heart responds to effort.

After a preliminary EKG that gave us something to compare the results to, Mr. Thayler signed a release—the risk of a life-threatening problem while a patient is on the treadmill is about 1 in 10,000—and a technician shaved the ten spots on his body where the electrodes would be attached. Stripped to the waist and wearing an old pair of tennis sneakers, Mr. Thayler was escorted to the treadmill by Jeffrey Cowen, a bearded, bespectacled second-year cardiology fellow who was then working in the stress lab.

"I'm here to make sure you're safe," Cowen said. "Just try to relax and get into the rhythm of the treadmill. And remember, if you have any pain at all, let me know right away."

The treadmill started up with a roar. Mr. Thayler wobbled, his arms grasping the handrails, until his legs found the pace. While he stared out the window at the rainy rooftops of upper Manhattan, the bottom half of his body marched along, stiff-legged but rhythmic. After one minute, his heart rate was up to 120. At three minutes, the treadmill abruptly upped its speed and its slope. Mr. Thayler had a few shaky moments before he once again found the right pace. Four minutes into the test, his heart rate was 138 and his blood pressure 170/100. About a minute later, he looked over to Cowen.

"I'm getting that tightness," he said over the noise.

Cowen checked the EKG reading on the console and saw that Mr. Thayler's ST-segments were drooping. Part of his heart wasn't getting enough oxygen and was signaling its trouble.

"How bad is the tightness on a scale of one to ten?"

"It's getting to be about a six."

Cowen frowned and stopped the test. "When the treadmill comes to a stop, just stand quietly with your arms at your side so we can get a clear cardiogram." This reading—with the distracting motion eliminated but the patient's heart still in an ischemic state—is often the most diagnostically revealing. After a few minutes on a nearby stretcher with a nitroglycerin under his tongue, Mr. Thayler reported that the pain had vanished. The electrocardiogram was back to normal, and the color had returned to the patient's face.

We met in my office the next day. Even on the beta blockers, it was clear he was having angina. I told him I wanted to increase the doses of his medicines. If they could control his symptoms, fine. If they couldn't, the next step would be angiography, to map the pattern of coronary blockages and perhaps guide the hand of the surgeon if bypass proved necessary.

CASE TWO: WITHOUT WARNING

Thomas Finder felt perfectly fine, which made matters all the worse. He played tennis during the summer and skied in the

winter. He was rarely sick, and certainly never suspected he had
a heart problem. And yet just moments after the sixty-one-year-
old executive with a computer corporation stepped onto a treadmill as part of his company's annual physical, the doctor
administering the test grew very concerned.

"Are you sure you feel okay?" Mr. Finder recalled being
asked. Almost before he could answer, he was ordered to stop
running. He insisted that he could go on. The doctor insisted that
he shouldn't. Mr. Finder's blood pressure, which should have
risen with exercise, had begun to drop precipitously. After the
fifth minute on the treadmill, it had dropped all the way from
130/85 to 100/50. To make matters worse, the EKG showed that
while his heart rate was rising, the ST-segments were falling.
All this meant the front wall of his left ventricle, the part of the
heart that does much of the work, wasn't getting enough oxygen.

"I know this is going to be hard to accept," I said when he
came to my office, "but you may have severe coronary artery
disease."

"How can you say that? I feel great, and I exercise all the
time."

"Yes, but according to the stress test, you don't have symptoms to tell you when there's trouble. You may think you're fine,
but you're not. The fact is, when you were on that treadmill,
your heart was starving for oxygen, and you didn't know it."

No doubt there are millions of people walking around with
"silent ischemia." A British study of thirty angina patients, in
fact, indicated that chest pangs accompanied episodes of cardiac
oxygen starvation less than half the time. And 10 percent of
angiographically studied coronary patients who don't have
symptoms turn out to have blockages of the left main artery.
This is the most severe form of coronary artery disease, since
that artery is responsible for most of the left ventricle, and a
single clog can cut off the supply of blood to that all-important

pump. Regardless of how a patient feels, surgery is recommended whenever there is significant blockage of the left main coronary artery.

Can the stress test be wrong? Any test can. Patients whose left ventricles have been thickened by hypertension often have falsely positive stress tests. Sometimes normal coronary vessels do not produce a uniform oxygen supply, resulting in EKGs that look as though the heart is suffering from ischemia. But in Mr. Finder's case, an error was unlikely. The reason has partly to do with Baye's theorem, which holds that the value of a diagnostic test for a disease has to do with the prevalence of that disease in a given population. In other words, if one were fishing in a pond well stocked with trout, a tug on the line would usually mean dinner. If the pond were sparsely populated, however, the same tug would probably turn out to be an old shoe. Since coronary artery disease is more common among older males, it follows that older males who have abnormal stress tests almost always turn out to have coronary disease. The tests aren't nearly as accurate for younger women, who have a much lower incidence of coronary disease. Even without Baye's theorem, the fall in Mr. Finder's blood pressure while he was on the treadmill indicated his heart muscle was temporarily weakened.

To supplement a stress test, we sometimes inject radioactive thallium into an exercising patient; this isotope follows the coronary flow and lights up the healthy heart muscle so we can see on a monitor any area that isn't getting enough blood. But if a patient has suffered a heart attack in the past, he'll have such a bloodless zone already. To tell whether that spot is from a current imbalance in supply and demand or an old heart attack, we have to wait several hours for the heart to rest, then repeat the thallium scan. If the spot is still there, it most likely represents an old infarction; if it's gone, we suspect that the hunger for oxygen has been resolved but that the muscle is in jeopardy.

The reason Mr. Finder didn't get a thallium scan is that it

reveals only the evenness of coronary flow, not its volume. So it's conceivable that a person could have severe disease of every coronary artery—a possibility in Mr. Finder's case—and nevertheless, because so much of his heart is being supplied by the affected vessels, still pass a thallium test.

Fortunately, another stress test, the rest and exercise gated cardiac blood-pool scan, ingeniously sidesteps this problem with computer graphics that would impress George Lucas. It involves injecting into a patient another radioactive isotope—technetium pertechnetate—which mingles with his blood. The patient is then placed on an examination table and a large, drumlike camera is positioned over his chest to record the radioactive blood as it flows in and out of the cardiac chambers. The camera's shutter is connected to an EKG machine and synchronized with the cardiac cycle, merging a series of heartbeats into an electronic cartoon that shows the movement of the muscle. The computer also calculates how much blood the left ventricle is able to pump.

Two sets of pictures are taken: one with the patient at rest and the other while he pumps bicycle pedals attached to the foot of the examination table. At rest, Mr. Finder's heart contracted vigorously, ejecting a normal 63 percent of the contents of the left ventricle with each beat. But when he pedaled with roughly the effort that made his ST-segments creep downward on the treadmill, a portion of the curving ventricular wall flattened like a tire. The ejection fraction, which should have risen with exercise, fell to 31 percent. This meant his stress test was no mistake. "The only way to find out how bad your arteries are," I told him later that afternoon, "is with a coronary angiogram."

In the cold language of the craft, cardiologists call it an invasive procedure. Actually, it is nothing short of a minioperation in which a catheter is slid all the way into a patient's heart so that pressures can be measured, blood can be sampled, and, most important of all, the coronary arteries can be viewed. Catheters had been inserted into the hearts of horses in the nineteenth century, apparently with no ill effects, but it wasn't until 1929 that Werner Forssmann suggested that they might also be used on humans. When his boss, the chief of surgery, refused to let him catheterize a patient, the young German physician went ahead and catheterized himself, inserting a rubber tube designed for the bladder into his arm and watching over a fluoroscope as it snaked its way through the subclavian vein and the vena cava into the right atrium, as a horrified nurse looked on. Forssmann lost his job but eventually won a Nobel prize.

Although the risks of serious complications are about one in a thousand, catheterization is not something to be taken lightly. The tubes can damage the blood vessels they pass through on the way to the heart or tear the coronary arteries. They can cause blood clots to form or dislodge pieces of atherosclerotic debris, which could travel downstream and cause a stroke or kidney failure, threaten a limb, or provoke a heart attack. Catheters can tickle the heart into an electrical disturbance or cause coronary spasm, for which nitroglycerin is always standing by. The procedure is expensive—about $1,500—and inconvenient, so we try not to send any patient to the cath lab who doesn't need to be there. "But," I told Mr. Finder, "in your case the risks of doing the procedure are less than the risks of not doing it."

The following Monday evening, Mr. Finder returned to Mount Sinai, was interviewed and examined by a series of interns, residents, cardiology fellows, and nurses, and was given yet another electrocardiogram, a chest X ray, and a battery of blood tests. He signed a consent form and was shown to a four-bed room along Madison Avenue, where he spent a fitful night. At eight the next morning, he was sedated with Valium and Benadryl and wheeled into a room that looks like a cross between a television studio and Dr. Frankenstein's laboratory. A hazy Mr. Finder was rolled to a table in the center of the room and strapped on, so he wouldn't roll off as it pivoted on its side. Sterile green drapery was placed over everything but his head, the bend of his right elbow, and a small patch of skin on his shaved right groin.

As nurses and technicians donned surgical masks and gowns and heavy lead aprons, K. Peter Rentrop, as lean and lanky as Ichabod Crane, injected Mr. Finder's right arm with Novocain and made a small incision just over the vein. With silk sutures he deftly lassoed the vessel and opened it with a tiny blade. A squirt of blood stained the arm of his blue cotton gown. Then he snaked a long, thin plastic tube into the incision. Since there are few nerves inside the blood vessels, the only sensation Mr. Finder felt was the pressure from Rentrop's fingers as the catheter slid like a knife through butter up his arm, into the right atrium, across the tricuspid valve, into the triangular cavity of the right ventricle, through the pulmonic valve, and into the pulmonary artery, all the while measuring pressure in the various parts of the right side of the heart.

Mr. Finder was given another shot of Novocain in his right groin, and a pigtail catheter tipped with a curlicue to prevent vessel tears was slid into place just above the aortic valve, where it recorded the central body blood pressure, the truest blood pressure reading of all. Rentrop gave Mr. Finder a dose of blood-thinning heparin to prevent clotting, and the table was turned on its side. Under the guidance of two X-ray cameras, the catheter snaked across the aortic valve and into the left ventricle. On the screen, the shadow of the undulating chamber could be seen, every now and then irritably throwing in an extra beat. Mr. Finder, by now accustomed to the procedure, gazed at the monitor along with everyone else.

"You're going to feel a warm flash," Rentrop said as he prepared to inject about half a highball of X-ray dye through the catheter. "It will only last a few seconds, and it won't hurt." The X-ray and video cameras were rolled into place. "Take a deep breath now, Mr. Finder." This got his diaphragm out of the way for a good picture. "Okay, shoot." The lights went out, the cameras whirred, the television screens brightened. Mr. Finder squirmed slightly as a strange but painless sensation of warmth coursed through his body. On the screen, his left ventricle could be seen contracting almost normally except for a small area on the front wall.

The pigtail catheter was replaced with one specially designed to find its way into the mouth of the left coronary artery. Twisting and turning the tube, Rentrop delicately guided it snugly into place in the tiny vessel, one of the end zones of the circulatory system. The table was rotated, and more dye was injected in small squirts. The cypresslike pattern of the left coronary artery and its branches appeared on the screen. "There, look at that," Rentrop said, pointing to a spot near the vessel's origin, where it suddenly narrowed almost to a close. Another blockage, not quite as severe, was visible farther downstream in the anterior descending artery. The problem lay in Mr. Finder's left main coronary artery. Bad news.

In less than an hour, the catheters were removed, and the procedure was over. For the next twenty minutes, Mr. Finder lay in an adjoining room as a cardiology fellow pressed his fingers on the femoral artery to prevent the punctured vessel from oozing. Then came six hours with a small sandbag on his groin. Since the dye acts as a diuretic, Mr. Finder was urged to prevent dehydration by drinking copious amounts of fluid, hardly a convenient activity when you're flat on your back.

Had he a less serious form of coronary artery disease, Mr. Finder would have been allowed to get out of bed that evening and leave the hospital the next day. But left-main disease is a time bomb only the surgeon can defuse, and I'm loath to let patients with it out of the hospital even for a few days when the blockage is severe. Without coronary bypass surgery, the current statistics gave Mr. Finder only a slightly better than fifty-fifty chance of surviving five years, and virtually no chance of surviving ten. With bypass surgery, he had an 80 to 90 percent chance of living five years, and a better than even chance of living a decade. Even in the normally contentious cardiological community, the verdict is nearly unanimous—the only treatment for left-main disease is surgery.

I was not quite sure Mr. Finder had accepted all that had happened to him. After all, only a few days ago he appeared to be the picture of health, and he had yet to feel any chest pain. But Rentrop's film helped me convince him that he needed a coronary bypass—and soon. We scheduled the operation for two days later.

CASE 3: PEACEFUL COEXISTENCE

Everything a patient says has to be evaluated with healthy skepticism. Perhaps the most obvious example is the answer "Not much" to the question "How much do you drink?" It's like that, too, with complaints of angina. Is the pain really from the heart, or from the myriad of other possible sources, including the mind? So I was very skeptical about the case of Isaac Feinstein, a seventy-year-old professor of sociology. A short, casual man given to turtlenecks, tweed jackets, and crepe-soled shoes (in the several years I've known him, I don't think I've ever seen him in a suit and tie), Mr. Feinstein had a heart attack in 1952 and has complained of chest pains ever since. The Q-waves on his electrocardiogram were virtual proof of the infarction, but despite more than three decades of subsequent heart pain, he had suffered no additional damage, a highly unlikely course.

My doubts that he really had angina were diminished somewhat when he told me his pain was precipitated by walking, especially in the cold, after eating heavy meals, and occasionally when he dreamed he was running or got hot under the collar. These are classic provokers of angina, occasions when the heart is compelled to increase its output and demands more oxygen in return. Generally Mr. Feinstein's episodes responded promptly to nitroglycerin, which in itself tended to support the diagnosis. Sometimes a patient will tell me that the discomfort is gone fifteen or twenty minutes after slipping a pill under his tongue, a time span inconsistent with nitroglycerin's action, which lasts only five or ten minutes. Then I suspect it isn't angina.

Nitroglycerin also helps relieve other aches—certain gallbladder and esophagus pains, for example—since it relaxes not only blood vessels but also some muscles in the upper intestinal tract. (This may be an accident of physiology, since gastrointestinal pain is frequently confused with angina.) Mr. Feinstein had already discovered the drug's wide-ranging applications. "Nitro," he told me, "is good for all sorts of things."

He was something of a nitro connoisseur, in fact. He relied mostly on nitroglycerin tablets, generally using fifteen to twenty weekly, but occasionally took isosorbide dinitrate, a long-acting form of the drug. He had also tried a sort of Vicks Vapo-Rub ointment of nitroglycerin, which is absorbed through the skin. About the only variety he hadn't tried was the nitroglycerin patch, which goes on like a Band-Aid and releases the drug steadily over twenty-four hours. Which may have been just as well, because there is some evidence to suggest that constant levels of nitroglycerin aren't as effective as short bursts.

It was a particularly severe episode of chest pain lasting about twenty minutes—the borderline between the reversible ischemia of angina and the permanent damage of a heart attack—that sent Mr. Feinstein to me, but it soon became apparent that, as in many victims, atherosclerosis was causing problems all over his body. For sixteen years he had experienced "angina of the legs," a tightness in the calf muscles resulting from blockages of the arteries supplying his lower extremities. The pain would get so bad it would cause him to limp and limit him to walking just a few blocks at a time. Then there were "ministrokes"— episodes of blindness, dizziness, and head pressure caused by the migration of atherosclerotic debris from the arteries in his neck into his brain. Atherosclerosis was probably also a factor in Mr. Feinstein's occasional impotence.

"We might be able to fix everything that's wrong with you,"

I told Mr. Feinstein when we sat down in my office after his physical, "but let's talk about what it would mean." The mini-strokes he was having would make cardiac surgery risky, so before we could operate on his heart, we would have to consider surgically repairing the arteries in his neck. Then, assuming we didn't give him a heart attack or a stroke in the process, we could go ahead with the bypass operation. But he still wouldn't have much mobility because of the pain in his legs, a condition called intermittent claudication after the Emperor Claudius, who limped. They would have to be operated on, too. "It's going to take about a year out of your life, and the risks that something could go wrong multiply with the number of procedures."

This kind of decision basically comes down to "Who is the patient?" Mr. Feinstein's age helped tip the scale against surgery. Operations are significantly more dangerous on older patients—the surgical mortality rate for coronary bypass is about 8 or 10 percent for a seventy-five-year-old—and whenever you take an elderly person "out of his life," even a minor setback can have serious psychological consequences. But even more important, Mr. Feinstein was quite productive—he taught a full schedule and had a book coming out—so he seemed to have adjusted to his symptoms. Had he been a fifty-six-year-old mailman, I would hardly have hesitated to recommend the surgical triple-header the case required—operations on the vessels feeding the head, the heart, and the legs. But since he was able to lead a full professional life, I steered him away from the operating room.

Mr. Feinstein once told me that, as a Jew in Germany before World War II, he had usually carried a gun. The idea was not to kill the Nazis, but to kill himself if he was caught. He had a similar attitude toward illness—he could live with symptoms, up to a point. He wasn't looking for a risky cure; he just wanted to make sure things wouldn't get worse. "It's been thirty years like this, so what am I going to take a risk for?" he said. "I don't want to die from improvements. Anyway, who doesn't have pain?"

The solution seemed to be medication, and I had a particular drug in mind. Calcium blockers have been used in Europe for nearly twenty years, first to treat high blood pressure and later for vascular spasm as well. They are a little like nitrates, in that they dilate blood vessels, and a little like beta blockers, in that they reduce the work load of the heart. But calcium blockers wouldn't make Mr. Feinstein's leg pain worse, as beta blockers might by constricting his blood vessels and cutting the circulation to his calves.

Calcium is an essential part of the heart's battery acid; the flow of calcium ions controls the heart cells' electrical and muscular activity. Calcium blockers interfere with the movement of these ions in that mysterious instant when the current triggers a contraction. In so doing, the drug relaxes cardiovascular cells, dilates blood vessels, slows the heart's rate, and reduces its force.

It was my hope that calcium blockers would reduce Mr. Feinstein's pain and enable him to get around better. I started him on nifedipine, one of the three calcium blockers then available, and carefully monitored his progress. What follows are excerpts from my case notes.

August 7, 1981: After two months on nifedipine, 10 mg three times daily, patient swims and rides a stationary bicycle for 40 minutes. Walking still limited by claudication. Using one nitroglycerin a day. No episodes of blindness since beginning antithrombotic therapy with aspirin and dipyridamole.

October 13: Reports considerable improvement in angina after four months of nifedipine. Uses only two to three nitroglycerins weekly. Intermittent claudication still prevents him from walking more than three to five blocks without discomfort, but is able to force himself to proceed. Managed 30 blocks yesterday. Occasional dizziness, but no transient blindness.

November 20: Complains of increasingly frequent episodes of chest pain, now a more diffuse, tensionlike discomfort involving shoulder blades and arms. Mild exertion produces shortness of breath. Pain is more erratically responsive to nitroglycerin and at times awakens him from sleep. In the past, angina had become worse in colder weather. Remains on 10 mg nifedipine three times daily. Patient is concerned but not distressed. On examination, the chest is tender and the pain is reproduced exactly by pressing on sternum and upper ribs. Possibly arthritis? Shortness of breath suggests congestive failure, and the chest X-ray supports this. The EKG looks the same as in the past. If angina, it is feasible that this destabilization of the pattern, now requiring 4 or 5 nitroglycerins daily, relates to onset of colder weather. Patient must be watched closely lest symptoms accelerate. Put him back on isosorbide dinitrate [a long-acting nitrate]. He will watch his salt intake and I suggested a small dose of diuretic medication for lung congestion.

December 22: Still having chest pain, now clearly sounds like angina. Gated cardiac blood-pool scan on Dec. 10 showed a small region of damaged muscle. Ejection fraction in the range of 40 to 45 percent. Still actively engaged in academic work and awaits publication of new book in a few months. Disturbing to witness patient's increasing functional limitation. Am reluctant to hospitalize, but it could be necessary if a true pre-infarctional syndrome emerges.

January 4, 1982: Telephone call to report that symptoms have lessened a bit, and he's getting outdoors more. Medications continued.

March 1: Patient returns for re-evaluation. Angina now stable. Still takes two nitroglycerins daily, but no major episodes of pain. Occasional shortness of breath relieved by furosemide [a diuretic]. Has had two brief episodes of partial blindness. Troubled by leg pain after walking one block, but can walk up to 20 blocks by starting and stopping. Surgical risks are substantial, though he is eager to obtain relief of claudication. Now quite prolific at his work, with new book on subway crime just published.

July 6:   Patient bothered by claudication and two episodes of blindness. Angina occurs about once a week, lesser forms of chest pressure more frequently. Consumes one nitroglycerin a day. Swims and bicycles. Stable. Reluctant to recommend multiple surgical procedures that would be required for vascular reconstruction at productive time in his academic career. Option remains open if symptoms worsen. Meanwhile, suggest conservative approach.

By this time, I was beginning to understand how Mr. Feinstein could have had thousands of episodes of angina, and taken thousands of nitros, without permanently damaging a single heart cell since his heart attack thirty years ago. The reason, I think, is that he has developed a highly effective collateral coronary circulation, tiny auxiliary vessels that connect areas of the heart with good blood flow to zones where the flow is inadequate, thereby spreading the wealth. These vessels seem to increase the blood flow enough to protect a heart from cell death, though not enough to prevent ischemia or angina. Mr. Feinstein's collaterals may not have been fully developed when he suffered his heart attack, or perhaps they kept the damage to a minimum (it was a relatively small infarction). Anyway, they seemed to be protecting him rather well now.

September 9:   Patient recently hosptialized following episode of vertigo. Possibly he might have had some ischemia of brain. Again, no permanent damage done. I am reassured. Feeling out patient again about surgery, he tells me he doesn't want to jeopardize productivity so we decide to continue on present conservative course.

January 12, 1983:   Angina stable. When he writes, words sometimes seem to shift on the page, but he has no other visual disturbances. Leg pain on walking about as before. Impotence is becoming more annoying and relations with wife strained. I explained that this was probably due to the same blockages that were causing his leg pain, and that an operation to fix it would have the same risks and unfortunately be far less certain to work. His medications and psychological factors might also be involved. I encouraged him to think of other ways to show his feelings for his wife and be more creative about sex to relieve marital tensions.

June 3:   Two or three episodes of the eye problem, the last yesterday. Angina and leg pain stable. Declines to take blood thinning drugs, but may have to if situation deteriorates. Am still reluctant about surgery. Advised to keep taking an aspirin a day.

September 8:   Patient stable, working. Physical examination unchanged. EKG and lab data satisfactory. Tolerates medicines. No new symptoms.

Now that I had a feel for Mr. Feinstein, and vice versa, we both agreed that we were on the right track with a medical approach. With an elderly patient who is stable, and who also suffers from other complications of atherosclerosis, the surgical risks are higher and the benefits lower—especially if, like Mr. Feinstein, the patient is able to live with his symptoms. Even if his condition were to destabilize, I would still be extremely hesitant to recommend surgery. But I don't think that will happen. Mr. Feinstein has settled into a pattern that should continue for a while. If all goes well, he will not need to see me more than two or three times a year.

CASE 4: A SHORT FUSE

When I first met Deborah Falk, she had already been assigned a curtained-off cubicle in Mount Sinai's Rose Coronary Care Unit. She was fifty-eight but looked much older. Her face was pale, her forehead beaded with sweat. From the chart at the foot of her bed, I pieced together her story. Mrs. Falk had first felt a pressure under her breastbone about three weeks earlier while at work (she was a hairdresser). Gradually, the episodes of pain became more and more frequent and were brought on by less and less activity. The night before I saw her, she had suffered an attack that woke her from a deep sleep. Her family physician told her to get to the hospital right away.

Soon after her 5 A.M. arrival at the Mount Sinai emergency room, she had another attack. An electrocardiogram revealed depression of the ST-segments and inversion of the T-waves, indicating she was flirting with a major heart attack. Nitroglycerin calmed her pain, and she was wheeled to the eighth floor of the Annenberg Building and into Bed 4 in the CCU. Before coronary care units were built, the prognosis for victims of severe coronary disease was bleak. If they survived the initial attack, physicians would put them in private rooms, only to find the next morning that they had died from ventricular arrhythmias. In the Rose Unit, as in other CCUs around the country, each patient's EKG is monitored at a nursing station staffed around the clock. When trouble occurs, alarms sound, and help is at the bedside within seconds. Besides correcting electrical irregularities, coronary care units have enabled us to limit the size of heart attacks. Indeed, these units are vital in controlling unstable angina and preventing it from deteriorating into a heart attack. I hoped that would be the case with Mrs. Falk.

At the nursing station, I read the chart filled out by the cardiology fellow on call when she arrived.

Physician's Orders

September 12, 1983
05:45

1. Admit Rose CCU

2. Diagnosis: Unstable Angina, rule out myocardial infarction

3. Allergies: none reported

4. Activity: bedrest

5. Diet: 2 gram sodium, 1,400 calorie, low cholesterol

6. Vital Signs: temperature q 4 h [every four hours]; pulse, blood pressure, respirations q 2 h

7. Lidocaine, 2 mg per minute i.v. infusion

8. Heparin, 5,000 units i.v., 600 units per hour intusion

9. 12-lead EKG on admission, daily, and in event of chest pain

10. Portable chest X-ray

11. Routine admission blood studies plus CPK and LDH iso-enzymes and SGOT stat, in 6 h and at 08:00

12. Nasal oxygen, 2 liters per minute

13. Valium, 5 mg p.o. [orally] q 6–8 h, prn [as needed for] sedation

14. Colace, 100 mg tid [three times a day], as needed for softening stools

15. Nitroglycerin, $\frac{1}{150}$ grains sublingually prn angina and call M.D.

16. Isosorbide dinitrate, 20 mg p.o. q 4 h while awake

17. Nitroglycerin, 2% ointment, 1 inch topically q 4 h while asleep

18. Propranolol, 20 mg p.o. q 6 h

We asked Mrs. Falk not to do anything for herself. We wanted her to go in slow motion, even when she wasn't in any pain, to keep her heart's oxygen demand as low as possible. She was put on a nitrate, a beta blocker, and later a calcium blocker. We carefully explained the importance of her signaling the nurse if she had even the slightest chest discomfort.

Mrs. Falk's first day in the Unit was quiet. After she spent a fitful but painless night, the doses of medications were stiffened. That afternoon she was allowed to sit up in a chair; she promptly had another attack. With morphine and nitroglycerin, the pain went away, and her EKG returned to normal. Then, just before dinner, she had yet another bout with pain. The medicines were cranked up to maximum doses, and she was put on intravenous nitroglycerin, the best alternative to direct coronary injection.

In addition to its obvious therapeutic value, the peace and quiet of the CCU is to a cardiologist what a couch is to a psychiatrist. The hushed, librarylike atmosphere encourages patients to think about their illness and what is triggering it. Sometimes, the emotional underpinnings of coronary disease are obvious. That was apparent in Mrs. Falk's case when, the next day, she suffered another attack right after a visit from her husband. Later, she told me she had gone through menopause and feared that her husband was losing interest in her. On top of that, her youngest son had left for college. When women (or, for that matter, men) find themselves on the far side of middle age, coping with feelings of empty nests and emptiness, latent coronary artery disease can burst forth with a vengeance.

On her third day in the CCU, Mrs. Falk had an attack that, unlike her earlier brief episodes, stretched to about half an hour. How could we tell if she had crossed the line separating angina and infarction? When a heart cell dies, some of its contents spill into the surrounding tissue and eventually enter the bloodstream. These include the enzymes creatine phosphokinase (CPK), lactic dehydrogenase (LDH), and serum glutamic oxalo-acetic transaminase (SGOT). Theoretically, we can tell how much of the heart has been damaged by how much of these substances appear in the blood. But since they are also present in other parts of the body—CPK in skeletal muscles and in the brain, LDH in liver, lung, and red blood cells, and SGOT in liver cells—we must look for subtypes of these substances, or isoenzymes. For example, the isoenzymes of CPK are designated BB for brain, MM for skeletal muscle, and MB for heart muscle. There is a certain amount of CPK in the blood at any time from the usual wear and tear of life, but no more than 2 percent should be CPK-MB. We know a heart attack has occurred if, after about six hours, the total amount of CPK goes up, and the proportion of CPK-MB rises. Such measurements are added to clinical observations and the electrocardiographic data. To use the Chinese menu school of cardiology, one from Column A, one from Column B, and one from Column C equal a heart attack.

In Mrs. Falk's case, the EKG went back to normal after the prolonged episode, but the enzymes indicated infarction. It wasn't a full heart attack, not yet at least, but it wasn't far from one. This is an intermediate coronary syndrome that Michael D. Klein, director of the CCU at Boston University Medical Center, calls "infarction in progress." How long can it go on? Weeks. The popularly held concept of a heart attack as an abrupt event is not always accurate.

Since Mrs. Falk was completely inactive, her heart's demand for oxygen was constant. Therefore, the change in her condition must have been the result of a change on the supply side. In other words, something about the plaque in her arteries had changed for the worse. Perhaps bleeding or oozing had swelled the blockage, or maybe a blood clot or a piece of atherosclerotic debris had showered downstream like a cluster bomb, cutting off small twiglike arteries and causing tiny heart attacks that were nibbling away at the muscle. A more likely possibility was a spasmodic opening and closing of the coronary vessel near the obstruction. This condition, first described by Myron Prinzmetal in the 1950s, results in an intermittent supply of blood that is often inadequate to sustain heart cells.

Whatever was causing Mrs. Falk's attacks, it was clear that

the drugs she was taking weren't effective. Here she was, already pale and groggy from the highest doses of medicines that we could give, barely lifting a finger and still having heart pain. What makes patients like Mrs. Falk especially hard to treat is that you have to be so careful explaining to them their condition. If they can have an attack just lying there, there is no telling what damage bad news from their doctor might cause. All you can do is watch the monitors in the CCU and break it to them gently and gradually. That is what I tried to do with Mrs. Falk. "Frankly, you're on enough medicine. I don't think we're going to get anywhere by pushing the doses higher, and I don't imagine you want to stay hooked up to that IV," I said to her when I stopped by to see her during her fourth day in the Unit. "Fortunately, we have a machine that can help."

Then I proceeded to tell her about the intra-aortic balloon pump. The balloon itself is a long, narrow plastic tube that is inserted into an artery in the groin like a catheter and slid up into the aorta near the heart. Timed to inflate between heartbeats, it pushes the blood in the aorta backward into the coronary arteries and forward to the rest of the body. Then it deflates as the heart contracts, clearing the way for the blood flowing out of the left ventricle. (In fact, the suction action as the balloon deflates tends to pull the blood out of the heart.) Thus, the balloon decreases the work of the heart. Some believe it also increases blood flow through the coronary arteries. In any event, it improves the balance of oxygen supply and demand.

Unfortunately, the pump part of the balloon is a Maytag-sized contraption that sits at the foot of a patient's bed, thumping away as it tracks the cardiac cycles. The balloon doesn't hurt once it is in place, but the pump is a big, noisy, and somewhat disturbing presence, and we often have to sedate patients quite heavily when we put them on it so they won't move around and tear the groin artery. Sometimes, to remind them to keep still, we loosely tie an ankle to the bed frame. Clearly, this is not something patients want to endure for any length of time. Not that they have much choice. The balloon, like any foreign object in the body, can generate dangerous blood clots, and it can also damage the aorta. Because of this, the record stay on a balloon is seventy-two days.

Mrs. Falk was reluctant, but not because of the inconvenience and risk. Her reaction puzzled me until I remembered that, in one of our first conversations, she had referred to her angina as being like "little menstrual period pains that come and go." It now seemed a very revealing comparison. Her symptom had become associated with her lost menses and youth, and she was determined not to give it up a second time. "I think you're feeling older than you really are," I told her. "You really do have a lot to live for." It may not have been the most insightful pep talk, but I kept it up until it worked, and she agreed to be hooked up to the balloon.

Two days later, still strapped to the contraption, Mrs. Falk was wheeled into the cath lab, where Rentrop confirmed my fears. Her right coronary artery was almost completely blocked —98 percent—near its origin, with diffuse atherosclerosis downstream. Her left main coronary artery was clear, but both the circumflex and anterior descending branches had major obstructions, 80 and 90 percent respectively. The angiogram also showed an area of sluggishly moving muscle at the tip of the ventricle, but, all things considered, Mrs. Falk still had a reasonably healthy heart. Had the configuration of the blockages been less complicated, we might have considered angioplasty, a newly developed procedure in which an inflatable catheter is slid into the mouth of the coronary artery and through the obstructed segment, then expanded to press the plaque against the wall of the artery, opening up the vessel. The technique, a relative picnic compared to the trauma of surgery, is largely limited to straightforward cases of coronary disease involving an evenly developed blockage near the beginning of a major artery. Even so, angioplasty can trigger coronary spasm, cause a dangerous shower of atherosclerotic fallout into the tiny coronary vessels down-stream, or tear the arterial wall. About 6 percent of the 17,000 or so patients undergoing angioplasties each year end up being rushed to the operating room, and such emergency bypasses are considerably riskier than nonemergency procedures. (For more on angioplasty, see Chapter 13.) In Mrs. Falk's case, though, the complex, multivessel pattern of atherosclerotic disease and her tenuous state made coronary bypass surgery the first and only choice.

"You're in danger of having a major heart attack," I told her, before explaining the ins and outs of bypass surgery, "but I'm optimistic an operation can prevent it, relieve your pain, and get you back on your feet. There's a sizable risk, but it's not as great as the risk you seem to face without it."

Having spent several days on the balloon pump, Mrs. Falk readily agreed.

In retrospect, I now see that Mrs. Falk's bypass was a fore-gone conclusion. Although unstable angina can sometimes be quieted with drugs, many patients eventually come under a sur-geon's scalpel. It is really a question of time—and how much of it drugs can buy—before bypass surgery.

6

Should You or Shouldn't You?
The Bypass Dilemma

BEFORE THERE WAS BYPASS surgery, the options for treating patients with the cardinal symptom of coronary heart disease, angina pectoris, were few. There was nitroglycerin, which the afflicted had been taking under their tongues for more than a century. Doctors also ordered their patients to take it easy. And sometimes they even prescribed a move to Arizona or Florida to escape the cold, which makes the chest pain worse. Before there was a Sunbelt, there was an angina belt.

What happened to these coronary victims, though usually not a pleasant story, has at least provided us with a sense of the natural course of the disease and a yardstick against which modern treatments can be measured. After years of scrupulous record keeping, cardiologists figured that one out of every six male patients with chest pain died by the end of four years. On the other hand, 14 percent of the time for men and 19 percent for women, pain that had been occurring for at least two years simply went away, all by itself. (Of course, until the 1960s there was no way of knowing whether such pain was due to coronary disease or some other cause.) Of patients that survived heart attacks, prima facie evidence for the presence of a coronary blockage, nearly one in five was dead after four years. And although the incidence of coronary atherosclerosis was lower for women, the disease carried a higher mortality rate.

Only with the development of modern diagnostic techniques did clinicians come to appreciate the complexity of coronary disease. There are three major arteries that serve the heart. Any of them can be blocked at any point along its path—the combinations are infinite. What's more, the impact of a blockage can range from a slight ripple in the flow of blood to a total shutoff. Take two patients with comparable lesions, and one can feel fine while the other suffers. Sometimes the pain never surfaces, while in other cases it culminates in a crushing heart attack. And then there are those who simply, and suddenly, drop dead.

In general, the more vessels blocked, the more heart muscle jeopardized, the worse the outlook. Patients with an obstruction in just one artery have a better than 90 percent chance of surviving five years even if they receive no treatment. With three vessels obstructed, however, the chance an untreated patient won't survive a decade approaches 50 percent. Without doubt, the worst single spot to have a blockage is in that portion of the left coronary artery before it divides in two, while it is still the Alaska pipeline of the heart's fuel supply. A clot here can threaten a massive amount of heart muscle, often with fatal results. (Blockages in both of the left main's tributaries are not as dangerous as a single one in the main trunk, since both are unlikely to shut off the blood supply at the same time.) Overall, fewer than 10 percent of patients with cardiac pain have left-main time bombs ticking in their chests, but for them the prognosis is bleak. If untreated, about half will be dead in five years. The ten-year mortality approaches 100 percent for especially difficult left-main cases, twice the rate for patients with triple-vessel disease.

These discouraging figures gave cardiac surgeons a powerful incentive to intervene, but there was a long tradition standing in their way. From the days of Hippocrates, the first surgeon, until the turn of this century, the heart, seat of life, was forbidden territory. "Surgery of the heart has probably reached the limits set by Nature," was the way Stephen Paget, the great British surgeon, put it in 1896. "No new method and no new discovery can overcome the natural difficulties that attend a wound of the heart." That same year, however, Dr. Ludwig Rehn, the German pioneer, described the first successful suture of a heart laceration. A decade or so later, Rehn had improved his technique and reported a survival rate of 40 percent in 124 cases. The era of cardiac surgery had belatedly begun.

Surgeons were soon honing their new craft on the battlefields of World War I. In 1923, Elliot Cutler, a professor of surgery at Harvard Medical School, operated on an eleven-year-old girl whose mitral valve had been damaged by rheumatic fever and gave her four and a half more years of life. When his next half dozen patients died, Cutler abandoned his efforts. Fifteen years later, another Boston surgeon, Robert Gross, successfully repaired a congenital defect in a seven-and-a-half-year-old girl, renewing interest in the field. Another World War intervened, and Dwight Harken pushed the frontier of cardiac surgery forward, removing shell fragments from deep inside the hearts of wounded soldiers.

In peacetime, surgeons opened another front in the battle against cardiac disease—improving the supply of blood to the heart muscle. In the United States, Claude Beck, and in England, Laurence O'Shaughnessy, sewed tissues from the neighboring pericardium and chest wall muscles to the surface of the heart in an effort to get blood to flow from one to the other. It was a more sophisticated approach than previous efforts, in which asbestos or talc was applied to the heart or its surface was scraped in hopes the irritation would stimulate the growth of new vessels. But perhaps the best that could be said for all these procedures was that patients generally survived. Meanwhile, the death toll from coronary disease continued to rise.

In the mid-1950s, Robert P. Glover, a surgeon at Philadelphia's Episcopal Hospital, turned his attention to the internal mammary artery, a vessel that runs along the chest wall and infuses the pericardium, which he believed could be used to improve the heart's blood supply. Tying a knot around the artery's lower end, he theorized, would increase pressure in the vessel and cause blood to back up, forcing some of it into the muscle of the heart. Thus, with a relatively simple, almost risk-free procedure—the artery could be reached with a shallow incision that required only a local anesthetic—Glover and his followers claimed angina pectoris could be relieved 90 percent of the time and eliminated entirely in almost half their patients.

A few years later, skeptics compared a group of patients undergoing the Glover procedure with another group which, unbeknownst to them, was given a sham operation in which small chest incisions were made but the mammary arteries were left undisturbed. The relief rates for both groups were identical—about 35 to 40 percent. One patient treated with the fake surgery told researchers he felt fine, only to die the very next day. Needless to say, the questionable ethics of placebo surgery make studies like this a rarity in medical literature.

Incidentally, that 35 percent placebo rate also applied to a variety of other medical treatments pressed into service in the fight against the coronary epidemic, including drugs that dilated blood vessels, tranquilizers, X rays, heart-muscle extracts, hormones, blood thinners, vitamins—even cobra venom. Placebos are safe and cheap and have been used effectively, if deceptively, for hundreds of years. But their benefits are almost always short-lived, a fact that led Armand Trousseau, the nineteenth-century French physician, to recommend that "you should treat as many patients as possible with the new drugs as long as they still have the power to heal."

No sooner was the Glover procedure unmasked than Arthur

Vineberg, a Montreal surgeon, proposed implanting the same mammary artery directly into the heart muscle like a garden hose in soft earth, theorizing that it would sprout new coronary branches. The reaction of the medical community again was skeptical, but Vineberg somehow found more than a hundred willing patients. In 1962, F. Mason Sones, Jr., the father of coronary angiography, tested a Vineberg veteran and to nearly everyone's surprise discovered that the procedure had in fact increased the supply of blood through the development of collateral vessels (although, apart from the placebo effect, it usually failed to relieve angina).

The pioneers of coronary surgery, of course, were forced to work on a moving target—the beating heart. It could not be interfered with for very long; six or seven minutes without blood flow and the patient's brain would die. In 1931, a Philadelphia surgeon named John H. Gibbon, Jr., had set out to find a way around the problem—a machine that could temporarily take over for the heart and the lungs and pump oxygen-rich blood throughout the body. The idea wasn't new. The first pump had been patented more than fifty years before, but perfecting it proved exceedingly difficult. It had to be of a design that wouldn't damage the fragile red cells and made of materials that wouldn't cause the blood to clot. And to take the place of the lungs, the machine had to duplicate the miraculous exchange of carbon dioxide for oxygen. Within a few years, Gibbon had built a model that could keep a cat alive for nearly four hours, but it was not until 1953 that his new device was successfully used on a human being—an eighteen-year-old woman whose heart was stopped for twenty-seven minutes, time enough for a surgical team to repair a congenital defect in the atrial wall.

One medical historian compared Gibbon's accomplishment to the development of the phonetic alphabet, the invention of the telephone, even the creation of a symphony by Mozart, but many of his fellow surgeons were less enthusiastic and explored other approaches. Some tried lowering the body temperature, which reduced the need for oxygenated blood from the heart. A more novel technique, cross-circulation, involved linking a patient's circulatory system to that of one of his parents or siblings. Thus, one heart would beat for two. Skeptics warned that the operation would be the first with a 200 percent mortality rate, but more than half the patients who underwent the procedure—and all of the donors—survived.

Eventually his colleagues became convinced that Gibbon was on the right track and set out to improve on the technology of extracorporeal circulation. One problem with the early pumps was their reliance on a system that bubbled oxygen through the blood. The process was not nearly as efficient as that which takes place in the lungs, and the bubbles, if allowed to enter a patient's bloodstream, could be lethal. Mechanical oxygenators using perforated disks to spin the gas through the blood were an improvement. Modern pumps, which rely on membrane oxygenators that work on the natural principle of osmosis, are better still. And on the way are centrifugal pumps, which are much more gentle, reducing trauma to the blood's cells.

Like anesthesia, cardiopulmonary bypass machines bought time, although the devices available in 1967 could only sustain patients for an hour or so before damage to various organs began. That was long enough, however, for René G. Favaloro, a surgeon at the Cleveland Clinic, to usher in the era of coronary artery bypass graft surgery. At that time, surgeons were unroofing the coronary arteries, stripping out the plaque, and repairing the vessels with pieces of the patients' own veins, but the results left much to be desired. Instead of simply patching the arteries, Favaloro believed a tubular section of saphenous vein, a spare vessel removed from the patient's leg, could be used to "jump" over a coronary blockage, the same way other surgeons at Cleveland had been detouring around obstructions in the kidney arteries. The technique worked, but only in cases where the position of the blockage allowed room on either side for a graft to be connected. It didn't take long for Favaloro to come up with a crucial modification: Instead of jumping over the blockages, he began *bypassing* them, attaching one end of the vein graft to the aorta, the main passageway from the heart, and the other to the diseased coronary artery beyond the atherosclerotic narrowing.

Ask Favaloro how it feels to have developed what is now the most common major operation performed in the United States, and he will start by telling you about Alexis Carrel. In 1894, Carrel was a young intern in France when Sadi Carnot, the President of the Republic, was stabbed by an Italian anarchist. The blade slashed a large blood vessel in Carnot's abdomen, and although surgeons could repair the skin and muscles, they were virtually helpless when it came to injured veins and arteries. Carnot died, and a frustrated Carrel decided to devote his life to the infant specialty of vascular surgery. He made his own needles and sutures, and borrowed techniques from an embroideress. In little more than a decade, he had not only learned how to repair ripped vessels but could also sew artery to artery, vein to vein, or vein to artery, and he could make these connections side to side, end to end, or end to side. Sixteen years after Carnot's death, he actually performed coronary bypass surgery on a dog, connecting the descending aorta to the left coronary branch. (When the dog died, Carrel blamed himself for taking too much time sewing—five minutes, about the time it takes an experienced bypass surgeon to make a similar connection today.) Indeed, before winning the Nobel Prize in 1912, he had even transplanted canine kidneys and, yes, a heart.

But Carrel was an experimenter, and it took clinicians several generations to take his discoveries from the bench to the bedside. In the coffee shop of the New York Hilton on a stopover between lectures, Favaloro, a massive man who does his operating these days in Buenos Aires, where he is head of the Institute of Cardiology and Cardiovascular Surgery at the Guemes Hospital and professor at El Salvador University School of Medicine, picked up the story.

"When I started at Cleveland in 1962, I used to spend a tremendous amount of time in the cardiac catheterization laboratory, where Mason Sones must have had 15,000 films already. I looked at the movies, and I realized there were two kinds of patients: one with diffuse disease and one with localized obstruction. So we used the Vineberg procedure for the diffuse disease and the patch-repair technique for the localized obstruction. The patch technique was good for the right coronary artery but was a total disaster for the left. I did everything you can imagine— even cooled down the heart—but even with all kinds of variations, in a patient with left-main obstruction, there was so much ischemia that 15 or 20 minutes of total occlusion was too long. The operation was beautiful, but the patient didn't recuperate.

"In May I performed the first [bypass] operation on a 51-year-old patient—I can't remember his name. I did a bypass to the right coronary artery. There were no problems at all.

"The first double bypass was in March 1968, and we repeated it in December. By then, we had done 171 operations. Mason [Sones] was always holding me back. He questioned how long the grafts would last, whether they would be vulnerable to thrombosis. I kept pushing—it was more than my Latin temperament. When we reviewed the mortality of the patients on the waiting list, it was higher than the operative mortality. We were behind about three months.

"I went to Houston that year to show the films of my first cases. All [Denton] Cooley said was, 'You have something there. Keep up the good work.' He wasn't impressed. [Favaloro would later discover to his amazement that the first bypass had in fact been improvised in 1964—but not reported until 1973—in Houston by H. "Edward" Garrett, a member of Michael DeBakey's surgical team, when a vein patch operation went sour and the vessel fell apart. And of the nearly 900 papers attributed to Cooley today, several dozen are about bypass.]

"The next year, at the Sixth World Congress of Cardiology in London, they made the mistake of scheduling the discussion on coronary bypass surgery in a small room. Well, one hour before it started the place was jammed. There were people on the floor, everywhere. They closed the door, and the doctors were shouting and screaming outside, like at a football field in Argentina. They pushed so hard they broke the door down.

"Charlie Friedberg said it was difficult for him to accept that the operation could be done with a low mortality. But I said, 'The doors of the Cleveland Clinic are open. Anyone can come and see it.' And in 1969, I had about 500 visitors at Cleveland to see the work. Patients were coming from all over the country, too. Cleveland was the Mecca."

Whether bypass surgery was an accident whose time had come—as in Houston—or an idea that changed the face of coronary care—as in Cleveland—Favaloro and others were soon able to perform the procedure with relatively little immediate risk. Patients at some other hospitals, however, ran more than a 10 percent chance of dying on the table, and in the early days heart attacks during and after bypass surgery were not uncommon. At some institutions, the risk was far worse. In 1976, *The Boston Globe* reported that half the patients undergoing certain types of cardiac surgery including coronary bypass at the Malden Hospital in Massachusetts since 1969 had failed to survive. That was five to ten times the mortality rates of other Boston-area hospitals at that time. Surgeons at the 280-bed facility averaged eleven open-heart operations a year despite a recommendation by the American College of Cardiology that hospitals performing such surgery have an annual caseload of 200 to 300. The importance of choosing a hospital carefully was underscored again in 1980, when cardiologists at the University of California at Davis reported a bypass mortality rate of 17 percent at a time when most major medical centers had their rates down to 1 percent. The result was seventy-three malpractice suits and a $500 million class-action suit alleging fraud.

If the risk at most hospitals was low, surgeons insisted the payout from their handiwork was high. They claimed their procedure was able to relieve the often incapacitating chest pain far more effectively than the medicines then available. One study of five hundred bypass patients at the Baylor College of Medicine, where DeBakey held sway, indicated that after five years 51 percent were completely free of pain and 42 percent were improved, while only 7 percent were unchanged or worse. After ten years, the figures were 48 percent, 41 percent, and 11 percent, respectively. By 1972, nearly three dozen articles had been published in medical journals implying that patients undergoing bypass surgery also lived longer than those treated medically. The five-year survival rates for a thousand males with single- and double-vessel disease operated on by the Baylor team were 90 to 95 percent, depending on the health of the heart muscle, and about 5 percentage points less for those with three blocked arteries. A study at the Cleveland Clinic reported a five-year survival rate of 88 percent for patients with blockages in their left-main arteries, vastly better than would have been expected with medical therapy despite a higher surgical mortality rate for these cases than other patterns of disease.

Even critics of bypass surgery—and there were many—didn't contest its pain-relieving power. But the claims that it could prolong life were based mainly on historical comparisons with the dismal experiences of patients living out their lives in the angina belt. While the surgeons were busy operating, beta blockers were coming on the market, offering for the first time an effective alternative to the blade.

In *The Annals of Thoracic Surgery* in 1972, Thomas C. Chalmers, then of the National Institutes of Health and later president of Mount Sinai Medical Center and dean of its medical school, noted that the case for bypass was made largely with studies that were, "by their very nature, more likely to be enthusiastic than negative in their conclusions. Physicians and surgeons are not likely to report new and dramatic therapies when they have resulted in disaster for the first few patients."

The only way to settle the issue, according to Chalmers and many others, was with a randomized trial from which patients with varieties of coronary artery disease already known to do best with either medical or surgical treatment would be excluded. This would let researchers concentrate only on those in the gray zone, who would be assigned by chance to either medical treatment or surgery.

Randomized trials aren't perfect. For one thing, it's hard to be sure all variables are equally distributed. Some also believe randomized studies tend to favor medical treatment, just as nonrandomized studies are biased to favor surgery. Their reason has to do with the concept of "operability": Some blockages are easier to fix with bypass than others, and some patients are healthier than others. As it happens, the people who are likely to do well with surgery are also the ones with the best prognosis with medicines. In nonrandomized studies, as in everyday medical practice, patients selected for surgery are generally more "operable" than those picked for medicine, thus tend to do better. But in randomized studies, a patient a surgeon rates as only a "maybe" might arbitrarily be sent to the operating room. Thus, less-operable patients can be assigned surgery and more-operable patients given medical therapy, skewing the results.

In medicine, however, there is always room for a second opinion. In this case, there are those who feel that sicker patients are syphoned off to surgery by worried physicians who refuse to allow them in randomized trials. Several medical centers, including the Oregon, Montreal, and Texas heart institutes, launched randomized studies of their own, only to run into this "referral bias." Partly as a result, their samples were so small that tiny statistical differences told more about the local surgical talent than anything else.

If ever there was a health care organization equipped to deal with these problems, it was the Veterans Administration, with its large supply of patients unlikely to look elsewhere for treatment. Between 1970 and 1974, thirteen VA hospitals randomly sent to surgery or assigned to medical care 686 men, all of whom had angina and obstructions of one or more coronary arteries. The surgical patients reported a 60 percent improvement in anginal pain, compared with a mere 7 percent reduction in symptoms for medically treated patients, but the seven-year survival rate for the bypass patients was 77 percent, scarcely better than the 70 percent achieved by the medical group.

Surgeons were quick to criticize the VA's relatively high operative mortality rate of nearly 6 percent. If several of the hospitals with especially bad figures had been erased from the study, they asserted, the surgical survival rate would have been far higher. But doctors on the other side noted that 12 percent of the VA patients had blockages in their left-main arteries, a condition that was even then believed to respond better to surgery. When the left-main medical patients were excluded, the edge in survival with bypass surgery evaporated. There were also questions about the consistency of care from hospital to hospital. At the VA center in Hines, Illinois, for example, surgically treated patients had survival rates similar to those at the other institutions, but the rate for medically treated patients was significantly lower. And how representative was the VA's patient population, with its high percentage of "arteriopaths," as one prominent cardiologist labeled its cigarette smokers and alcoholics? At the very least, one might suspect there would be problems getting some patients to take their medicines, which can be difficult even under normal circumstances. When the argument died down, all the VA study seemed to prove was that medical statistics can be just as slippery as any other kind, if not more so.

As the VA trial was winding down, a dozen European countries were gearing up their own bypass study with a pool of 768 males, each with at least 50 percent blockages of two or more vessels and angina for three months or longer. Bypass was shown to be as effective in relieving symptoms as it was in the VA trial. Compared to medical therapy, surgery also seemed to lengthen the lives of patients with triple-vessel disease, but not those with single- or double-vessel blockages.

This time, surgeons complained that patients in the European study suffered an unexpectedly large number of heart attacks while in the operating room and had more blockages of the left anterior descending artery, sometimes known as the widow-maker because it serves a huge amount of the heart. But perhaps the biggest objection to the European study was the large number of "crossovers." Some patients had heart attacks and other coronary events before their scheduled surgery; those who died were regarded as "surgical" deaths even though they never got to the operating room. Crossover works both ways, and there were also patients initially assigned to medical therapy who later needed surgery, died after it, and were counted as medical deaths.

Riding headlong into the midst of this confusion came an American cavalry drafted by the National Heart, Lung, and Blood Institute that included not only federal bureaucrats but also surgeons and cardiologists. The Who's Who of medical centers participating in the Coronary Artery Surgery Study included the University of Alabama in Birmingham, Albany Medical College, Boston University Medical Center, Loma Linda (California) University School of Medicine, Marshfield (Wisconsin) Medical Foundation, Massachusetts General Hospital, Mayo Clinic, Miami Heart Institute, Institut de Cardiologie de Montreal, New York University Medical Center, St. Louis University School of Medicine, St. Luke's–Roosevelt Hospital Center in New York, Stanford University Medical Center, the Medical College of Wisconsin, and Yale University School of Medicine. Each carefully monitored all potential bypass patients from 1974 to 1979. To be included in the study, patients had to have mild to moderate angina or have suffered a heart attack that left them with no residual symptoms, have a passably strong heart muscle and operable vessels with at least one 70 percent blockage. It was conceded that surgery was better for patients with blocked left-main arteries or severe angina, so these patients were excluded. In the end, there were 780 patients assigned to either medical or surgical care. By compiling a registry including 1,319 patients who could have been randomized but for one reason or another weren't and more than 20,000 patients who didn't qualify for the study, researchers were able to double-check their findings in a way those who conducted the other studies were not.

How do you persuade a heart patient to let a coin toss decide his treatment? I put that question to Thomas J. Ryan, chief of cardiology at Boston University and a member of the study's steering committee, who in 1984 became president of the American Heart Association. His answer: Not very easily. Ryan describes himself as "nothing more or less than a New York Irishman who fell upon Jesuit training" but appears a quintessential Brahmin, with graying temples and a deep, resonant voice capable of reassuring the desperate. In any event, he is the kind of physician who commands instant respect. Even so, he recalled that many of the more educated Bostonians "came in hard charging and eager for surgery" before he had a chance to present the alternatives. It showed how far heart surgery had come since 1955, when Albert Einstein, the century's premier scientific mind, suffered a ruptured aortic aneurysm but rejected Michael DeBakey's advice to have an operation and died.

Once enrolled in the study, the patients were followed for five years. "We were seeing them every six months, so they became a cadre of patients that we were very close to," Ryan said.

"There was a special appointments secretary calling them, and if there was a little personal problem she worked out the kinks. Parking, things like that. The participants received treatment that they hadn't received before in the medical system."

When it was done, the ten-year effort confirmed what the VA and European trials had concluded about surgery and pain: Bypass relieved angina 70 to 85 percent of the time. In contrast, only 25 percent of the triple-vessel patients treated with drugs became pain free. Survival rates, on the other hand, were virtually identical after five years: 92 percent for surgical patients, 90 percent for medical patients—a statistically insignificant difference. For those with normal heart muscles, the surgical and medical five-year-survival rates were both 95 percent; with impaired pumps, the surgical patients had a slight but inconsequential edge. The only patients in the study—and remember that those with left-main blockages and severe or unstable angina were excluded—for whom surgery seemed to prolong life were those with both triple-vessel disease and abnormal heart muscles.

For others, the closeness of the surgical and medical survival rates suggests that there is little to lose in trying a medical approach first. "We were really testing two strategies," said Michael B. Mock of the National Institutes of Health. "You go to immediate surgery, or you have medicine as long as your symptoms are controlled." Medications might buy a patient time, delaying the first bypass operation and possibly eliminating the need for an encore. Second go-arounds, which are increasingly common, are much more dangerous.

But there is a limit to this delaying tactic: Each year nearly 5 percent of the patients in the medical group of the Coronary Artery Surgery Study have required surgery. If that rate holds, about half the entire medical group will join the surgical brigade within a decade.

Big as the federally funded study was, it wasn't big enough to satisfy everybody. Critics, including Favaloro and J. Willis

Hurst, the chief of medicine at Emory University in Atlanta, are troubled by the fact that the study ended up enlisting only a third of those patients who fit its criteria. Did some referral bias slip through? And even if the study had snared them all, how representative would these patients have been of the total coronary population? The 780 randomized patients, according to Hurst, fit into categories that represent "only a small percent of the people who are being operated on, perhaps 6 to 8 percent." He and others fear the results from this narrow spectrum of cases will be applied too broadly. Moreover, the survival rates of the medically treated patients, which were considerably better than those in the VA and European trials, may have been unrealistically high, Hurst says, because the randomized patients constituted "a subset already known to be good survival risks." "The people who designed the study knew good risk from poor risk," he argues, "and so they picked them out carefully."

Hurst edited one of the two standard cardiology textbooks. The other is the work of Eugene Braunwald, chairman of the department of medicine at Harvard, who ringingly endorsed the Coronary Artery Surgery Study before more than ten thousand heart specialists at the 56th Annual Scientific Sessions of the American Heart Association in Anaheim, California, in November 1983:

> Will the frequency of the procedure continue to increase? Probably not. . . . I suggest that after 15 years of increasing enthusiasm for CABG, if appropriate education of health professionals and the public concerning this procedure is carried out, the pendulum will swing back to a more appropriate equilibrium. I believe that this operation should and increasingly will be restricted to patients in whom intensive medical therapy has failed or in whom improved survival after surgery has been unambiguously demonstrated, rather than as a panacea for coronary artery disease.

In medicine, as in everything else, time marches on. Surgical techniques improve, but medical therapy does also. In a way, any study becomes invalid the minute it is completed. While the Coronary Artery Surgery Study was under way, operative mortality dropped from 5.6 to 1.4 percent, but medical mortality fell from 3.9 to 1.7 percent a year. Surgeons are also sewing in more bypass grafts these days than they used to—the average is up to 2.7 per heart—which may further increase survival rates, and there are drugs to help keep those grafts unclogged that weren't widely used when the study was carried out. Similarly, the medical patients in the study weren't getting the latest heart drugs —calcium blockers—which might further prolong their lives. Indeed, coronary bypass surgery, once considered a radical treatment, is now being challenged by newer and less invasive techniques such as angioplasty, in which arteries are unblocked without opening the chest.

Part of the problem in evaluating the use—or abuse—of bypass surgery is its mystique. In primitive cultures, surgery often had more to do with ritual than with health. To some critics, there was also an element of ritual in the national enthusiasm for bypass, as if the telltale scar running down the front of the chest were a medical status symbol rather than the stigma of disease. It would not have been the first time patients had flocked to a treatment that had attained great social significance despite uncertain clinical value. In the 1950s, surgeons were performing on the order of 50,000 tonsillectomies annually. In some wealthy communities, 20 to 30 percent of all children underwent what was later called unnecessary surgery. Today, it is relatively rare.

Even among procedures of accepted merit, researchers have found startling differences in frequency. A recent Massachusetts study, for example, indicated that Holyoke residents had gallbladder operations at only one fourth the rate of residents of Hingham, that people who lived in Dedham had their prostate glands removed less than half as often as those living in Brookline, and that, in sixteen communities examined, the rate of Caesarian sections varied from 22 to 48 percent. In some cases, access to health care varied widely. But, according to John E. Wennberg of Dartmouth Medical School, a consultant to the study, it also showed "the intellectual confusion and chaos that sits at the root of much medical practice. Most people assume there is much more science in medicine than there is."

"I don't think it's the case that surgeons have been out plying their trade needlessly on a helpless population," says Ryan of the bypass backlash. "I don't think the layman has to feel exploited. The surgeons took an operation that initially had a 5 percent mortality rate and brought it down to 1 percent, and they did it quickly. It's not that the surgery has failed us in any way, it's that medical therapy is making people do just as well. If patients can cope with their symptoms and the medicines they're taking, we don't have to go around holding our breath that they may be at a higher risk of dying. That's a piece of information that was hard to get and extremely encouraging for those of us who are out there toiling in the fields of patient care."

Even before the results of the Coronary Artery Surgery Study were released, the press, which had been avidly chronicling the bypasses of the rich and famous, seemed to lose some of its enthusiasm. "There's absolutely no question that bypass surgery is successful for many patients," was the way Tom Jarriel, a correspondent for ABC News, introduced a segment on bypass surgery on the network's newsmagazine, *20/20*. "But we found serious questions about when it's necessary, and where it's done. In the enthusiasm over bypass surgery, it's easy for patients to overlook these questions, because they don't hear about the failures as much as they do about the noteworthy successes." And after the study, a headline in *The New York Times* asked, "Is Bypass Surgery Necessary?"

The answer is yes, but not for everyone. Coronary artery bypass surgery is a magnificent example of technological medicine, the culmination of a century of surgical advances. Like any medicine, though, it can be ineffective, or even dangerous, when prescribed for the wrong patients. There is no doubt that bypass surgery prolongs the lives of patients whose left main arteries are substantially blocked—like Thomas Finder—and of patients with at least 70 percent obstructions of all three arteries and mildly damaged heart muscles. They should certainly have surgery. (And, by the way, there are two reasons to wait for vessels to become 70 percent blocked rather than rush in when they are, say, 40 percent obstructed. The first is that smaller blockages don't reduce coronary blood flow. Remember, that's what coronary reserve is all about. Also, atherosclerosis progresses at a more rapid rate in bypassed vessels.)

For patients with other types of coronary blockages—even those with three diseased vessels and who still have normal hearts, a group often automatically referred for surgery—symptoms are the key. If angina is debilitating and cannot be tamed with drugs, bypass surgery has proved an effective way to relieve it. Indeed, for patients with paralyzing and uncontrollable pain, like Deborah Falk, there's simply no choice but to operate. Generally, others should try to delay surgery as long as they can. Sometimes, as in the case of Isaac Feinstein, a combination of medication and adaptation can forestall an operation for many years, if not forever.

If and when it does come time for bypass surgery, there are new data that can help doctors and patients more accurately weigh the risks and benefits. For example, although the overall surgical mortality rate was 1.6 percent, the 24,959-patient Coronary Artery Surgery Study registry indicates that the mortality was 5.2 percent for those over age sixty-five and 9.5 percent for those over seventy-five (the latter figure was more than the mortality over two years without surgery). Age itself, however, isn't to blame for the higher risk. It's the other health problems elderly people often have—diabetes, heart failure, or circulation problems elsewhere in the body. With a less than 0.5 percent operative death rate versus a lifetime of symptoms, young patients would seem much more likely to benefit from bypass surgery, except for that second-bypass problem. And since most vein grafts don't stay open more than ten years, a young patient can outgrow the benefits of his operation. In fact, nearly half relapse within five years of surgery.

The surgical mortality was also three times higher for females than males and relief of angina less impressive. For women, the mortality for single-vessel disease was 1.4 percent; with double-vessel disease, it was 2.4 percent; with triple-vessel disease, it was 2.8 percent; and it was 4.4 percent for those with left-main disease. With a severely damaged heart muscle, the surgical death rate soared to 6.7 percent.

In my view people with angina that is rapidly getting worse despite medications should have surgery without delay, if only because the emergency operation that many of these patients will eventually face can be much more risky than an elective procedure. Although a study has not yet been devised to identify them, I also believe there are anatomic patterns like left-main disease that do better with surgery in good hands. An example is the patient with total occlusions of two coronary arteries whose heart relies on a critically narrowed third vessel. Then there are cases that are too special to be easily incorporated into a formula. I once had a patient with triple-vessel disease but fairly well-controlled angina. Ordinarily, I would have been in no rush to send him to the operating room, but he happened to be in the merchant marine and was off at sea six months at a time. It seemed better to get his surgery over with and let him take his risk up front, rather than leave him to face distress an ocean away from help.

7

On the Altar of the Surgeon
A Triple Bypass, Moment by Moment

THOUGH MOST PEOPLE CONSIDER it open-heart surgery, the heart is never entered during a bypass operation. Its beat is stopped, however, which is one reason the procedure is among the most obtrusive affairs in medicine. It affects not just the heart but the entire vascular system—and vice versa. Before a patient is rolled into the operating room, we make sure we know everything about him, right down to a runny nose or a loose tooth. Every detail is pieced into a complicated mosaic of clinical information from which we can predict how a patient will—and won't —react to the surgeon's blade. This means patients must spend a day or two before an operation being poked, prodded, and grilled by what seems like an unending parade of specialists, for it is characteristic of medicine that cardiologists, anesthesiologists, hematologists, and surgeons have different interests, and usually don't trust those outside their field to look after them.

Like most patients, Walter Stein, a stocky, sixty-one-year-old salesman from Westchester, New York, wasn't aware of all this when he checked into Mount Sinai one sticky June afternoon. He was thinking of the sharp chest pain that had suddenly asserted itself after a decade of good health, of the heart attack he had been told he had suffered, and of the shortness of breath that had stalled his recovery, prevented his return to work, and brought his life to a standstill. Coronary artery bypass graft surgery, he hoped, would get it moving again.

Even before Mr. Stein lumbered into the ground-floor admitting office, suitcase in hand, Bruce P. Mindich, one of four cardiac surgeons on the Mount Sinai staff, had sent down printed orders outlining the series of preoperative tests Mr. Stein would undergo. They included an electrocardiogram, blood samples to determine kidney and liver function and cholesterol and mineral balance, a blood-cell count, and a urinalysis. Forward and sideways chest X rays were also taken, and four units of blood cross-matched to Mr. Stein's type were put aside in the hospital blood bank. After an admitting clerk recorded his vital statistics, Mr. Stein was deposited in a wheelchair for the subterranean trip through the medical center and up to a four-bed room on the third floor of the Housman Pavilion, overlooking Central Park.

Mr. Stein had just finished unpacking when a nurse arrived to fill him in on the ward routine and check his temperature (it was 97.9), blood pressure (144/78), pulse (72), respiration (18 breaths per minute), and weight (214 pounds, a figure from which the doses of medicine given during and after surgery would be calculated). Delving into his medical history, the nurse learned about Mr. Stein's recent heart attack and the shortness of breath that made it hard for him to walk up even a few stairs. She also learned he was allergic to dogs, cats, and pollen, and lately had been constipated.

One of the next visitors was a scrub-suited resident, a short young man with dark hair and a mustache to whom Mr. Stein recounted more details of his heart attack and the subsequent coronary angiogram performed at a hospital near his home. Although the angiogram revealed blockages of his coronary arteries, Mr. Stein had not suffered the classic symptom—angina pectoris—that usually accompanies them. Apart from a brief episode of chest pain in 1971, the rest of his medical history, which included the repair of a detached retina in 1941 and the removal of a rectal polyp in 1965, was unremarkable, at least to the resident. Mr. Stein told the young physician that he was a "social drinker" and a reformed three-pack-a-day smoker who had gone cold turkey immediately after his heart attack. The resident asked whether Mr. Stein had ever had allergic reactions to anesthetics, a tendency to bleed, or ailments of the kidneys or lungs, all of which would have had a bearing on his candidacy for surgery. Mr. Stein said no. He also said he had not taken any aspirin for more than a week, as he had been instructed. Even a single pill can increase a patient's tendency to bleed. As Robert S. Litwak, the chief of cardiothoracic surgery at Mount Sinai, likes to put it, one aspirin is like one sperm.

The resident checked the results of Mr. Stein's admitting tests and, finding no abnormalities, recorded all he had learned on the patient's chart. He kept Mr. Stein on the standard combination of coronary medicines that his family doctor had prescribed—nifedipine, propranolol, and nitroglycerin—and added a sleeping pill and Valium to relieve any anxiety Mr. Stein may have been feeling in his new surroundings. He also put him on a low-sodium diet, prescribed a stool softener and milk of magnesia for his digestive difficulties and, as is usual in cardiac cases, cefazolin, an antibiotic. He ordered that Mr. Stein not be fed after midnight the following evening, the night before his operation, and that he should be scrubbed and shaved. With that, he left, to be followed immediately by Anthony Squire, a dark-haired, wiry junior cardiologist with a wry demeanor, who put Mr. Stein through his paces all over again. Then he walked down to my office to fill me in before I paid a call on our newest patient.

"I've seen your records," I told Mr. Stein when I entered his room an hour or so later, "and heard all about you from Dr.

Squire. But I'd like to go over it again, if you don't mind. I want to hear it in your words." I wanted to be sure that nothing was left out or garbled in the translation. So many factors can affect a patient's ability to withstand surgery, and the operating room is no place to learn about them. So for the fourth time that day, Mr. Stein found himself recounting his medical history.

The next morning, about the time Mr. Stein was brought his orange juice, corn flakes, and coffee, Squire and I met on the eighth floor of the Annenberg Building. There, in a large meeting room, about two dozen attending cardiologists and residents, cardboard coffee cups in hand, were gathered for the morning conference. We use these daily sessions to talk over cases and compare notes. There are old timers and young whippersnappers, conservative physicians and aggressive clinicians. Cardiologists never have a shortage of opinions.

While I sat in the audience, Squire walked up to the front of the room to present Mr. Stein's case. He was first up not because it was particularly complicated—it wasn't—but because the chest X ray, electrocardiogram, and angiogram were handy. "This sixty-one-year-old white male was free of symptoms until 1971," he began, "when, after moving his family from one house to another and lifting heavy packages all day, he had sharp chest pains in the evening. He was hospitalized for several days and told that he had a 'heart spasm'—we're not sure what that meant. Anyway, it was a short hospitalization of only two or three days, and it's not clear whether he suffered an ischemic event. He remained asymptomatic until the winter of 1983, when he began suffering exertional dyspnea when climbing stairs, which he attributed to the cigarettes he chain-smoked. After a particularly strenuous day lifting boxes while arranging a supermarket display, he noticed an achiness in his left arm and shoulder that extended to his chest. At first, he thought it was indigestion, but when antacids didn't help, he went to the local hospital emergency room. The cardiogram was unremarkable.

He was given medication—again, he's not certain what it was—and admitted to the coronary care unit, where he stayed for two days and was told that his blood enzymes were elevated. He was discharged from the hospital twelve days later without any symptoms or medications. A Holter monitor was subsequently obtained—we're not sure why—and on the basis of the findings he was told to return to the hospital for cardiac catheterization. He said he did not have any chest pains or palpitations but still suffered shortness of breath.

"The past medical history was noncontributory. The family history includes coronary disease in his father and a paternal uncle. Here's what I found on the physical exam: a rather obese man, appropriately anxious. The heart rate was 70 beats a minute, blood pressure 140/75 in both arms, sitting. He was breathing comfortably at 14 breaths a minute and afebrile. He had no skin lesions, and no lymph nodes were palpable. The head, eyes, ears, nose, and throat were remarkable only for arcus senilis. I heard no bruits over the carotid arteries. The thyroid gland did not seem enlarged. The chest showed increased expansion due to chronic lung disease, with soft wheezes and rhonchi. There was no venous distension, and the arterial pulse contour was normal. The precordial impulse was not displaced. The first and second heart sounds were normal. There was an S-4 gallop but no murmurs, click, or S-3. The abdomen was obese but otherwise benign. The extremities showed no cyanosis, clubbing, or edema. The peripheral pulses were intact. Neurological examination showed no abnormalities. Admission blood test results were normal, except for cholesterol, 262."

He then signaled for the chest X rays and electrocardiogram to be shown at the front of the room and continued his narration. "The films show a normal cardiomediastinal silhouette. The lung fields suggest chronic pulmonary disease. There is no evidence of congestive cardiac failure. The cardiogram shows no evidence of a transmural infarct. This is a subendocardial infarction by what we can judge now. We don't have the results of the Holter, but he reports that it showed abnormalities consistent with ambulatory ischemia."

Then Squire called for the angiograms, and the branchlike patterns of Mr. Stein's coronaries appeared on the screen. They showed 85 percent narrowing of his left main coronary artery just before the vessel divided into its two main branches, the left anterior descending and the left circumflex arteries, which were themselves blocked downstream. The LAD was 80 percent obstructed, and there seemed to be another 99 percent lesion of its first diagonal branch. My guess was that this blockage was what caused Mr. Stein's heart attack. The circumflex gave rise to a small second posterolateral branch, which was 90 percent occluded. But because these deposits were spread out along the narrow vessel lining, I wasn't sure whether the artery was "bypassable." The first posterolateral branch also had a 90 percent lesion near where it began, but looked like a good candidate for a graft. The other major vessel, the right coronary artery, had mild atherosclerosis, not enough to require surgical intervention. The motion picture of Mr. Stein's left ventricle showed a hint of weakness along part of the front wall.

"In summary," Squire went on, "we have a sixty-one-year-old man who has a history of cigarette smoking, is obese, sedentary, has a family history of coronary disease and elevated lipid levels. Physical exam shows no signs of cardiac failure. Chest X rays reflect lung disease, but this does not seem too severe. Angiography shows double-vessel disease in addition to a left-main lesion, with preserved ventricular function. We suspect recent subendocardial infarction involving the anterior wall related to disease in the diagonal branch of the LAD. Jon, do you have anything else to add?"

"Only that I'm bothered by lack of collaterals in this fellow," I said. In cases like this, where the blood supply to one side of the heart is reduced, nature often steps in to provide nourishment from the other side through auxiliary channels. Unfortunately, the film showed that none of these channels had developed in Mr. Stein's heart. "I agree, by the way, that his heart, rather than lungs, seems the cause of his shortness of breath."

There was some discussion about whether Mr. Stein's circumflex branch could receive a graft, but no real debate about what to do. Mr. Stein had the most compelling reason for bypass surgery—a major blockage in his left main artery. Statistically, his chances for survival were very bad without an operation. The films also showed that while a section of his left ventricle was beating sluggishly—that was the part damaged by his heart attack—the overall condition of the pumping chamber was good. That meant it would better withstand the stress of an operation.

After the meeting, I spotted Mindich walking toward me in the hall. "I saw Mr. Stein and reviewed his films," I told him. It's always a challenge for me to compress into a few moments with a busy heart surgeon the essence of a case, so I rely on cardiological shorthand. "He had a subendo last month, and his study showed an 85 percent left-main. There's also significant disease in the LAD and a good diagonal as well as tight lesions in the posterolaterals, but one is a small vessel and may not be do-able. There isn't much disease in the right, and the LV is good."

"When do you want him done?" Mindich replied.

"He's stable, ready to go. How about tomorrow?"

Later that day, I stopped by Mr. Stein's bedside. We chatted about some of the factors that may have contributed to his condition. High blood pressure was not a problem, and although Mr. Stein said he once had a positive urine test, diabetes didn't seem to be either. The same could not be said of Mr. Stein's long-standing obesity, which was aggravated by his sedentary life. I concluded my visit with a brief physical exam, which failed to turn up anything to alter the preoperative assessment. After reviewing the increasingly thick packet of reports in a blue loose-leaf binder bearing Mr. Stein's name, I added one more medicine to the regimen—an antithrombotic agent intended to help keep open the new vessels that would soon be sewn on his heart.

I was followed by a hematologist, who pricked Mr. Stein's forearm and determined that it took the normal amount of time to stop bleeding. He also took a sample of blood back to the lab for further tests of its coagulative ability. Then came an anesthesiologist, who noted Mr. Stein had some nasal congestion but no loose teeth, either of which could complicate matters in the OR. A nurse from the cardiac intensive care unit gave Mr. Stein a rundown on what to expect in the days after surgery, a session that helps to reduce postoperative anxiety. Then the chief surgical resident, a tall, dark-haired man with a stern, almost military bearing, reviewed Mr. Stein's chart to make sure all lights were still green. Before he left, he asked Mr. Stein to sign an "informed consent" form warning of "attendant discomforts and risks" and of "unforeseen conditions which might arise" during and after surgery. The form included a reminder that "no guarantees or assurances concerning the results of the procedure" had been made.

Among the last visitors that evening was an orderly who scrubbed Mr. Stein with Betadine, an antiseptic solution that turned his skin a sickly mustard hue, and shaved him from chin to toe. He was asleep a short time later, thanks to a "sleeping cocktail" of barbiturates.

Awakening at about 7 A.M., Mr. Stein learned he would be the second case of the day. He spent several hours alternately pacing the hall and reading a mystery novel, although when questioned a few days later he was at a loss to remember its title. A nurse gave him some Valium, packed his belongings, and sent them to the intensive care unit. Attendants arrived at about 10:30, tied a surgical cap on his head, and helped him onto a stretcher. They wheeled him to the basement, southeast along a busy corridor to Annenberg, into a stainless steel elevator

reserved for surgical patients and up to the suite of three cardiothoracic operating rooms on eight, where he was parked in the
hallway. He lay abandoned for more than an hour, drowsy but
conscious, while doctors and nurses, some of them the very
people who would soon be operating on him, passed back and
forth, barely giving him a glance. Scrubbed, shaved, stripped of
all worldly possessions, and swathed in surgical cotton, he
stared groggily at the ceiling, trying not to think and, thanks to
the drugs that were tightening their grip, succeeding.

Heart surgery usually conjures up images of gleaming amphi-
theaters with rows of seats filled by white-coated medical students. Operating Room Number 2, a twenty-by-twenty-foot
chamber with scuffed linoleum tile floors and battered steel cabi-
nets, testifies to the fact that it is now an everyday occurrence.
In fact, a bypass operation had ended in that same room moments before Mr. Stein was rolled into position outside its door.
Two nurses and an anesthesiologist were preparing for the
room's second case. The scrub nurse, a lean, angular, and intense young woman named Judy Harrow, had already lined up
endless rows of stainless steel clamps and forceps on carts that
would be wheeled into position alongside the operating table,
placing each instrument in its proper place much like a bartender
arranging a bar. The setup for heart surgery is medicine's most
extensive, but Harrow can finish it in half an hour flat. "I was
trained to hustle all the time," she says. "That way, when you
really have to, it's no big deal."
    Mr. Stein is fetched from the hall and wheeled in. The table on
which he lays is positioned over the pedestal in the middle of the
floor and raised into place, sparing the surgical team the formi-
dable task of lifting his chunky body. Electrodes are attached to
the back of his shoulders to monitor the electrical activity of his
heart, which will be displayed on a television hanging from the
ceiling and printed out next door in the monitoring room, where

the permanent surgical log is kept. "Will you give me your arm, please," the anesthesiologist gently asks through a heavy Greek accent, strapping on a standard-issue blood pressure cuff. Mr. Stein is composed and still. His eyes are closed. Soon, he is told, he will be given something to put him to sleep. A nurse records the time—12:10—in the surgical log. The operation has officially begun.

"You are going to feel a little pin prick," the anesthesiologist's assistant says, searching for a vein in the right arm through which the first intravenous needle is threaded. The line is connected to a bottle of sugar solution used mainly to keep open a fluid path deep within the patient's body. A few moments later, the anesthesiologist uses the hookup to administer a hypnotic solution of Valium and morphinelike Fentanyl. Mr. Stein becomes groggier.

"I'm going to paint your arm with a cold solution now, Mr. Stein," says the cardiothoracic resident. After applying more Betadine, he begins inserting another line into an artery at the left wrist. One end goes up the vessel, the other is attached to a plastic tube filled with a solution containing heparin, an anticoagulant, and leading to a transducer. This measures blood pressure, beat by beat, which is displayed as a wave on an overhead monitor and as a digital figure on an adjacent screen. The central venous pressure line is inserted at the bend in the left elbow and slid into the large vein near the heart to measure blood pressure and serve as the "ultimate IV," enabling the anesthesiologist to administer drugs almost directly into the heart on a moment's notice.

A black rubber mask is placed over Mr. Stein's face. "I want you to take some deep breaths," the anesthesiologist says. "This is just oxygen." It also contains nitrous oxide. "That's good," the anesthesiologist says comfortingly a moment later. "Everything is fine. Just take another deep breath, please. Very good. Now take another." He squeezes a black air bag, filling Mr. Stein's lungs. "Excellent, Mr. Stein," but Mr. Stein, of course, can't hear him. He is asleep.

The anesthesiologist, who had been so gentle while his patient was conscious, now pulls Mr. Stein's head back so that the blunt blade of the L-shaped laryngoscope can be placed down his throat. This straightens his airway, enabling the half-inch-wide endotracheal tube to be inserted past his vocal cords. A balloon on the lower end of the tube is inflated, securing it and creating an airtight seal. After pumping the air bag a few times and listening to Mr. Stein's chest with a stethoscope, he nods, indicating that the tube is in position. A smaller tube is placed in Mr. Stein's nose and inched down to his stomach to vent digestive fluids and gases. His eyes are taped shut to prevent them from drying out (anesthetized patients don't blink), and the tube is taped around his mouth. Once secure, it is used by the anesthesiologist to deliver more anesthesia, this time augmented by pancuronium, a muscle paralyzer.

"There is no neck here," he complains as he searches for a spot at which to tap Mr. Stein's jugular vein. It is indeed a difficult target, given the patient's position and portliness. The anesthesiologist backs off, and the surgical resident locates the vein, deftly inserting a catheter into the right side of the neck, then securing it with a few sutures. It is the sixth tube that has been inserted into the patient thus far—two in his left arm, one in the right, one in his neck, one in his mouth, and one in his nose. The seventh, a Foley catheter, is inserted through the penis into the bladder so that the urine can be collected in a calibrated bag. A temperature probe is inserted into the rectum. Mr. Stein's body, naked and prostrate, looks even colder in the 63 degree chill of the OR.

The surgical assistant begins painting the torso with still more Betadine and doesn't stop until he reaches the ankles. Mr. Stein is then draped in green cotton cloth, leaving exposed only the surgical fields—the left leg and the chest. More drapery is hung over the patient's head, obscuring it from everyone but the anesthesiologist, who is stationed at the head of the operating table.

The surgical resident traces the path of Mr. Stein's saphenous vein along the inside of his left leg with a black felt-tipped pen and, with his assistant, makes four diagonal incisions along the thigh and calf. Together, they work their fingers deep into the flesh, freeing the vessel from surrounding tissues and cauterizing bleeding tributaries with an electric surgical soldering iron called a Bovie. The smell of burned flesh fills the room. The assistant soon takes over the process, taking about an hour to remove a foot-long segment of the vein from the leg and tie off the ends of the remaining vessel. Lying in a stainless steel bowl, the vein resembles an elongated, translucent earthworm.

The resident moves to Mr. Stein's chest and with a curved blade begins a shallow incision from the base of the neck down the front of the chest using short strokes. A thin red line forms in the knife's wake. He slices deeper through an inch of rubbery yellow fat, using the Bovie to seal the tiny oozing vessels. They won't be missed, since this part of the chest has an abundant supply of blood.

Soon the breastbone, a gleaming white quarter-inch-thick plate, comes into view. Mindich, however, is not yet in sight. In fact, he is in a neighboring OR, hard at work on another bypass patient. But Mr. Stein is in experienced hands: The chief surgical resident himself is a veteran of six years of training as a general surgeon and another two years as a cardiothoracic specialist. He is passed a small surgical jigsaw with which he will make the most dramatic incision of the operation. He inserts the blade at the neck and, with both hands, yanks it down Mr. Stein's chest, splitting the bone like seasoned pine. "Jerk it," he says to Judy Harrow, and together they pry Mr. Stein's chest apart with their hands. A Favaloro retractor is inserted, holding Mr. Stein's body open and forcing his ribcage upward to form a rectangular surgical field nine inches long and six inches wide. In the center is the pericardium, a glimmering sheath of tissue veined like a leaf, marking the boundary that surgeons had so long feared to cross. Within it lies Mr. Stein's still-beating heart.

Fresh from the scrub sink, Mindich strides around the operating table and is helped into a green surgical gown and translucent rubber gloves. The level of tension in the room rises perceptibly. The boss has arrived, and everyone has snapped to. There is a natural authority about Mindich, despite his youthful, angular features and slight build, and, as is soon apparent, a natural ability. Like many in his line of work, the Bronx-born Mindich cannot remember a time when he did not want to be a surgeon. "I was always fixing things," he once recalled. "My father was very mechanically inclined, and I used to work with him all the time repairing everything from the machines in his dry cleaning store to the family Chevy. We were always working with our hands." And Mindich kept working with them, completing Downstate Medical School and taking his internship at Brooklyn Jewish Hospital in the middle of the impoverished Bedford-Stuyvesant section of New York City, where he remembers treating three or four stab and gunshot wounds each night. "I had my hands on more people's hearts than most heart surgeons," he said one day during a rare lunch away from the hospital. Of course, repairing a stab wound is a far cry from the delicate business of bypassing coronary arteries. "When I first began to see it, I didn't believe it," Mindich said of the procedure. "I thought, how are they going to keep those tiny little grafts open? But little by little, I came to realize that this is for me."

Following a cardiac surgical residency at Mount Sinai, he was appointed an attending surgeon and passed his certifying boards before he was thirty, an uncommonly young age. Mount Sinai, like other centers, was still at the beginning of the learning curve of grafting. Patients were rolled into the OR early in the morning and weren't rolled out until midnight. Mindich recalled one case in which he did a relatively simple single bypass, only to watch the patient suffer a heart attack when the graft prematurely closed. The young surgeon knew there was a better way and arranged a trip to the Cleveland Clinic to learn it.

Mindich moved into a hotel across from the famed center and soon found himself operating twelve to fourteen hours a day, five days a week. He learned how to tell which patients would do well in the OR and which would not, how to locate the tiny, almost invisible coronary arteries in seconds, how to estimate the temperature of the heart by observing subtle changes in the muscle's color. "It was the difference between doing two a week and fifteen a day," he said. "They had a specific technique, and it never varied. Every case had a surgeon, a resident, and two physician's assistants, and they all knew their jobs. It was boom, boom, boom—a ballet of fingers."

On his way back from Cleveland, Mindich took a detour for several months at the University of Alabama in Birmingham, where cardioplegia—the technique of stilling the heart and reducing its hunger for oxygen with an icy potassium solution— was then being improved. He returned to Mount Sinai with his skills honed but hardly in demand. "The first month I think I only did four or five cases. Nobody wanted to send me a patient." It proved a temporary problem, however, and within five years his caseload had grown to an annual total of seven hundred, about seventy percent of which were bypasses. These are figures few surgeons in the country can match. Mindich's indefatigability, combined with his age—he still has twenty-five or more years in the OR ahead of him—is the subject of no small amount of talk around the hospital, much of it from nurses and technicians whose energies he has stretched to the limit, and who do not always forgive his occasional outbursts of temper. He says his biggest problem is how potential patients react when confronted by a surgeon who looks as though he should still be dissecting frogs. "If they don't infarct right away when they see me," he says, "I know they'll hold up well in surgery."

Youth has not prevented Mindich from developing the ego for

which his older and more prominent surgical colleagues are noted. It makes clinical sense, he argues. "Nobody wants a surgeon who comes in and says, 'Well, I think you'll be okay.' You want somebody who says, 'It's going to be fine.' I don't lie to my patients. I try to quote them an accurate risk figure. But you have to let them know you're making the right decision in going to surgery. You have to tell them, 'You're going to be fine.' You have to be confident. I operate on seventy-year-olds without blinking. I do eighty-year-olds. I have even done some ninety-year-olds. I think I've only rejected two or three cases for surgery, and those people had other health problems. Like all surgeons, I'm either at the top of the medical pyramid or the bottom, depending on your perspective. The only thing I really decide is whether or not the patient is a candidate for surgery, and when I can do him."

When can be a problem for the young surgeon, who spends most of his workday in the OR. He is not by nature a hand-holder, and his consultations with patients, when he has time for them, are invariably perfunctory. Indeed, his first sight of Mr. Stein came about an hour into the operation, when he stuck his head through the door, saw that all was as it should be, and left. In keeping with the custom of the top practitioners of his craft, he didn't return for another half hour, during which time the harvesting of the saphenous vein was completed and Mr. Stein's chest split. (Once, when Mindich miscalculated the time and found himself handling the saw, he complained, "You can bet Denton Cooley doesn't have to do this.")

Now, with the left side of Mr. Stein's chest raised by the metal Favaloro frame, Mindich starts to work with the Bovie, freeing the left internal mammary artery, Vineberg's artery, from its bed in the chest wall. This vessel will soon be pressed into service supplying a key part of Mr. Stein's heart. "It takes a few extra minutes to take down the LIMA, but it's well worth it," he says, sealing off the tiny bleeders as he cuts away the oozing strip of fatty tissue containing the vessel. Recent evidence backs him up. LIMA have been shown to stay open longer, although patients often experience more incisional pain in the first days after surgery.

"When does your shift end?" he asks Judy. Correctly sensing that he is really asking if she will be available to help on his next case, which at that moment is being wheeled into the neighboring operating room, she tells him she'll go on overtime at three. "I'll be out of here by then," he says, leaving the issue temporarily unresolved.

A bundle of clear plastic tubes, which will connect the patient to the heart-lung machine, are deposited on Mr. Stein's chest. With well-practiced motions, Mindich cuts the lines to the proper length and clamps them in place on the drapery. He stares down into the surgical opening and slices through the pericardium, exposing the heart. It is a moving pink mass, covered with creamy fat, as big as four clenched fists. Reaching into the cavity, he cups his right hand underneath the heart and gently raises it from its bed. On the left ventricle, the crucial chamber, he can see a small area that is moving sluggishly but shows no sign of the brownish discoloration that would have indicated that extensive damage had been done during Mr. Stein's heart attack. The surgeon is pleased. "A little bit of infarct there," he says, "but there's still some viable muscle. It will pump better after we give it more blood."

It is time to attach the patient to the heart-lung pump. Mindich picks a spot on the front of the aorta and sews two neat rows of purse string sutures in a circle a half-inch in diameter. The loose ends are gathered and passed through soft, green plastic tubes to identify them and hold them in place. He creates the same kind of snare on the wall of the right auricle. Mindich orders a precalculated dose of heparin added to Mr. Stein's blood as it flows through the mechanical pump. After making a small incision, he stabs one of the clear plastic pipes through it and pulls the purse strings tight, locking the pipe into place in Mr. Stein's heart. This will carry venous blood, its oxygen spent, from the patient to the heart-lung machine. He attaches another of the pipes to the aorta to return bright red oxygenated blood from the machine to Mr. Stein's circulatory system. Blood enters the first section of the tubes, and Mindich and his assistant carefully search for air bubbles, which could be lethal if allowed into the bloodstream. When the surgeon is satisfied, the pipes are unclamped, and the red fluid flows quickly to the machine which is stationed on the floor of the OR directly behind the surgeon. With a countdown worthy of NASA, the heart-lung pump is switched on, and its four rotors start to turn. A clock in Mindich's mind clicks on, too. The less time a patient spends on the machine, he knows, the better.

Another dose of heparin is added to Mr. Stein's blood. The idea of operating on a patient whose blood is not allowed to clot—in effect, an artificial hemophiliac—is anathema to many surgeons. But clotting is as much the cardiac surgeon's enemy as bleeding is the general surgeon's. Clots can block circulation or damage organs. It is a peculiarity of heart surgery, moreover, that, as the patient bleeds, his blood can immediately be sucked back into the pump, filtered, and returned to his circulatory system, reducing the need for transfusions.

The machine is still turning slowly. Nothing has been done to interfere with the patient's heart, so the pump is still an adjunct. That is about to change. Mindich glances up at the scope. He sees that Mr. Stein's temperature is 36 degrees Centigrade, a little cooler than normal but right for a patient whose open chest is letting a lot of body heat escape. Mean arterial pressure is 86. "Go to twenty-five degrees," Mindich says, ordering the technician operating the pump to cool the blood as it spins through the rotors. Thus begins what medical textbooks call systemic hypothermia—the lowering of the body's temperature to slow its metabolism. When they are cold, organs need less oxygen, and the effects of its deprivation are diminished.

To slow the heart, Mindich takes a more direct approach. He clamps the aorta, blocking the flow of blood and isolating the heart from the rest of the vascular tree. Then he jabs a short, stubby needle into the giant vessel below the clamp. Through it flows cardioplegic solution used to still the heart and bring muscular activity to a standstill.

"Fifty ccs going in to test the line," the pump operator announces. Almost immediately, Mr. Stein's heart slows. Mindich orders another 800 milliliters from a frosty bottle hanging over the heart-lung machine. The heart begins to contract erratically, then comes to a halt. It lies paralyzed in midbeat, bloated with unpumped blood. To get at the areas of muscle supplied by the soon-to-be bypassed coronary arteries—if blood can't get through, cardioplegic solution can't either—Mindich uses a small needle to inject the icy fluid directly into the vessels below the blockages. When he is finished, he checks the rapidly paling muscle with a needlelike temperature probe to make certain he hasn't missed any spots.

The heartbeat indicator reads 0. The organ has stopped, ready for the surgeon's touch. Bloodless, motionless, and rubbery, it is an ideal target. Once again Mindich reaches into the chest and lifts the heart from its nest, this time narrating the anatomy. "Here's a huge right," he says, pointing to Mr. Stein's relatively healthy right coronary artery, "and a very small left first posterolateral," a branch of the left circumflex coronary jeopardized by the left-main lesion. "That's not worth it," he goes on, knowing he must sacrifice a small area of Mr. Stein's left ventricle.

With a Number 15 blade, he cuts into the muscle to expose a pale yellow streak on the back of the heart where the major posterolateral branch of the circumflex artery runs. Then he scans the surface of the ventricle for the left anterior descending artery. "The distal LAD looks pretty good," he says when at last he finds it. "We'll put the graft here."

"What's the temperature?" Mindich asks.

"Twenty-five," he is told.

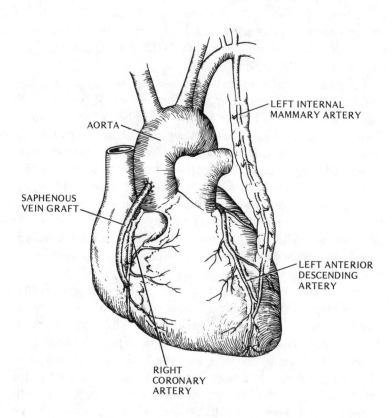

A DOUBLE BYPASS: Surgeons have used a piece of saphenous vein from the leg to detour around a blockage in the right coronary artery. An obstruction in the left anterior descending artery has been circumvented with the left internal mammary artery, a vessel that runs behind the breast. Seven or more such bypasses can be connected during a single operation.

"And the flow?"

The machine is pumping three liters of blood a minute through Mr. Stein's body, the technician says. Mindich is satisfied. After two hours of work, the patient's heart is finally ready to receive the new grafts. Mindich's eyes take a quick tour around the OR, making sure nothing is out of place. Expectedness is a surgeon's best friend.

Mindich is passed the saphenous vein from its bath in a basin of fluid on Judy's table. He inspects it carefully, then turns it upside down so its one-way valves, which help propel blood from the leg, will not interfere with the flow to the heart. He trims one end of the vein into an elliptical opening that will mate with a similarly shaped hole he has cut in the posterolateral circumflex artery on the back of Mr. Stein's heart. There is no small talk from the surgeon now. The outcome of the operation—indeed, the patient's life—will depend on the quality of his handiwork. Holding a curved surgical needle at the tip of long-handled forceps and passing it from one wet-gloved, slippery hand to the other, he sews a series of tiny stitches with gossamerlike plastic filament first in the cocktail-straw-sized vein, then in the barely visible artery. "You can't make them too far apart, or too close together," he says later. "You can't take too big a bite from the vein or go in too close to the edge. There are lots of things that can go wrong, but only one that can go right."

It takes eight turns of the suture to join vein to artery. When Mindich is done, he casually throws in a series of one-handed knots it takes residents a year or more to master, then takes a probe and slides it up and down the vessel "just to be one hundred percent sure I haven't oversewn it." He lifts the top of the vein and shoots cardioplegia solution through the graft into the recipient artery. "This happens to be a very nice vessel," he says, admiring his work, too. The entire procedure has taken six minutes.

Another segment of the saphenous vein is similarly attached to the diagonal branch of the LAD. The ends of both grafts are left connected to heparin-filled syringes.

"He's a little acidotic," says the anesthesiologist, who has just received the latest blood-gas report from the laboratory. "I'm giving him bicarbonate."

"What's the urine?" Mindich asks. The circulating nurse goes to the bag hanging from the operating table and calls out, "One hundred twenty-five for the hour."

Mindich turns back to Mr. Stein's heart and focuses on the distal LAD—his next, and in many ways most important, target. "There's a lot of disease in this vessel. But this will turn out to be a very nice internal mammary," he says, picking up the LIMA, which he has left clamped. "See how big it is."

"Twenty-eight degrees, please," he tells the technician at the pump, and asks Judy for the finest 7-0 sutures. "The internal mammary artery is much more delicate than the saphenous vein," he says. "Still, I like the LIMA for the LAD. It provides a lot of flow." Once the connection is complete, he unclamps the LIMA, and his point about blood flow is quickly proved. On the surface of Mr. Stein's heart, branch after branch of tiny vessels immediately turn bright red.

"What's the time?" Mindich asks. He is told that the heart muscle has been deprived of blood for twenty-one minutes. Right on schedule.

What remains is for Mindich to sew what will be the upper ends of the saphenous vein grafts to Mr. Stein's aorta. He applies a half-moon-shaped clamp to the massive vessel, isolating a quarter-sized area where the veins will be attached. "Any time you clamp the aorta you do some damage," he says. "The hope is that it isn't much." He punches two tiny circular holes into the vessel through which blood will flow into the new conduits to the heart. Before he begins to sew, he checks the path the vein segments will travel, choosing a more circuitous course behind the heart to avoid kinks. "The more bypasses I do, the more I see how much nicer a lie you can get if you bring it around under. The chances of it staying open are improved, and that's the name of the game."

It is now 2:25. Everything is going so smoothly Mindich starts to sing "Smoke Gets in Your Eyes," which is playing on the OR radio. The mood in the room seems to lift, but only temporarily. The surgical team has come to the last hurdle—getting the patient off the pump. It can be like trying to start a car on a bitter winter morning. Will the battery be strong enough? Will Mr. Stein's heart turn over? Sometimes the stiff, cold muscle must be shocked back to life with two electrical paddles the size of silver dollars. Sometimes, especially after a long and complicated procedure, it can take hours to wean the patient from the machine. But as it turns out, Mr. Stein has spent barely an hour on the pump, and his heart has already started to revive. The muscle, pale only moments ago, is now a healthier pink, and spasmodic beating has begun.

Mindich checks the grafts. Bulging with blood, there are no leaks or kinks. He is ready to attach the pacemaker wires to the right atrium and ventricle. Thin plastic tubes to monitor the pressure in the right and left atria are next to be implanted.

I made it a point to keep track of Mindich's progress throughout the afternoon. At around 2:35 I went into the monitoring room to watch him finish. Using the microphone, I asked him how it was going. "No problems, but I couldn't do the distal circ. I gave him a LIMA to the LAD and vein grafts to the diagonal and the big lateral. He's coming off fine."

With arms crossed, Mindich turns from the patient to watch the scope over the table that tracks the state of Mr. Stein's cardiovascular system. The mean arterial pressure is 58 millimeters of mercury; the left atrial pressure is 4. "That's a little low," Mindich says, "but we'll just give him more volume." More fluid is added to the pump, and the blood pressure begins to rise, but not enough. A pacemaker is brought to the table, and Mindich connects it to the two atrial leads. "After a bypass, a little faster rate is always helpful," he says, setting the dial. The heart rate instantly rises from 46 to 90 beats per minute. The mean blood pressure reaches 72. "That's more like it," he says, spinning clamps in his hands as though they were six-shooters.

The white and orange pacing wires are lying in a tangle in the incision. "Neatness is not my forte," Mindich remarks as he works his way through the strands, isolating one bunch from another and, with a large-bore needle, poking them through the wall of Mr. Stein's chest. He takes one last look at his handiwork and is satisfied the connections are tight. The place on the aorta where the cardioplegia needle was inserted is now oozing slightly, but no suturing is needed. Protamine, an antidote for heparin, is given. Soon, the bleeding stops. Mindich examines the trimmed branches of the LIMA and seals them with surgical clips. As Judy passes him the clip holder, one of the tiny metal fasteners pops out of her grasp and across the surgical field. "The Flying Wallendas will now appear," he snaps, eyes glaring over the top of his mask. Judy backs away from the table, head bowed.

Mindich picks up the Bovie and reaches inside the wall of the chest, cauterizing any vessels that are still bleeding. "I think it's pretty dry," he says after a while. Clear plastic tubes a half-inch in diameter are placed over the front surface of the heart and in the left chest cavity to drain any bloody fluid after the incision is closed. The surgeon orders another 100 milligrams of protamine and leaves at 2:59, the predicted time, for the operating room next door, where another heart awaits him.

Mindich's departure signals the beginning of the operation's final phase—the closing. The circulating nurse begins the first of two sponge counts. The surgical assistant has completed suturing Mr. Stein's left leg, wrapped it in cotton gauze, and covered it with an elastic bandage. Releasing the Cooley retractor, the resident brings the two sides of Mr. Stein's chest together and lines up the rough edges of his breastbone. With about a dozen stainless steel sutures, he wires the sternum shut. The subcutaneous tissues are closed in layers, and word is sent down the hall to the cardiac intensive care unit that another customer will soon be arriving. By 3:16, the skin incision has been sewn shut and the surgical drapery removed, revealing Mr. Stein's face for the first time since the operation began. It looks swollen. In fact, his whole yellow-tinged body has a lifeless pallor more characteristic of a morgue than a recovery room. But the monitors tell a reassuring story. The heart rhythm is still driven by the pacemaker, and the arterial pressure is steady at 73. The left atrial pressure is 12, the right atrial pressure 9. According to the latest blood-gas report from the lab, the patient's respiratory system is fine. In short, Mr. Stein is doing well.

The anesthesiologist puts away his syringes and makes the final entries in his log. His patient is now breathing pure oxygen, but the effects of the anesthesia will linger for some time. Judy is gathering the dozens of instruments used during the past three hours, a comparatively swift job as bypasses go. The resident turns to the foot of the table, where the fluid from the patient's chest is being collected and measured. In the first ten minutes after the chest was closed, 40 ml of blood have drained —not bad, but not good enough for him to be moved. As they wait and watch, the resident tamps the chest tube with the handle of a clamp to prevent clots from clogging it. Over the next ten minutes, the bleeding rate slows to a satisfactory 20 ml.

It takes most of the available hands to move Mr. Stein's bulky body from the operating table to the bed wheeled in from the CICU. The appropriate label has already been taped to the frame —"Stein, W. 6/6 CABGx3" ("cabbage times three" in hospital slang). It is a short fifty-foot trip to the CICU but a potentially dangerous one, since most of the elaborate monitoring devices must be temporarily disconnected. The anesthesiologist leads the way out of the OR at 3:58. The double doors to the CICU are swung open, and the team is directed to Bed 3, where two nurses and a biomedical technician are waiting.

8

Big Brother Is Watching
The Intensive Care Unit

SURGEONS, NO MATTER HOW skilled, temporarily leave their patients worse than they find them. This is especially true of cardiothoracic surgeons. Even with efficient heart-lung machines and modern anesthesia, the plain truth is that hearts don't like to be handled. In fact, they can get downright irritable. Cardiac intensive care units were developed to help patients who have undergone the trauma of heart surgery through the first potentially difficult days. Virtually all the marvels of modern medicine are instantly available in such units, around the clock. Diagnostic devices. Computer monitors. Hundreds of medications. Specially trained nurses and technicians. Physicians can order any test, any piece of equipment, and no one thinks twice about the cost. Unlike the rest of the hospital, the bureaucracy is minimal—patients get what they need, and they get it as fast as humanly possible.

The CICU is also a very artificial environment. Much of the time patients aren't awake. Even after they regain consciousness, they can barely communicate through the thicket of tubes and lines and the cacophony of alarms and buzzers. Night flows into day, and one day flows into the next. Patients become disoriented, depressed, and sometimes even worse. Overworked doctors are assisted by a staff whose responsibilities overlap with machines and each other. All this, needless to say, is not always conducive to the rational practice of medicine.

If there is a slow time in the Mount Sinai CICU, it is on Monday mornings. Many of the previous week's cases have been moved to a regular ward to continue their convalescence. The few that remain have been wheeled to "the suburbs" at the far end of the one-hundred-foot room to await transfer. At the start of one recent week, in fact, most of the Unit's eighteen beds were empty, quiet testimony to the reluctance of surgeons to practice their craft on weekends. (According to an article in *The Journal of Anaesthesiology*, even "emergency" cardiac surgery is more likely to occur on a Thursday or Friday than a Saturday or Sunday.) A dozen or so nurses in a pastel rainbow of green, blue, and yellow scrub suits are gathered around the desks in the center of the Unit. Usually an edgy and occasionally cranky group, the staff is subdued and relaxed, taking advantage of the lull to catch up on paperwork and small talk and to check the assignments on a bulletin board listing the names of patients and—in a subtle reminder of their often precarious condition— their religious affiliations.

Just before noon, the week's first case—a sixty-eight-year-old gray-haired banker named Edward Fowler—is rolled out of OR 3, along a short corridor, and through the double doors into the CICU. A portable EKG monitor nicknamed "the goat" bleats out his heartbeat, reassuring an entourage that includes an anesthesiologist, a surgical resident, and a physician's assistant.

"Bed 4," someone shouts, and the caravan takes a sharp left, heading for an alcove where Barbara DeVries is waiting. A two-year intensive care veteran, she came to the CICU directly from college but, like the other forty-eight nurses on the staff, trained for six months more before qualifying as a "primary" nurse. She will plan every aspect of Mr. Fowler's nursing care and make sure it is followed, for as long as he is in the Unit. She will also keep Mr. Fowler's family informed of his progress, a job that sometimes is nearly as taxing. DeVries has been checking with the OR from time to time during the morning to see how her patient is doing. She knows that the operation has gone relatively smoothly, that Mr. Fowler's heart is being paced electronically, and that he is receiving the vessel-dilating drug nitroprusside to control high blood pressure, all standard procedure but nevertheless relevant to the postoperative game plan. Meanwhile, Jesse Qualls, a biomedical technician, has punched Mr. Fowler's vital statistics into the bedside computer.

As Mr. Fowler is rolled into place—like all patients, he was put in an intensive care bed in the OR to eliminate another transfer of his cold and heavy body—Qualls and DeVries join the surgical team hooking up the various monitoring lines to the electronic surveillance system that will keep track of Mr. Fowler's heart, lungs, and various other organs. The information is relayed to the main computer one floor below, where it will be electronically processed for display on the television screen above the patient's bed. The anesthesiologist, who has been squeezing a black rubber air bag to fill Mr. Fowler's lungs, connects the endotracheal tube to the mechanical respirator that will supply him with oxygen for the next twelve to twenty-four hours. Qualls punches the desired respiration rate—sixteen breaths per minute—into the keyboard, and the ventilator settings flash on the screen. Once the respirator is set, DeVries takes a sample of arterial blood from the line in Mr. Fowler's wrist and sends it to the neighboring lab. The results, flashed on the monitor five minutes later, confirm that the ventilator settings are correct and indicate that she can begin to lower the amount of oxygen Mr. Fowler is receiving. Prolonged exposure to excessively high concentrations of oxygen, she knows, can poison the lungs.

From time to time, DeVries milks the translucent rubber tubes running down Mr. Fowler's chest, making certain they are clear of clots so the oozing tissue around the surgical wound can drain into a bubbling collector at the foot of the bed. She also keeps a close eye on her patient's blood pressure, trying to control it by regulating a pump delivering more nitroprusside through an intravenous line. Soon, another computer specially designed by technicians on the Mount Sinai staff will be wheeled to the crowded bedside to take over the task electronically.

About forty-five minutes pass before Mr. Fowler is fully connected. Once his postoperative bleeding, breathing, and metabolism have been assessed, DeVries attaches him to a standard electrocardiograph, the same instrument that helped identify his heart problem. I try to time my arrival at the bedside to that initial EKG, which will provide the first clue as to whether a patient has suffered any heart damage in the OR. "Supervised" heart attacks are generally better tolerated than those that occur outside the hospital, perhaps because the heart is saturated by the icy cardioplegic solution that diminishes its hunger for oxygen. But they aren't always easy to diagnose, since even uncomplicated surgery can affect an electrocardiogram. In Mr. Fowler's case, though, there was no evidence of infarction.

An hour after his operation, the patient was still unconscious. I would have been alarmed had he been otherwise. The temperature of his arms and legs was equal, from which I could deduce that the circulation in his limbs was fine. Peering under his eyelids, I found his pupils like pinpoints, a sign of the anesthesia. (Dilated pupils would have suggested brain damage.) Placing my stethoscope on his chest, I could hear air moving through the passageways of his respiratory tract, indicating the lungs were fully expanded. The heart was muffled, but I could make out the scratchy sound of the chest tubes rubbing against the pericardium. There were no abnormal murmurs. Urine flow was excellent.

Tapping out several codes on the keyboard, I checked his oxygen supply and asked DeVries to instruct the computer to adjust the respirator for deeper breaths. The fluid-balance record showed more was flowing out than in, as Mr. Fowler's kidneys cleared the cardioplegic solution from his bloodstream. "Let's forward-load him," I said, instructing DeVries to add fluid intravenously, "and he's going to need more potassium. How's the bleeding?"

"Still pretty wet, but slowing," she said after checking the chest tubes.

"All right, go ahead with aspirin and dipyridamole down the nasogastric tube. Why don't you also start digitalis? He looks good, and I'm sure his heart rate and blood pressure will come around over the next day or so. And you can let his family come in. I've already filled them in."

The CICU visitors' lounge at Mount Sinai is a tiny, smoky room just outside the Unit's double doors. It has a color TV, a few aged newspapers and magazines, and not much else to distract an assortment of anxious relatives and friends who, on this muggy summer afternoon, included three generations of Fowlers—wife, mother, and son. DeVries did her best to prepare them for the sight of a loved one slightly bloated and a ghastly yellow from the antiseptic, cold, lifeless, and entangled in an ominous clump of tubes and wires. Some visitors have been known to scream at the sight. Others shake with fear. I recall one case where a son fainted, only to have his mother, who had undergone surgery the previous day, try to get out of bed to help him up. Another patient's wife, on hearing that surgery had gone well, proceeded to have a heart attack herself (she eventually had successful bypass surgery, too), which triggered a round of chest pains in the couple's daughter and son (one required tranquilizers, the other merely reassurance). Still another woman visited her husband just after his triple bypass, left for a glass of water, then returned and stayed for almost an hour

—at the wrong bed. As a precaution, DeVries talked the youngest Fowler, who was thirteen, into staying behind.

As the two Mrs. Fowlers approached Bed 4, both were pale with worry. "He's doing fine," DeVries kept repeating, but confronted with the sight before them, they weren't sure they could take her word for it. Clearly, being cooped up for hours with a roomful of nervous people doesn't help matters. But CICU nurses go through such scenes countless times and are well prepared. DeVries pulled the blanket from Mr. Fowler's left side and put the wife's hand in her husband's. Reassured at the unmistakable feel of life, Mrs. Fowler allowed her other hand, which had been raised to her mouth, to drop to her side. DeVries repeated the process with Mr. Fowler's mother, then firmly suggested that the women come back the next day, when the patient would be awake and at least minimally communicative. The wife agreed, started to walk away, then turned back toward the bed. "It's okay to give him a kiss," DeVries said.

After the family left, DeVries briefly outlined what Mr. Fowler was likely to go through in the next few days: "In the coming hours, I'm going to monitor his urine output, watch the pressures in various parts of the heart, and basically just wait for him to wake up. Patients are usually cold for four to six hours. If he starts to wake up and shiver too early—they start coming around when they reach about 35 degrees Centigrade, which is just below normal—it increases the metabolic rate and blood pressure. Most patients become hypertensive an hour or two after surgery, and if the blood pressure goes too high, they'll bleed too quickly and could blow a graft. Usually they also need fluids—we give a solution of albumin, the protein part of plasma. I also watch the potassium level in the blood and continue the antibiotics we started before surgery.

"When he's unconscious, I have to do everything for the patient. Once he starts waking up, though, I'll let him become more independent, as long as it's not going to hurt him physiologi-

cally. If he wants to sleep and his oxygen level is low and he's
got a lot of junk in his lungs, he's not going to have a choice
about clearing them out. He's going to have to do his deep-
breathing exercises, no matter how much it hurts. And it does.
But if he's really exhausted, I might let him rest for an hour
first.

"During the first night, as patients regain consciousness, we
start taking them off some of the medicines. At four or five in
the morning, all the nurses start getting their patients up and
washing them, and it's wild in here. Then, if they're doing well,
we'll take out the endotracheal tube. After that, it's usually time
for rounds with the doctors. The daily blood tests, cardiograms,
and X rays come next. In the afternoon, if the blood pressure is
under control and the chest-tube drainage is low, they'll take the
atrial lines out, and we'll work on the lungs a lot, slapping their
backs to loosen the phlegm. They're still fuzzy from all the pain
medicine, but we'll get them out of bed and sit them in a chair
for a little while. The next day the chest tubes should come out,
followed by the IVs, one by one as they're no longer needed.
Then they're ready to go."

If he is like most patients, the first thing Mr. Fowler will
become conscious of is the endotracheal tube. It will prevent him
from talking, irritate his vocal cords, and feel, quite understandably, like it's been rammed down his throat. Many times, patients try to yank the tube out themselves, one sign that they
may be strong enough to breathe with just an oxygen mask. We
usually remove it early on the morning after, but even a short
experience with an endotracheal tube can leave the voice hoarse
and the throat sore.

One virtue of the endotracheal ordeal, besides assuring the
supply of oxygen, is that it tends to distract patients from the
nasogastric tube, which allows immediate access to the digestive
tract and would, under other circumstances, be extremely difficult to ignore. A similar relationship exists between the chest

tubes and the chest incision. Although intravenous narcotics are given just before the drainage tubes are removed, the process can still be painful. Once they are out, however, chest discomfort usually diminishes, though it can still hurt when patients cough and breathe and when the nurses bang on their backs to loosen secretions that accumulate in their lungs. Partly because there's so much else that hurts, and partly because they are relatively shallow, the leg incisions don't bother patients after the second postoperative day.

While the Foley catheter is in place, patients constantly feel as if their bladder is full, and even after it is withdrawn they often feel a burning when they urinate. On the other hand, the intravenous lines and pacemaker leads, though they look frightening, are generally painless. And since blood samples can be drawn through the arterial line, patients are spared countless needle punctures.

Although patients usually feel parched—their mouths, after all, have been open for twenty-four hours—surgeons don't like them to be given too much fluid for fear they will become waterlogged. Too much to drink can also cause vomiting, which is extremely painful under the circumstances. And it is a blessing indeed that patients usually don't confront the need for a bowel movement for several days.

Heart surgery can sometimes lead to more serious complications, though just how often they occur depends on the condition of the patient and the skill of the surgeon. Many hearts leave the OR beating too slowly, a hangover from cardioplegia or preoperative beta blockers, which control angina by governing the speed and force of the heart. Drugs, disturbances of body chemistry, or simply the wear and tear of surgery also can affect the sinoatrial node, the quarter-inch nerve center on the back wall of the right atrium, which initiates the electrical impulse that makes the heart beat. If, for example, an oxygen mask inadvertently slips off, or the blood becomes overly acidic or has too much potassium, this natural pacemaker could be knocked out of commission for a few days.

The same factors can also cause short circuits between the atria and ventricles. This condition, called heart block, can vary in severity from a slight delay between the action of the upper chambers, which collect the blood, and that of the lower ones, which pump it to the body, to a total breakdown in communication. In that event, nature provides a backup—a built-in "escape rhythm" causes the ventricles to beat thirty to forty times a minute, regardless of how often they receive signals from the atrium. That is enough to keep a healthy person alive, but it doesn't meet the needs of a patient just subjected to surgery. What do we do? We could treat heart block with drugs, but they can be difficult to control given the organ's constantly changing metabolic environment. Electronic pacemakers are easier to handle, and they can instantly be attached to patients with the wires already affixed to the surface of the heart in the OR.

Even more problematic than the heart that goes too slow is the one that goes too fast. Rapid heart action, or tachyarrhythmia, may range from isolated and relatively harmless extra beats to salvos of premature contractions all the way to total electrical disorganization—fibrillation—which leaves the heart muscle wiggling like a bag of worms. Atrial fibrillation can be tolerated if the ventricles can be kept under control; ventricular fibrillation, on the other hand, is deadly if not immediately halted. Fortunately, a jolt of electricity delivered through the chest wall can erase this disastrous rhythm and give the sinoatrial node a chance to reassert itself. The energy needed can range from a thump on the chest, which generates a single joule, to 400 joules delivered with paddles from the crash cart.

Even if the heart's electrical system is working properly, the organ can break down mechanically, especially if the muscle has not been sufficiently insulated with cardioplegic solution during surgery or if a newly grafted vessel prematurely closes. Either way, the left ventricle will not get enough oxygen, which impairs its ability to suck blood in and pump it out. This leads to congestive heart failure—not enough blood flows to the body, causing it to back up in the lungs. Cardiologists have developed a host of remedies, including diuretics to help the body purge liquids, stimulants to make the heart beat more forcefully, and blood vessel dilators to ease circulation. The heart that can't relax enough to draw in blood can be forward-loaded with intravenous fluids that prime the pump (as Mr. Fowler's was). The heart that's too relaxed can be revved up with adrenalin, dopamine, or that age-old tonic, digitalis, a derivative of foxglove, which Sir William Withering brewed as a tea to treat his patients in the eighteenth century. Although it is by far the weakest of the three drugs, "dig" is the only one that can be given orally, hence its long-standing popularity. It is also used as an antiarrhythmic agent, but, either way, it stays in the system for many days and cannot be removed.

Sometimes inadequate circulation is not the fault of the heart at all but rather of blood vessels that can't maintain adequate pressure. For this, constrictor drugs are given, including the same Neo-Synephrine used for runny noses.

If these medicines fail, pumps to assist the heart can be called into action, but only temporarily. The most widely used, the intra-aortic balloon pump, is slid into an artery at the groin and up to the main vessel behind the heart to help pull the blood from the ventricle and push it into the rest of the body. However, the balloon takes its toll on the vascular system and sometimes generates potentially lethal blood clots, so it can only buy a limited amount of time, usually a matter of days. The same is true with more direct methods of cardiac support, experimental ventricular assist devices connected when the chest is open. These machines, prototypes for artificial hearts, are in use at several medical centers but are still far from fully developed.

Since 20 percent of the blood pumped by the heart goes to the kidneys, we keep a close eye on them as well. Sometimes, especially with diabetics, we expect problems. We know the kidneys are in trouble if we don't see a high urine flow after surgery, since the concentrated cardioplegic solution acts as a diuretic for the large volume of fluid the patient has received while on the pump. Kidney failure after cardiac surgery can be an ominous development. We don't hesitate to put bypass patients on dialysis when necessary; they have been given many kinds of drugs in a relatively short period of time, and getting them out of the body is essential.

Liver failure is much less common and usually the result of hepatitis or a toxic drug reaction. Heart failure can in rare cases lead to jaundice, but the yellowish cast that colors some patients for a few days after surgery, like the hue of a fading bruise, is more often the result of the body's harmless recycling of pigment derived from blood cells damaged during the operation.

During all surgery performed under general anesthesia, some of the microscopic air sacs of the patient's lungs collapse and fill with fluid. This makes breathing difficult and increases the risk of pneumonia. In bypass cases, these problems are compounded by irritation of the lining of the lungs and soreness of the chest caused by the incision and the tubes used to drain the tissues around it. As for the heart-lung machine, it can damage surfactant—the surface-active ingredient that allows oxygen to pass from the lungs to the blood without fluids leaking the other way. There's always a tenuous balance where the capillaries meet the air sacs, and if the blood pressure in these vessels rises above a critical level, leakage is more likely, and the lungs will be flooded, a dreadful condition known as pulmonary edema. Lung problems, of course, can be much more severe in smokers.

A natural barrier prevents many of the drugs we give to help the heart from entering and poisoning the brain, and antidotes are available to reverse the effects of narcotic anesthesia quickly. But while improved surgical techniques have reduced the likelihood of strokes, they have not eliminated them. The most common causes are bubbles of air, blood clots, or particles of fatty deposits loosened from the aorta, which travel to the brain. If you look hard enough, you are likely to find at least some microscopic debris in the gray matter of most bypass patients, especially those who stayed on the pump a long time. The operation is riskier for those with preexisting cerebral vascular disease, for whom a drop in blood pressure that would be harmless for a normal person could be devastating. High blood pressure can also pose problems, as can the steady flow of blood from the bypass pump to an organ that is accustomed to receiving it in waves.

When a patient first wakes up in the Unit, usually after about eight hours, nurses watch carefully for any signs of abnormal behavior, from problems with movement and coordination to signs of disorientation, memory loss, or confusion. Sometimes such difficulties are an understandable reaction to the ordeal of surgery or to the sensory overload of the CICU, where the lights are always on and alarms are constantly sounding. Some windows at Mount Sinai offer beautiful views of Central Park, but few CICU patients are in any shape to notice, much less enjoy them. "I couldn't tell if it was two in the morning or four in the afternoon," said one typical patient. "I didn't know if it was Thursday or Monday. I wasn't even close."

It was probably no accident that coronary surgery did not flourish until the start of the electronic era. Computers are uniquely suited to monitor and record the often complex reactions of the heart, lungs, brain, and other organs to the trauma of the surgeon's blade. Nor does it seem entirely coincidental that heart surgeons, perhaps more than any other kind, are familiar with and appreciative of technology. After all, they owe much of their livelihood to the development of the heart-lung pump.

Among the first institutions to recognize the value of electronic monitoring was the Pacific Medical Center in San Francisco, where during the mid-1960s more than a dozen software experts from IBM worked with Dr. John J. Osborn to develop the first computerized cardiac intensive care unit. As its volume of coronary surgery increased in the early 1970s, Mount Sinai sent a young biomedical engineer named Richard deAsla to study Osborn's unit. Upon his return, he built his own two-patient monitoring system that was linked to San Francisco by telephone for a twenty-two-month trial.

A decade later, Mount Sinai has become a technological leader in its own right, thanks largely to deAsla, now the medical center's chief cardiothoracic engineer. (The Mount Sinai CICU also has on its staff a physician with a doctorate in engineering, who specializes in critical care, Anthony Benis.) DeAsla is constantly on call, watching over the $50,000 or more of electronic and mechanical equipment likely to be clustered at each patient's bedside and the IBM 1800 mainframe one floor below that receives the data, "massages" it, and sends it back to the CICU monitors in the form of lists, graphs, and tables. Just what gets looked at depends on who's doing the looking: The nurses tend to focus on immediate measurements; the handful of residents watches the short-term trends; while most of the senior physicians concentrate on the twelve-to-forty-eight-hour patterns, which is understandable since they are reviewing a total of up to eighteen patients at a time.

In truth, there is a great deal of material from the computer that no one looks at. Each week, megabytes of data are purged from the system because not even deAsla can figure out what to do with them. Other information might be valuable if someone had time to study it, so deAsla has programmed the computer itself to look at some of it. If it detects adverse trends in a patient's recovery, it sounds an alarm. "The system was not intended to bring to our attention catastrophic events like cardiac arrest," deAsla said one day, sitting in his cubbyhole of an office lined with shelves of electronic gadgets. "For immediate problems like that, we still rely on the bedside alarms. The computer warning system goes off only after certain variables are out of limits for five minutes. It is designed to catch problems before they become life-threatening events.

"The next stage is the actual control of drug administration, using a computer in what's known as a closed-loop system. We're already doing this to control postoperative hypertension with nitroprusside. The computer measures the patient's blood pressure once a second, and adjusts the drug infusion rate every ten seconds. Our studies show that without doubt it's superior to manual control. I tell the nurses the machine isn't smarter, it's just very dedicated to a single task.

"In principle, you should be able to close-loop many systems. Another direction that we could go in is toward artificial intelligence, systems that are programmed to measure multiple variables, draw conclusions, and advise the medical staff only when things are outside preset limits. There are many clinical problems that can be diagnosed strictly by the numbers. Others are not so straightforward, and it's important to realize that. There was a paper written about fifteen years ago about the limits of computers that was illustrated by pictures of two children. Anyone could see that one was terribly sick and the other was well. Now how do you feed that information into a computer? It's a very sticky problem."

Another is money. The technology employed in even an advanced intensive care unit is no more sophisticated than in a Pac-Man game, but the lack of a consensus from hospital to hospital on equipment, combined with the litigiousness of medicine, make an intensive care unit an extraordinarily expensive undertaking. Still, deAsla and Benis have been busy designing a new system for Mount Sinai, with even smarter bedside terminals and a more powerful electronic Big Brother downstairs to watch over them.

"Do these machines save lives?" deAsla asked himself.

"That is becoming an increasingly difficult question to answer. Many hospitals doing coronaries have mortality rates of less than one percent, so measuring any change requires an enormous number of patients, and by the time you went through them, there would have undoubtedly been advances in anesthesia or drug management, so you wouldn't really know what you were measuring. Subjectively, though, we think the Unit's worth it."

The best way to see the CICU is the way the physicians who work there do, on rounds. As the liaison cardiologist to those undergoing open-heart surgery at Mount Sinai, I go through the Unit bed by bed and try to talk to the patients, even if they aren't always able to talk back. The computers are a great help, of course, but you have to use your eyes and your ears and your stethoscope to get a true sense of each patient's condition. Whenever I hear anyone describe a case as routine, my warning lights flash. Nothing is routine in the CICU.

I usually begin at about 9 A.M., and on one typical morning I was accompanied by Tony Benis, Norman Riegel, a cardiology fellow in his final year of training, Fulvio Mazzucchi, a cardiothoracic fellow studying intensive care medicine, several residents and medical students, a physician's assistant assigned to the CICU, and Sylvia Jacobs, the nurse in charge on that shift. Our first stop was the bed of seventy-three-year-old Florence Mowser, who had suffered a massive heart attack (her second) three months earlier. When high doses of medicine had failed to relieve increasingly severe angina, she had been transferred to Mount Sinai, where we put in an intra-aortic balloon pump to ease the strain on her heart and reduce the pain. Tests determined that her left ventricle was badly damaged and her arteries were blocked, and to make matters worse, she had developed an aneurysm on the left ventricular wall. All in all, she was a poor surgical risk. On the other hand, there was little alternative, so

Mindich had operated the night before, giving her three grafts and repairing the aneurysm.

Mazzucchi, a medical man trying to survive among the surgeons, filled in the details. "She came out of the OR at about seven-thirty on intravenous nitrates [drugs that keep the pressures inside the heart under control], dopamine, and heparin [to keep clots from forming on the balloon pump, which she still needed]. She is heavily sedated and has a low blood pressure. I think she's deteriorating."

One look at the bedside monitor convinced me that he was right. The chaotic pattern of the electrocardiogram revealed that the upper chambers of Mrs. Mowser's heart were fibrillating, and the abnormal rhythm made her already critical condition worse. I decided to try to erase the rhythm electrically even though the procedure was risky because of the postoperative irritability of her heart. I sent for the crash cart and checked the timing of the shock against her EKG. "Don't touch anything connected to her," I warned the others. (As an intern, I once saw a bystander drop to the floor during an emergency resuscitation, when the current flowed into his body through the bed frame he was leaning on. Fortunately, we were able to resuscitate him along with the patient.) Placing the paddles on the patient's chest, I gave her 400 joules, enough to power a 100-watt lightbulb for four seconds. Her back arched, and her arms rose from her sides and came together, as though she were hugging a child. Looking at the monitor, I saw the signal change to atrial flutter, a slightly more organized rhythm but far from satisfactory. I gave her another jolt. The signal disappeared off the top of the screen, and her pulse stopped. After a few anxious seconds, a normal heart rhythm started, slowly at first, then picking up speed.

By this time a crowd had gathered at the bedside, not because of the rarity of the procedure—I probably do it several times a month—but because of the realization that something might go wrong, a fear that attends even simple medical tasks in the Unit. "That's it. You've got it," said Dick deAsla, who had stationed himself by the balloon pump when he saw what was happening. Soon, Mrs. Mowser's blood pressure rose, and the heart chamber pressures fell toward the normal range. To be on the safe side, I asked the nurse to increase the digoxin Mrs. Mowser was receiving to control the heart rate if the atrial fibrillation recurred.

Mrs. Mowser's neighbor in the next bed, a fifty-three-year-old woman, barely noticed the commotion. Awake but drowsy, she was making a remarkably smooth recovery from an operation to replace an aortic valve that had been severely damaged by rheumatic fever.

In Bed 4, Tony Piero, a forty-nine-year-old mailman who had had a quadruple bypass forty-eight hours earlier, was also doing well, with the exception of slight fever and a fast pulse. Tylenol would lower his temperature, and once his fever was under control, his heart would slow. "How do you feel?" I asked him. He ran his left hand down the front of his chest and mouthed the word "pain." "You're doing well, but I really want you to work on your breathing. I'm going to have the nurse give you a little more pain medicine, but I don't want you to take so much that you fall asleep. Don't stop working on your coughing and deep breathing." Chest exercises were especially important for Mr. Piero, because I had heard some congestion at the base of his right lung and wanted to head off the risk of pneumonia. "It might be a good idea to get him out of bed and into the chair," I told his nurse, "so he'll breathe more deeply."

Bed 5 belonged to Sanjay Gupta, a devout Hindu whose quest for spirituality had over the past few years been periodically interrupted by chest pains and, his tests indicated, a myocardial infarction. An angiogram revealed triple-vessel disease—all three coronary arteries were blocked. Nevertheless, Mr. Gupta had been almost oppressively cheerful throughout his preoperative stay. "The whole experience I am going through has been like one great Disneyland," the soft-spoken Indian told me when I looked in on him the night before surgery. "All this time I have been smiling, but the real test will be whether I can still be this cheerful in two days."

I had tried to warn Mr. Gupta that all bypass patients experience a certain amount of discomfort and pain. Now, eighteen hours after he received three grafts, he was awake, alert, and already off dopamine and nitroprusside. I sat him up to listen to his lungs—they were clear—and checked the bedside computer. Blood chemistry, fluid balance, chamber pressures, chest-tube drainage all were in the acceptable range, and the morning's EKG showed no signs of new heart damage. Still, his cheery resolve seemed to have given way to a vulnerable look made all the more touching by the presurgical removal of most of his long, wispy beard. When I bent down to ask him how he felt, he clutched my hand and wouldn't let go. My guess was that the anesthesia or medications given him had impaired his ability to put mind over matter, and he was feeling far more earthly discomfort than he had expected.

We didn't stay long at the next bed, assigned to a Middle Eastern woman in her early twenties, whose blocked mitral valve had been successfully repaired and who would soon be leaving the Unit. The prospects were considerably less optimistic for Eugene Burns, a massive fifty-eight-year-old lawyer next door. Mr. Burns had arrived at Mount Sinai with two blocked arteries nine days earlier and had undergone an angioplasty that had failed to open one of them. Bypass surgery followed, but shortly afterward Mr. Burns's blood pressure dropped precipitously, one sign of tamponade, the compression of the heart by an accumulation of blood that, instead of flowing through the chest tubes, has clotted in the pericardial space. There wasn't time to move him back to the OR, so his chest was opened, drained, and closed in the Unit. Remarkably, Mr. Burns resumed his recovery and four days later was sent to a regular ward, where he was soon back on his feet. However, his EKGs suggested problems with his grafts, and sure enough, a coronary angiogram showed that all three had closed. Far worse, he suffered a rare reaction to the dye used during the angiography and went into shock. He was rushed back to the OR, where for the third time his chest was opened. The grafts were replaced, but the surgical team had difficulty getting him off the pump— hardly a surprise given what he and his heart had been through —and had to put him on an intra-aortic balloon pump. Now, twenty-four hours later and well past the time when he should have awakened, Mr. Burns remained unresponsive, the respirator still pumping his huge chest up and down. This is an example of what Mount Sinai's chief cardiothoracic surgeon, Robert S. Litwak, calls the beget syndrome, as in "one problem begets another."

In Bed 8, Colonel George Nessen, USAF Ret., has flown in from Denver and was now three days into his recovery from his second coronary bypass operation. The return trip to the OR had become necessary when grafts placed five years earlier, when he was fifty-six, had closed and angina had recurred. As with many re-ops, prolonged postoperative bleeding had been a problem at first, but from the look of things, I now expected his recovery to be as smooth as those of his former CICU neighbors, an assortment of bypass cases who went under the knife on the same day and who had already been transferred, leaving the next few beds vacant. Given the surgical schedule at the hospital, I knew they wouldn't remain empty for long.

Moving around the corner of the Unit to Bed 14, we learned the story of Benjamin Kessler, a fifty-nine-year-old luncheonette owner. While vacationing with his family in the Poconos, Mr. Kessler suffered repeated episodes of upper abdominal pain and was admitted to a small local hospital. The doctor treated him at first for pancreatitis, but he failed to respond. When he also complained of palpitations, the family requested that a cardiologist be called. A review of the EKGs showed severe abnormalities, and the diagnosis was changed to unstable angina. He had been transferred to Mount Sinai by a helicopter that landed in Central Park five days earlier, and intravenous nitroglycerin was given, relieving his pain. The next morning, he went to the cath lab, and triple-vessel disease was found. He had received five grafts on Monday, and his postoperative course was smooth.

"Show the doctors how good you are with the spirometer," said his nurse, handing the patient a small plastic tube used to measure the strength of his breathing. "His only problem is some numbness along the side of his right arm, but this seems to be getting better."

Mr. Kessler struggled with the machine and raised the little ball about a third of the way up the tube. After congratulating him on his progress, I performed a short physical examination during which I found that a nerve in his neck had been slightly irritated when his ribcage was opened in the OR. This explained the numbness, which I assured him would go away in a few days. Since the computer data, lab reports, X rays, and electrocardiograms were all in order, I suggested that he be transferred to the ward.

Next was an elderly black woman who had received two grafts three days earlier; she was doing well enough to be transferred were she not a Jehovah's Witness. It is a tenet of that faith not to accept transfusions of blood or blood products, which can make surgery risky. We operate on many Witnesses at Mount Sinai and often keep them in the CICU an extra day or so. The staff knows that their wishes are to be honored no matter what the medical consequences. We do ask that they sign a form absolving the hospital of responsibility.

Bed 16 was actually a crib, and in it was eighteen-month-old Joshua Stone, whose congenitally deformed heart had required surgery. He was now well on the way to recovery, and his nurse seemed to be enjoying his company. Patients like Joshua can lift the spirit of the entire CICU. On the other hand, patients who linger in the Unit for months can sap morale and leave the staff feeling helpless.

For several weeks, a string of such patients had ended up in Bed 17, near the double doors. It appeared the present occupant, Mollie Carnofsky, would continue the trend. The frail eighty-four-year-old woman had been operated on two weeks earlier to remove a tumor from her heart, had developed pneumonia, and nearly had died because of infection. With intensive antibiotic therapy and vigorous lung workouts, she seemed to be rallying, which surprised me, considering her age and condition. But she still spent a lot of the day moaning, "I'm going to die," over and over again, much to the consternation of everyone within ear-shot.

In the eighteenth and last bed was Nathan Gerstein, a seventy-four-year-old retired machinist, who had had a quadruple bypass four days earlier. His heart had gone into atrial fibrillation, which several different medicines failed to correct, but since it still managed to supply his body with an adequate flow of blood, I elected not to try to jolt him out of it as I had with Mrs. Mowser. I was more concerned with his sluggish mental state and wondered whether he had suffered a mild stroke. The disorienting world of the CICU is not the best place for patients such as Mr. Gerstein, and I hoped he would soon be well enough to be transferred to a regular ward, where he would fare better psychologically.*

The mental fuzziness experienced by Mr. Gerstein is by no means uncommon in the CICU. A 1971 study found that the incidence of psychiatric complications, less than 0.1 percent

---

*Mr. Burns bore out our pessimistic assessment a few days later, when infection supervened and he died. Mollie Carnofsky, on the other hand, made a steady recovery. Mr. Gerstein would return to the Unit when the cause of his problems would finally become clear: An infection of the breastbone along the surgical incision had enveloped his heart, requiring emergency surgical drainage. After a long course of antibiotics, he recovered.

after general surgery, was 15 percent after cardiac procedures such as bypasses (and 57 percent after open-heart surgery such as valve repair). The problem is variously known as postoperative delirium, ICU syndrome, or even "pump head," but by any name, it is characterized by depression, anxiety, and impairment of orientation, memory, and judgment. Just how much these difficulties result from the distracting world of the CICU and how much they are caused by the trauma of surgery is not clear.

Writing on the psychiatric complications of cardiac surgery, Stuart H. Bartle, a psychiatrist at Mount Sinai, described the reaction this way:

> The initial insult appears to be neurologic, usually occurring during cardiopulmonary bypass, most likely secondary to microembolic phenomena. In these cases, careful neurologic examination in the immediate postoperative period frequently will show a deficit, often a gross one not routinely detected because the patient's immobilization and endotracheal tube present obstacles to neurologic assessment. The minimal deficit is a cognitive one. People are usually ashamed of any defective thinking, however, and do not spontaneously disclose it. Conscious of a defect in their thought processes but feeling the need to hide this from the staff, their sense of isolation increases. They try to be hyperalert (to compensate for defective perceptual ability), causing further physiologic stress. They lose sleep and become more anxious, with increasing fears of losing control. If everything else goes well, they eventually may recover. They may succeed in hiding the defect from the staff and may even forget it themselves, although a high percentage of patients will recall some aberrant thinking before discharge.
>
> If, however, greater stresses are placed on people with certain pre-existing psychological [problems], the process may go on to produce last-ditch psychologic defenses; i.e., paranoid delusions, hallucinations and escape into a full-blown psychosis. Additional psychologic stress would result from: 1) drugs caus-

ing drowsiness and thus threatening alertness; 2) any complication that delays recovery and that can be misinterpreted as
further evidence of imminent death or permanent disability; 3)
an ICU environment preventing rest, with the resultant tremendous sensory overload; 4) any perception or misperception of
something occurring or heard on the ward, for example a
patient's death, a misunderstood remark; 5) difficult communication because of a tracheotomy or aphasia, which prevents
patients from getting their needs met, threatens their sense of
control, and increases their sense of isolation, and 6) poor
postoperative relationships with members of their family. The
major pre-existing psychologic factor that increases the stress
on their defenses is the expectation of a bad outcome; this
often results from identification with a relative or friend who
has died after an operation, frequently based on unconscious
fantasies of guilt and punishment.

Fortunately, these problems almost always respond to prompt
treatment in which tranquilizers, talk, and tender loving care
can figure prominently. Nurses, who have far more contact with
patients than physicians, are invaluable in this. But nurses themselves are also subject to considerable ICU stress. Their sometimes hazy lines of responsibility plus the pressure of caring
only for the critically ill plus the frequency of death seems a
formula for psychological trouble. Perhaps no one knows this
any better than Edith Deasis, who came to Mount Sinai as an
intensive care nurse in 1974, became senior clinical nurse two
years later, and in 1980 took over as supervisor. At that time, the
nursing shortage plaguing hospitals across the country was
reaching near catastrophic dimensions in the Mount Sinai CICU,
where there was a skeletal staff of eighteen, thirty below the
normal complement. Even shored up by per diem and private
nurses, the Unit was stretched almost to the breaking point.

"Nursing in the CICU is much more difficult than on a regular
floor," Deasis says. "The patient-nurse ratio is only one to one

—it's five to one on a regular ward—but in here you have to be alert all the time, because patients can suddenly die in front of your eyes. The physical activity is less, but the emotional and mental toll is enormous."

The frequently short and unhappy career of an intensive care nurse was outlined by Janet Boller in the professional journal *Focus*. Inexperienced nurses, typically fresh from school and in their early twenties, take six months to a year to master the technological demands of the Unit. Then, as they reach proficiency, they are saddled with increasingly difficult cases, and the pressure of constant exposure to the critically ill and dying mounts. Often they feel overworked and underappreciated, frustrated, and restless. Many wonder whether the effort and energy they have invested in intensive care nursing have been worthwhile. Some go on to other types of nursing. Others return to school. Still others leave the profession altogether. "I challenge any intelligent and motivated individual to work 12 to 18 months continuously as a staff person in any busy ICU," Boller writes, "without developing symptoms of . . . burnout."

In an effort to ease the stress and reduce the turnover, Deasis instituted programs such as peer teaching, where the more experienced nurses train newcomers. She also let nurses undertake research projects, gave them a voice in scheduling—she introduced flexible shifts of seven and a half, ten, and twelve hours—and encouraged them to attend a weekly session with a social worker and a psychiatrist, which I suspect is devoted in large measure to the difficulties of getting along with physicians.

Not that doctors, especially residents, don't have their own problems in the Unit. If modern physicians have become gadget-dependent, intensive care units turn them into technocrats. But even the wealth of sophisticated medical technology can't solve every problem. Indeed, having at hand all the appropriate physiological facts, only to discover that one's own brain works far more slowly than the equipment that supplies those facts, can be unnerving. I have seen more than a few residents humbled.

The answer, I believe, is to concentrate on the patients, not the information processors. The longer you work in an intensive care unit, the more you realize that it comes down to human issues, and human beings. So you talk to the patient, you talk to the family, you think, you look, you meditate. CICU workers have become accustomed to instant answers. I spend a lot of time just saying, "I don't know, I have to think." It really catches the staff by surprise, and it may be the most important thing they learn.

9

Patient, Heal Thyself
First Steps to Recovery

To WALK ACROSS THE plaza from the new Mount Sinai of Mrs. Annenberg's tower to the old Mount Sinai of the Stella S. Housman Pavilion is to travel back in time. Except for the bright racing stripes lining the walls, color-coded to identify the different floors, the somber brick landmark doesn't look too different from the way it looked during the Great Depression, when it was home to victims of influenza and tuberculosis. Some members of the Board of Trustees would like to raze the fifty-five-year-old structure, no doubt to make room for another glass-and-steel hulk. Mount Sinai fund-raisers have gathered hundreds of millions of dollars in construction pledges, but regulators have been hesitant to let them spend the money, fearing that the hospital's costs, of which the government pays a big chunk, would soar. So the old Housman wards remain, including the ones on the third floor that have been pressed into service for one of medicine's newest epidemics: status—post CABG.

Though many hospitals put bypass patients in wards nearly as well-equipped as intensive care units, there is a certain spartan logic about Housman 3. The bathroom in the hall gives patients an incentive to get up and start walking. The four-bed rooms provide built-in companionship. Patients on Housman 3 heal the old-fashioned way. Instead of twentieth-century technology, the staff relies on tincture of time—leave it alone and let it get better.

And it usually does. Bypass patients, unlike victims of cancer and other progressive diseases, have a natural tendency to improve. A properly planned and executed surgical wound incorporates the mechanisms of its repair at the moment of its execution. In response to the trauma of the blade, cells called fibroblasts infiltrate the area around the incision and produce strands of collagen to knit the edges together. It takes longer for the superficial nerves to recover from injury, but their malfunction temporarily provides the soothing blessing of numbness. When enough new tissue has formed to make the connection complete, the body switches off the repair mechanism and goes about its ordinary business.

This is not to say that getting better is automatic. It is good to remember that no physician, no matter how knowledgeable, can recover a patient. Patients must do their own recovering, and at any point in the process a host of confounding physical and psychological factors can intervene. Still, in the low-tech world of Housman 3, it is a physician's assistant, rather than a physician, who most often gives nature a helping hand, using a roster of medications so standard they are outlined on preprinted discharge orders issued on transfer from the CICU: digitalis, to control common arrhythmias; vitamins and iron, to help rebuild the battered blood; and an antibiotic to finish the battle against infection that was started before surgery.

None of these is so important that it won't be stopped if side effects develop. That also goes for the aspirin and dipyridamole used to keep the newly installed coronary grafts wide open. Before this regimen was developed, about 10 percent of the grafts became clogged by blood clots before their owners left the hospital. With the two drugs, the problem has been reduced manyfold, clearing the way for the wall of the transplanted vein to thicken gradually into a reasonable semblance of a coronary artery.

The electrical disturbances of the heart rhythm, so common during the stay in the CICU, tend to quiet down on Housman 3. But it's not unheard of for a person making good progress to get to the fourth or fifth day after surgery and suddenly feel weak, sweaty, and dizzy, the result of atria racing out of control. Most of the time, the heart can easily be coaxed back into the normal rhythm with pacesetting impulses delivered through the temporary electrodes that were implanted in the operating room.

How does it feel to get over heart surgery? It hurts much worse than any angina that may have prompted it. Just the fifteen-minute wheelchair ride from the CICU is enough to knock you out for the rest of the day. Then there's the pincushion syndrome: From toe to head, you will become increasingly aware of a multitude of aches and pains from the needles, tubes, and incisions that the god Morpheus clouded from your consciousness during the early days of recovery.

With so many places hurting at once, you'll hardly notice that the foot on your surgical leg has puffed up to a 14 triple-E, especially with the distraction of the red-black scar along the inside of the thigh and calf, which commemorates the harvesting of the saphenous vein. Since it's merely a superficial vessel, it won't be missed. (The deep veins that are the conduits back to the heart have hardly been touched.) But the tiny lymphatic channels that were disrupted when the vein was removed were the homeward pathways for fluids, and those fluids now have no place to go but down.

The ankle isn't painful, at least compared with the leg, but nothing heals when it is swollen, so we'll wrap it in an elastic stocking. While you are on your back, you'll be spending most of the time with your leg elevated and gravity lessening the swelling. This reduces the danger of blood clots, which can break loose from surgically irritated leg veins and travel to the lungs. Pulmonary embolism kills about 50,000 hospital patients a year, making it among the most lethal of surgical complications, but bypass patients, who are more mobile than most, seem to be at lower risk.

In any patient who has undergone major surgery, fluid migrates out of the cells and into what is called the body's third space—the space not in the body's cells or in the circulation. Along about the third postoperative day, this fluid is drawn into the circulatory system and delivered to the kidneys, which add it to the urine. That means frequent trips down the hall to the bathroom, and that can present another problem, since there is often a terrible burning sensation after the bladder catheter is removed. (This is less an issue for women because of their shorter urethras.) Pyridium, an anesthetic that numbs the urinary tract, also turns the urine fire-engine red, enabling enterprising patients to make small fortunes from wagers in the ward's communal john. What are the odds on having scarlet urine?

On the other hand, there is the problem of urine retention. The bladder, like the heart, can be stretched so much that it loses its elasticity, and antiarrhythmic drugs and pain-killing narcotics can make things worse. It sometimes takes a while for bladder tone to be restored. If you can't manage to empty your bladder within eight hours after the catheter's removal, you'll face the truly disturbing prospect of having it reinserted, this time while you are awake to experience it. That tends to concentrate the mind on this most basic bodily function, and the resulting anxiety often makes the task of urinating even more difficult.

Given the anesthetics and narcotics, which depress the gastrointestinal tract, and all the missed meals, bowel movements aren't an issue in the first few postoperative days. But a few days after your arrival on Housman 3, the moment should come. If not, we start with milk of magnesia, then move on to an ominous-sounding cocktail known as the black-and-white, one part cascara and one part magnesia, or even stronger measures.

Hospital cuisine hardly makes anyone's mouth water. Even if it did, the combination of such stomach-gnawing medications as aspirin, iron, and antibiotics would almost certainly squelch a budding appetite. Still, nourishment becomes increasingly important. Surgery has broken down a lot of tissue, and your body needs fuel to rebuild. If you're not eating enough, we'll provide supplements and encourage visitors to bring snacks. When pressed, we might even turn the other way while a corned beef sandwich slips in, sodium notwithstanding. (On my first rotation as a third-year medical student, I once found a bag of them under a patient's bed.)

If you have gallstone trouble, bypass surgery can aggravate it. Even if you don't, it may seem as if you do because the chest incision can reach the top of the abdominal cavity and irritate the peritoneum, a cardinal sign of gallbladder disease. As in the CICU, you'll frequently be reminded to cough in order to clear your lungs. If it hurts too much, we'll give you extra pain medicine. There will be chest X rays every other day to check for collapsed airways or signs of pneumonia. If you've been a smoker—and many patients have been, since smoking is linked with coronary disease—you'll probably have more problems clearing your lungs. Of course, you'll probably also be a better cougher.

Your chest will be sore all over, but the sharpest pain will emanate from a point just under the throat, where the incision has been pulled together like a Windsor knot. When you cough or turn suddenly, it may feel as if your chest is about to burst open. It won't. The bone-to-bone connection is held together with eight or ten steel wires. The stability of the chest incision, called a median sternotomy, enables bypass patients to get on their feet much faster than, say, someone who has just had a gallbladder removed. And the chest incision hurts far less than the soft tissue wounds of abdominal surgery, which are sensitive to the slightest push and pull.

Behind the vertical chest scar sits the pericardium, the sac around the heart that was cut open during the operation and sewn shut after the grafts were connected. It is similar in composition to the lining of a joint, and feels somewhat arthritic after surgery. Through the stethoscope, the inflamed pericardium sounds like sandpaper as it rubs against the beating heart. Sometimes, this irritation causes fluid to collect beneath the membrane. Postsurgical pericarditis can be a nuisance, since it often leads to chest pain that is hard to distinguish from a patient's worst fear—a recurrence of angina, the condition the operation was designed to eliminate. Like arthritis, pericarditis can be treated with aspirin or a host of new anti-inflammatory drugs. Occasionally, a more severe case develops with fever, pain, palpitations, and shortness of breath. Then we call out the heavy artillery—cortisone.

The most dreaded complication of the chest incision, as the case of Nathan Gerstein illustrated, is an infection of the space around the heart called mediastinitis. It can spread to the breastbone and reduce it to the consistency of pea soup. So much pus can collect that the heart itself can become compressed, requiring an emergency operation to reopen and drain the chest and a long period of recuperation back in the CICU, on a respirator and undergoing intensive antibiotic therapy. Fewer than 1 percent of CABG patients fall victim to mediastinitis, but of that small number, few survive.

Your blood has not only been diluted with several liters of intravenous solutions during and after surgery but has also taken a beating from the cardiopulmonary bypass pump. Add to that a vampirelike series of blood-draining tests, and you have the makings of anemia. It takes weeks for the body to fill the deficit, so almost everyone leaves Housman 3 with an abnormal blood count. Although the normal hematocrit level (the ratio of blood cells to liquid plasma) is about 45 percent, you may come out of the operating room at around 25 percent and be up to only 30 or 35 percent when you are discharged. Essentially, it's a matter of balance. If your blood has too few red cells (a hematocrit of less than 25 to 30 percent), you'll feel weak, and your heart will have to work harder to supply enough oxygen to your tissues. If your blood is too thick with red cells (a hematocrit greater than 50 percent), your heart also will have to work harder to pump it through your body. As for white cells, a count that is too high could mean infection, while one that is too low could mean reduced resistance to infection. Similarly, too few platelets in the blood could lead to hemorrhage, but too many could clog the grafts.

Certain chemicals in the blood also rise after surgery, including bilirubin, a pigment related to hemoglobin, and alkaline phosphatase, an enzyme that leaks out of the cracked breastbone. Levels of electrolytes such as sodium, potassium, chloride, and bicarbonate need to be monitored and adjusted by the nurses, but there is less concern about low levels of calcium, phosphorous, and magnesium, which leach out of the blood as it travels through the bypass pump. Albumin, an important protein, almost always drops after major surgery, but plummets even more after bypass. A rise in blood urea nitrogen and creatinine, two wastes cleared by the kidneys, could indicate renal failure, a complication that could require dialysis.

Rather than give transfusions, we try to let Mother Nature build up the blood supply gradually. Screening has lessened the risk of some forms of transfusion-borne hepatitis, but there are new ones to worry about. Even more worrisome today is the specter of AIDS (acquired immune deficiency syndrome), a disease that destroys the body's ability to fight off infection, invariably with fatal consequences.

Since the development of bypass surgery in the 1960s, the rate of complications has steadily diminished. But when they happen, complications can vastly lengthen a patient's hospital stay and impair recovery. A 1981 study of 365 bypass patients at the University of California at Long Beach found that 27 percent had postoperative problems, about half of which were classified as major. Among those at high risk were people over sixty, people who spent a long time attached to the bypass pump, people who received more than five grafts, and people with diabetes. Similar results have been reported from other well-known bypass centers, including the Cleveland Clinic.

"Every affection of the mind that is attended with either pain or pleasure, hope or fear, is the cause of an agitation whose influence extends to the heart." Bypass patients are living proof not only of the truth of William Harvey's statement but also of its converse. Several studies have found small brain lesions and reduced regional blood flow in cardiac surgical patients, though they failed to detect any adverse effects. Another investigator found that the IQ of bypass patients drops slightly after surgery, only to return to preoperative levels in six weeks. The brain, used to the natural pulse of blood from the heart, may be foggy from the steady flow of the bypass pump. Anesthesia during the operation and the disorientation that follows it can leave a gap in the memory that rips at a patient's confidence. But more importantly, the entire surgical ordeal can expose the chinks in a patient's emotional armor and summon to the surface deeply rooted fears and anxieties. You can tell something is going on by the strange dreams common during the early postoperative period. Consider this example: "I was on a cruise and the ship was sinking and people were throwing furniture through the porthole . . . only they were coming toward my chest and toward my groin. I kicked so hard I woke myself up."

If one were to undertake a study of the psychological stresses after bypass surgery, leaving the intensive care unit for the ward would top the list. The CICU may be an unsettling environment, but a patient never gets the feeling there of being ignored. On Housman 3, the nurse-patient ratio is lower than in the intensive care unit, and the computer-patient ratio is lower still. "It's like being pushed out of the nest," a patient once told me. "Up there, you're never alone. Down here, you don't get more attention than anyone else. It can get scary, especially at night."

And if patients are buoyed in the CICU by the euphoria of survival—there are few greater joys than waking up after surgery—once they get to Housman 3 they are confronted with the depressing reality of putting their lives back together. Unrealistic goals can make matters worse. Patients who have long suffered from cardiac disease tend to expect less from surgery because they've adjusted to being sick. Sometimes, though, these cardiac veterans allow themselves the faith-healing fantasy that they will be able to throw away their pills after surgery. When they discover that they still need drugs—and sometimes still have pain—they can be crushed.

When the patient is struck by disease in youth, he often is defiant and angry. For the vigorous middle-aged patient who suddenly finds himself facing the surgeon after the onset and acceleration of angina, there is the "Why me?" phase, then the "Will I live?" phase, and then the "What will I do now?" phase. Finally come the questions "Can I work? Can I make love? Can I play with my children [or grandchildren]?"

Support from the family can take some of the bumps out of recovery; then again, if a patient's relatives have succumbed to heart disease, perhaps because advances like bypass surgery were not available in their day, a cardiac survivor syndrome can evolve in which patients feel guilty for their rescue, a reaction that interferes with the motivation to recover.

The psychiatric rites of passage through heart surgery were apparent several years before Favaloro sewed his first vein graft. In a paper titled "Emotions and the Outcome of Cardiac Surgery," published in the *Bulletin of the New York Academy of Sciences,* Janet A. Kennedy and Hyman Bakst divide patients into several "rudimentary but fundamental psychological categories."

Let's call Group I the Healthy Deniers. According to Kennedy and Bakst, they tend "to recognize the risks of surgery and the possibility of death, but the denial mechanism blocks out the fear of anesthesia, periods of helplessness and unconsciousness, and any idea of unpleasantness or difficulty in the operating and recovery rooms."

Group II are the Illness-Dependent. They "seem to have accepted realistically the limitations imposed by the disease. They accept or seem to accept the aid provided by medical staff personnel. They cooperate with procedures up to the point of catheterization and sometimes beyond it, but—they do not want rescue. They are addicted to a disease dependent way of life."

Group III are the Terrified. They "are characterized by a degree of panic that may effectively paralyze their long-term and short-term defenses, whether they are neurotic or healthy. . . . Quite simply, [they are] suffering from a conflict between a strong desire to be well and a no less strong dread of the terrifying prospect of surgery and all its implications of helplessness and the menace of immediate death."

Group IV are the Medical Addicts. They are trapped "by the recognition of the value of freedom from the crippling disease and the terror of giving up the secondary gain of dependency. . . . They demand too much medication, they pull out tubes, are sleepless, and if they do not die in the recovery room from exhaustion or psychosis, they will not use the rescue once they are discharged."

Group V are the Suicidal. "These patients find life intolerable. . . . Their wish to die is greater than their fear of surgery. In addition, they do not expect to be here to face any pain after the operation. If they are approved for operation, the rest of it, as far as they are concerned, will be taken care of for them. The surgeon will be the executioner. Here the psychiatrist must not be misled by a seeming readiness, even an eagerness, for surgery."

Monitoring the progress of patients in these categories during the surgical ordeal, Kennedy and Bakst gathered some intriguing findings. Preoperatively, the few medical complications were concentrated among the members of Group II, while psychiatric problems were most often found among those in Groups II and IV. As might be expected, there were a greater number of serious medical and psychological problems after surgery. The incidence of arrhythmias, shock, and similar difficulties was lowest among the members of Group I and Group III and highest among those in Group II and Group IV. The rate of serious psychiatric complications was also lowest in Group I, higher in Group IV, and highest in Group III, which the authors attributed "to the serious ambivalence in these latter two groups of patients, and the maximum strain thereby imposed on their psychological defenses." Group I had the fewest postoperative deaths, and Group IV had the most, "thus emphasizing the severe penalty paid by these patients for the combination of strong anxiety and weak motivation." The seasoned clinician listens hard to the Group V patient who before surgery exclaims, "I'll die if I go through with this," for he often turns out to be right. "It is our thesis," the authors conclude, "that the psychological and physiological states are inseparable, and that both must receive proper attention if the patient is to undergo surgery under optimal conditions."

Among those at Mount Sinai concerned with this task is Brenda Weiss, one of two social workers assigned to bypass patients. She helps them through the immediate postoperative difficulties, at the same time trying not to stir any neuroses that surgery may have brought to the surface. "You can't open up all that in a short hospitalization," she says. "I can pass along the warning down the line and make it part of a referral to a community hospital, but I can't resolve a complicated psychological disorder in the eight or ten days I have with patients."

Does this frustrate her? Certainly. But given the pressures of Housman 3, there isn't much she can do about it. "You can see the handwriting on the wall, sure," Weiss says, "but you don't look at the wall."

Weiss hears about troublesome cases from everyone—technicians and housekeepers, cardiologists and surgeons. She makes scouting rounds in the CICU, where she looks for such danger signs as an unusual flurry of activity around a bed or a particularly anxious expression on the face of a spouse. The primary source of information, however, are the nurses, who meet with her in a small lounge off the Housman 3 corridor every Tuesday morning at 11:30 to go over the entire roster of patients. Medical problems are discussed only incidentally; what matters is what is going on in the patients' minds. Here is how such a session sounds.*

WEISS. Let's review last week's cases. Mr. Johnson, how is he doing? Is he back to his grumpiness?

NURSE ONE. He's been just impossible about the food. He copes by being picky and grouchy.

NURSE TWO. What about his wife? I hear she's incapacitated in some way, and he's supposed to be taking care of her. He may need some extra help there when he goes home.

WEISS. Basically, his thing is control. It's been hard for him to accept his bypass, so he nitpicks about other things to get us running around in circles. His illness has really compromised his whole social situation.

*Compiled from transcripts of several sessions.

Now, I have some news about Mrs. Moloney. She had to go back to the OR for bleeding. [Groans all around. She had been on Housman 3 for several weeks and was a favorite of the staff.] What about Mrs. Abrahams?

NURSE THREE. She's doing much better. She had a psychiatric consult, and she's fine.

WEISS. Okay, I'm open for referrals.

NURSE FOUR. There's Mrs. Howell in Bed 3A. She's very apathetic. She's quite obese; she just lies there. She was very angry preop, very scared. I don't think she believed she needed surgery. She was focusing on the leg incision, and of course they had to use veins from both legs. She also had a very bad experience in the CICU. She was frightened of the X-ray machine. She thought it was going to fall on her. She was very glad to get to Housman.

WEISS. She didn't seem to be a problem for the staff up in the CICU, so I suspect this is a whole internal production.

NURSE FOUR. I had another patient who had a terrible experience in the CICU, and when she got down here, it just all poured out. She kept saying, "Please don't make me go back there."

NURSE FIVE. They feel so dependent on the nurses up there for survival that they don't dare say anything. Then they come down here and complain about everything.

WEISS. Okay, I'll stop by and talk to her. What about Mr. Mann?

NURSE SIX. He looks better now. I was wondering if we could get him off the floor for a walk.

WEISS. Bed 4A? Who's got Mr. Chudkov?

NURSE SEVEN. He's very anxious, very upset. He thought he was going to die. But today he feels a little better. He's from Russia, you know, and he has language problems.

WEISS. I think it would be good to have him screened, so I'll interview him this afternoon. 4C?

NURSE TWO. That's Mrs. Golden. She's leaving tomorrow.

WEISS. 4D? 5?

NURSE SIX. They're both being discharged home.

WEISS. What about Mr. Wallace? Is he still so depressed and anxious?

NURSE TWO. Yes, but I really think it has more to do with his financial problems than his bypass.

NURSE ONE. His wife and son visit every day, so that's helping. You know, she really thought he was going to die. Now she's so relieved and upbeat.

WEISS. I saw her over the weekend. She's very supportive. So, Bed C?

NURSE SIX. C's okay and D's okay.

WEISS. 6?

NURSE FOUR. She just came down from the CICU. Mrs. Terrence. She's in her late seventies. Very independent. Lives alone. Her family doesn't live that near, so she's going to need a home-health-care person. She won't be able to do her own shopping or cooking or take care of her apartment. Her private duty nurse told me she's very involved in a senior citizens' group. She went to dinners and dances and on bus trips. She said she's angry about the cost of the nurse. She can't really afford the $300 a day for very long.

WEISS. Well, she's going to need someone for at least two or three weeks until she can get back on her feet. But why does she need a private nurse now?

NURSE TWO. I don't know. And her insurance doesn't cover it. Her doctor told her to cancel it, but she didn't want to. She wants someone there all the time.

WEISS. That is a *bad* sign. It sounds like the beginning of some kind of pseudodependency. I think it would be worth my while to go and talk to her. She may feel that she needs the care and attention, but it could also be an exaggerated holding on. When you see it in the face of shrinking resources, it's a red flag. Maybe we can get her to drop the nurse during the daytime. Room 7?

NURSE SIX. Mr. Wright is coping very well. As long as his pain is under control, anyway. He's getting oxycodone and was fine all morning. He even shaved himself today.

NURSE ONE. Yes, he started physical therapy yesterday, and that did a lot for his mood. They had him moving his leg in ways that he didn't think it could. One thing that worried him was the confusion over whether the leg incision needed to be opened up and drained.

WEISS. It's the old problem of doctors working out the problem over a patient's bed, while the patient hangs on every word. Maybe we can get a muzzle for Dr. Mindich. Room 8?

NURSE THREE. 8A is Mr. Lowenthal. He's a routine case, going home tomorrow. 8B is Freund. He's doing okay, but he has a history of alcohol abuse.

NURSE FOUR. I thought he looked rundown. I knew it was something.

WEISS. Okay, I'll stop by. Now, I talked with Mr. Bernstein in 8C for a long time.

NURSE TWO. I know. You really picked him up.

WEISS. I dropped in for twenty minutes, and two hours later I managed to haul myself down the elevator. You can't get away from him. Seriously, this is a classic case. The illness and the surgery stirred up all kinds of unfinished business for him. He is the oldest survivor of three brothers. The others died at twenty-seven and thirty-five, not from heart disease. He has an ambivalent relationship with his mother. And his father, with whom he got along somewhat better, is dead. He told me he died of diabetes. I said, "You know, nobody really dies of diabetes." And he said, "Well, I guess he really died of heart trouble." He said he had to take six days off when his father died. He never mentioned anything about being sad. His response was to double up on his work load. He puts out some sort of magazine. This time, for the first time, he can't double up on his work load. He can't use work to put himself out of his misery. So he's lying there, and it's all coming bubbling up. I think the only thing to do is send him home with a referral to a psychiatrist.

NURSE TWO. It's really frustrating that we so seldom get psychiatry consults while they're here.

WEISS. Now, is Mr. Bartkowski still on the floor?

NURSE ONE. He's going tomorrow. I just don't feel that anything we're teaching him is sinking in. He seems so laid back, I don't know if he understands anything.

WEISS. Mr. Stanhope looks as depressed as ever.

NURSE SIX. Actually, he's much better. He's with Mrs.

Emory, and you can't go near them without multiple complaints. But they seem to be cheering each other up.

WEISS. Whatever works.

NURSE THREE. Mr. Chambers' family wanted me to put him in a private room, so the sons could stay here overnight. What do you think?

WEISS. Well, he has no extraordinary medical needs. It's more the psychological problem of disorientation and anger at being a patient. He's very upset. He has to be integrated more into being a patient. I don't know if putting him alone is really the right thing for him.
Are there any more referrals?

NURSE SIX. There's Mr. Sloane in 9B. I think he's hard of hearing. And he doesn't seem to have company very often. There is one woman visitor, but she never gets close to him, like maybe she's scared of catching something.

WEISS. I'll stop in. And Mr. Raybeck? The roster says he's supposed to go home tomorrow. He doesn't need any discharge services?

NURSE SEVEN. He still seems distant to me.

NURSE SIX. He's been that way since he's been in the hospital. And he's always trying to sneak a cigarette. He used to smoke two or three packs a day of Camels. . . .

WEISS. Clint Eastwood's brand.

NURSE SIX. . . . and when he got here he mentioned he drinks a lot.

WEISS. That would explain his being so distant. 9D?

NURSE TWO. He's okay.

WEISS. Room 80?

NURSE TWO. She wants a visiting nurse.

WEISS. She had a long course in the CICU, and I think she deserves one. And that brings us to 81.

NURSE FIVE. He looks like he's practically ready to go home. He even puts his jogging clothes on each day.

Rehabilitation: The word conjures up images of sweating people lashed to Nautilus machines. Obviously, the patients on Housman 3 aren't ready for anything this strenuous. But like their colleagues in coronary distress, the victims of heart attacks, bypass patients can benefit from a program of regular exercise, especially when it comes with education in how to modify the risk factors that contributed to their need for surgery. A well-designed rehabilitation program can speed the healing of body and mind, cut several days off hospitalization and several thousand dollars off the bill, and most important, set patients on the road to cardiovascular fitness.

The Mount Sinai rehab team is led by S. Robert Levine, an earnest young cardiologist with a "Gimme a Break" button on his lapel who conducts the initial exam and checks the patients' progress each day. Margaret Macari, the nurse-coordinator, oversees the work of the exercise therapists, Marilyn Steinmetz and Lydia Ayala. Brenda Weiss and her social worker colleague Connie Cotter handle adjustment problems. And nutritionist Susan Wiener tries to teach patients a sensible diet (although the hospital kitchen is still as likely as not to serve them a cholesterol-laden breakfast of bacon and eggs—I don't understand why).

In a way, rehabilitation begins even before surgery. Team members try to check in on bypass patients the day before their operations, evaluating their physical condition and any psychological factors that might impede recovery. Patients are coached in the deep-breathing exercises that they will continue every waking hour of their stay on Housman 3, along with a regimen of such muscle-flexing exercises as ankle twirls, knee bends, torso twists, hand clasps, and shoulder rolls. These simple exercises, besides reducing the risk of postsurgical blood clots, help bypass patients get back in tune with their bodies. Some patients hold their breath at the moment of peak exertion, instead of relaxing so their breathing can mesh with their bodies' demand for oxygen. Such out-of-phase breathing imposes stress on the cardiovascular system and on the chest incision, and it can make even gentle muscle flexing much harder.

We'll try to get you out of bed and on your feet as soon as possible after your arrival on Housman 3. For starters, there will be a warm-up consisting of a few minutes of the motion exercises, followed by ten minutes of walking and another ten minutes of stretching and deep breathing to cool down. Your vital signs will be frequently monitored, and if your heart rate increases more than thirty beats per minute or your blood pressure drops significantly, we'll stop the workout and try it again the next day. Otherwise, you'll walk, and we'll watch. And if you do well, we'll ask you to repeat the routine on your own later in the day.

About five minutes will be added to your routine on each of the five to seven days you are on Housman 3. We'll gradually throw in some stairs, three up and three down. By the time you are ready to leave, you will be walking for twenty-five to thirty minutes and climbing up and down a flight of stairs, twice a day. This is hardly the kind of regimen likely to produce a Jesse Owens, but that isn't its goal. Far from conditioning, the purpose of these exercises is to prevent *de*conditioning. After spending two weeks in bed, a patient will have lost 40 to 50 percent of his cardiovascular endurance, making it hard to coordinate the blood vessel constriction and hormonal and neurologic changes required for that complex hemodynamic process known as standing. The more highly trained an individual is, the longer it will take for him to get back into his former shape. On the other hand, because they so often have angina, many bypass patients aren't in very good shape to start with, so it doesn't take much deconditioning to reduce them to helplessness.

Toward the end of your stay on Housman 3, we'll put you back on the treadmill, but this time, you'll go at a low speed and relatively slight grade. Depending on how you do, we'll make up an exercise prescription for you to take home. If you are like most patients, you'll start with a routine slightly shorter than the one you have been doing in the hospital and increase it by five to ten minutes a week. By the fourth week, you should be up to an hour a day of exercise (half an hour of walking plus warm-up and cool-down periods) five or six days a week. We'll also give you a target heart rate—70 percent of the rate you achieved on the post-op treadmill—which should not be exceeded in the first two weeks. After that, the heart rate gradually gets higher. Above all, the program is flexible. If you're uncomfortable at the target rate, slow down. How you feel is more important than your pulse rate.

For the high-risk patient whose heart may still have ischemic zones, the benefits of exercise have to be weighed against the risks, which include abnormal heart rhythms and loss of pumping power. But for the typical bypass patient, the program is fairly safe; in a study of 13,570 patients in thirty rehabilitation programs, the complication rate was one every 26,000 patient-hours, and the mortality rate was one every 116,402 hours. Of course, it's still possible to find cardiologists with the once widely held view that exercise strains hearts that have just been operated on. Given the statistics, however, most of us no longer hold our patients back.

On the other hand, the actual benefits of cardiac rehabilitation remain to be proved. We know that patients enrolled in programs can stay on treadmills longer and have a greater sense of well-being than patients who aren't. But whether rehabilitation retards the progression of coronary disease or improves the physical outlook for bypass patients is unclear.

"We can't prove it prolongs anyone's life, at least not yet," Levine says. "But we can show a marked improvement in patients' feelings about themselves. And there is also a hidden agenda to rehab—to get patients to take responsibility for their recovery, to give them back some control over their lives. We're saying, 'This is a partnership. There are things that can be done to help your recovery, and together we're going to do them.'" In many ways, this is the essence of the Housman 3 experience, the logical extension of requiring patients to walk down the hall to the bathroom and giving them the responsibility of picking up their medicines at the nursing station, rather than having a nurse deliver them to the bedside.

As for compliance with rehabilitation programs once patients leave Mount Sinai, Levine concedes it is not what he would like. "Most patients do the exercises for a while," he says. "It's tough, though, once they start feeling better."

All in all, we believe almost all coronary patients would profit from this kind of program, though relatively few enroll in them, either in or out of a hospital. America has 14 million heart patients—people who have suffered heart attacks, had bypass surgery, or have symptoms of coronary artery disease—but only 7 percent of the nation's hospitals have rehabilitation programs. Where they do exist, they can be expensive—one Massachusetts hospital, for example, charges $3,000 for a twelve-week outpatient program—although insurance sometimes covers the cost.

Sensing a market, several private companies have jumped into the rehabilitation business. United Medical Corporation already has a hundred centers, and Cardio-Pulmonary Rehab has fifty. Given the prevalence of coronary disease, they have been attracting attention on Wall Street, where the stock of such firms has been highly touted. When researchers followed more than two hundred men for four months after discharge, however, they found that those in a supervised rehabilitation program did no better on the treadmill than those who undertook a similar program on their own. Moral: Do-it-yourself exercise is just as good as the store-bought kind.

Unless complications arise, you'll be ready to go home ten days after surgery, or just about the time you've adjusted to life on Housman 3. The night before graduation, the pacing wires, the last souvenirs from the operating room, are removed from your chest. A nurse will give you a brown paper bag with a week's supply of medicines—Tylenol and codeine for pain, digoxin to prevent arrhythmias, aspirin and dipyridamole to keep your new grafts from clogging, and iron to build up the blood. Checkout time is 11 A.M. As you pack, you may feel more than a twinge of uncertainty. Out the window, the view ceases to be a diversion and becomes instead a landscape of challenge, maybe a threat. You may even find yourself feeling the way you did a week and a half earlier, when you prepared to enter the hospital to embark on the bypass ordeal.

I try to have my last visit at a time when family members are present. It helps to have witnesses around, in case questions come up later. Having been through such scenes hundreds of times, I have developed a recipe for recuperation. "You can go outside right away," I will begin, "but take care to keep the sunlight off the incisions. The new skin can't take it. And avoid extremes of temperatures. Go to bed early and get up early. Even if you are planning to go back to work—and we hope you will—consider yourself a temporary retiree. Take naps twice a day, for sixty or ninety minutes each. Exercise three times a day, in the fresh air whenever possible. You'll be more sensitive to colds, so try to avoid people who have them. Eat three or four meals a day, and eat them slowly. Of course, don't smoke. Avoid tension; remember the things that bring you stress and try to step away from them.

"Space out your activities. Don't cram too much into one day and then try to make it up with extra rest the next day. It won't work. Be careful when picking up heavy objects, reaching over your head, or opening stuck jar lids or windows—beware of all the things that might make you grunt. You'll hurt in places not directly affected by the surgery, like your back and knees. And you may find that, after making steady progress for a few days, you'll go back a step. It happens to all patients. But if you feel crummy two days in a row, let us know.

"During the first week, you should stay close to home, so you can jump into bed if you need to. By the second week, you'll be ready to start visiting friends and resocializing. You may find it less taxing going out to lunch than dinner, but in any event, don't overeat, and stay away from alcohol. In the third week, you can resume driving, but try to avoid trips longer than an hour. If travel is necessary, get up every forty minutes or so and walk around for a bit. Plane trips are permitted, but again try to get up once in a while. Go to the park and do that twenty minutes of exercise. You can jog lightly or swim, but don't let it get too strenuous. Your chest will still be sore, but most of the time you won't need any pain medicine.

"By the fourth week, you should be doing everything you were doing before the operation except for vigorous athletics and work. As more time goes by, you'll keep feeling better and better. The tissues will mend, the incision will flatten and nearly disappear, and your strength will return. In a sense, recovery never ends. The concept of an end was invented by insurance companies and compensation lawyers."

Like Freud, bypass patients know that it all comes down to love and work, so I spend a lot of time on these subjects. "It's natural to feel a depressed libido. It will take time to reestablish a comfortable, intimate relationship with your partner. Sex is best when you are well-rested, in familiar surroundings, and with someone who is familiar. So it may not be the smartest thing to rush into a new affair. After three weeks, you should be able to have intercourse, although you may have to alter positions because of chest soreness. It may also be a good idea to start out with activities that don't have a goal of orgasm, which can strain the heart by raising the blood pressure and the heart rate.

"As for work, after you've been home for a month, you can begin to make plans, but I don't want you actually going back until at least the first week of the second postoperative month. Any earlier, and you are pushing too hard, slipping down the Type A slope. That could lead to a return trip to the hospital. Some resume much later, but most of the people who return to work do so within three months. It's best to start with three half-days the first week, then five half-days the second week, then some full days in the third week. It should take several more weeks to build up to a full schedule, and you shouldn't even think about more than a nine-to-five day for at least several more months."

Finally, I tell my patients that all Mount Sinai bypasses come with a lifetime warranty. It's my feeling that patients with post-operative problems should first try to reach their family physician or cardiologist, since these doctors are likely to be nearby and more familiar with the patient's background. But at Mount Sinai, we don't cut the umbilical cord to our patients, and we're open twenty-four hours a day, seven days a week, the way gas stations used to be.

It's not unusual for patients to start to cry while I'm delivering my spiel. The whole coronary event, from the first symptom to the diagnostic testing to the decision to have a bypass to the confusion of the CICU and the aches and pains of Housman 3, is finally hitting home, and they are overwhelmed. Some of them feel pushed back into the world of the healthy without symptoms that they may have used as a crutch. Getting better can be almost as stressful as getting sick, and recovery as much of a dilemma as disease. There is a built-in paradox about bypass surgery, which at once offers patients relief from pain and certifies an illness. We give our patients a new lease on life, but we are also reminding them that the atherosclerotic process goes silently, steadily onward.

10

Atherosclerotics Anonymous
Risk Factors and Relapses

BYPASS SURGERY OFFERS MANY patients a second chance. They have endured a coronary event, but their new vein grafts are starting from scratch. Surgery has left them in an artificial state of grace: The procedure has temporarily reduced cholesterol levels, subsequent bed rest has lowered the blood pressure, and patients are smoking less, if at all. Whether they stay that way is an open question, since bypass doesn't halt atherosclerosis— only circumvents it. The choices a patient makes can play a large role in determining whether the grafts will clog (and studies show 10 percent become blocked every year) as well as whether the unbypassed arteries will stay open. By cleaning up their acts, bypass patients greatly improve the odds of avoiding a heart attack or a second operation. In spite of the pain, the expense, and the risk—mainly because of scar tissue left from the first operation—repeat bypasses are on the rise across the nation. At Mount Sinai, for example, there are now two or three re-ops a week.

All of which is why we don't let bypass patients out of the

hospital without a crash course in coronary risk factors and how some of them can be changed. An ounce of prevention is always good medicine, even when it comes after a pound of cure.

THE UNMODIFIABLES—AGE, SEX, AND FAMILY HISTORY

Atherosclerosis begins in childhood, but, like all progressive diseases, it takes its toll as we grow older. This doesn't mean age confers absolute protection: Each year, 1 percent of all men between the ages of thirty and sixty-two experience symptoms of coronary artery disease for the first time, and nearly half of that 1 percent have heart attacks. Moreover, youth does not counteract the harmful effects of cigarette smoking or the risk of family history.

Unlike the impact of age, which is relatively easy to explain, the difference in coronary risk for males and females has been an enigma since Osler's day. The issue comes down to this: Are men in greater peril, or are women somehow protected? Males smoke more than females, have higher blood pressure, and have a less favorable ratio of harmful low density lipoprotein (LDL) to protective high density lipoprotein (HDL). Female hormones may alter cholesterol metabolism for the better or even retard atherosclerosis, but this hormonal advantage may be negated by use of oral contraceptives. Diabetes somehow cancels the protection that being female confers. And although the concept of a Type A personality was developed with men in mind, a corresponding female stress syndrome is beginning to emerge in the medical journals. As women come to make up a larger proportion of the hard-driving, cigarette-smoking, overeating population, it seems reasonable to expect that they will find themselves facing greater coronary hazard.

To an extent, all risk factors are an interaction of biology and circumstance, but the gender puzzle is particularly complex. All things being equal, females tend to lag about eight years behind males in the morbidity tables, and although the incidence of disease rises after menopause, women never reach the same rate as men.

Which brings us to the last of the unmodifiables—a family history of premature coronary disease, with the emphasis on premature. Since it is likely that half of anyone's relatives will eventually die of cardiovascular disease, it's not very meaningful when a patient says his grandfather died of a heart attack at eighty-nine. But when someone tells me his father had a heart attack at forty-six, it indicates a genetic disposition to coronary disease.

Physicians have long considered family history an important measure of atherosclerotic risk, but only lately has it become clear just how important it is. Studies have shown that the rate of heart attacks is two to four times higher among the immediate relatives of heart attack victims than among the immediate relatives of healthy control group members. Recent evidence from a California study of more than 4,000 men and women suggests that young males with heart attacks in their families have five times the normal risk of cardiovascular death, but that the extra risk fades as the men get older. Interestingly, no excess risk was found for women, no matter what their age.

THE MODIFIABLES
Hypertension

For years, researchers grappled with a chicken-and-egg dilemma: Did artery-hardening atherosclerosis cause hypertension, or did the wear and tear of high blood pressure lead to arterial disease? The Framingham study left no doubt that it was the latter. High blood pressure not only helps initiate this deadly disease, it feeds the fire of atherosclerosis by making the arteries more permeable to fat and causing the release of adrenalinlike compounds that make platelets stickier, trigger the production of certain prostaglandins, and stimulate smooth-muscle-cell proliferation. A high pressure throughout the system also forces the heart to work harder, increasing the potential for ischemia, heart attacks, and congestive heart failure. One of every six patients with coronary heart disease has hypertension; more impressive, one of every three patients with hypertension first comes to medical attention because of coronary heart disease, and two thirds of the hypertensive population die of coronary problems. Nor are the consequences of high blood pressure restricted to the heart. Hypertension is responsible for a two- to fivefold rise in the risk of death from all causes, including stroke, kidney failure, and aneurysms of major arteries. If it remains untreated, high blood pressure slices an average of twenty years from the lives of its victims.

The textbooks define normal blood pressure as 120/80 millimeters of mercury, but physicians generally settle for anything under 140/90, depending on a patient's age. Measuring blood pressure accurately is no simple matter, however, which is why the American Heart Association puts out a report on the subject every few years. Should a doctor use a standard blood pressure cuff on a fat arm, for example, it will yield a falsely high reading. Either a standard-size cuff must be used on the patient's forearm or a thigh-cuff on the upper arm.

To an extent, inaccuracy is unavoidable. Blood pressure varies not only from day to day and hour to hour but literally from heartbeat to heartbeat, so any single reading is really only an estimate. The degree of variability—called lability—increases with age and also with emotional stress (as when a doctor checks your blood pressure).

The first number, the systolic reading, represents the pressure in the cardiovascular system when the heart is pumping. To get it, the cuff is inflated around the arm until the artery running through it is completely blocked. Then the air is let out until the pressure falls to the point at which the force of the heart can push the blood beyond the cuff, producing a faint knocking noise called the first sound of Korotkoff. The point at which this sound disappears as the cuff is further deflated identifies the diastolic pressure, which is created by the elastic recoil of the aorta while the heart is relaxed and filling with blood.

Which is the important number? They both are. The higher either of them is, the higher the risk of cardiovascular trouble. (There is usually no danger from a lower-than-average blood pressure, though there is no evidence to suggest that the lower, the better.) Severe elevations of blood pressure can cause headaches, chest pain, and, rarely, shortness of breath, blurred vision, dizziness, or a feeling of pressure in the head. But the vast majority of the 60 million Americans with diastolic pressures above 90, now considered the low end of the high range, have no symptoms, which is why this silent killer is so hard to diagnose.

In fewer than 10 percent of the cases, the causes of hypertension can be traced to specific disorders: abdominal tumors; abnormalities of blood vessels, the nervous system, or hormones; toxic reactions to medications; heart problems such as a leaky aortic valve; hardened arteries; even excessive consumption of licorice. The other 90 percent of the cases are called "essential" hypertension, which is a medical euphemism for "we don't know what causes it." The leading theory is that a genetic defect impedes the pumping of sodium across the boundaries of the cells in the cardiovascular system, causing blood vessels to constrict and pressure to rise. Tense vessels in the kidneys lead to fluid buildup in the body, and even higher pressure.

Sodium in the diet turns up the heat under this biological pressure cooker, and in our fast-food society sodium is hard to avoid. Commercially canned green beans have 925 milligrams of sodium per cup, as against only 5 mg for a cup of fresh green beans. A frozen turkey TV dinner has 1,735 mg, compared with 210 mg for 9 ounces of roasted fresh turkey. Three ounces of ground beef has 57 mg, while similar portions of pork and bacon have 565 mg and 1,400 mg respectively. Three pieces of Kentucky Fried Chicken with gravy, cole slaw, and a roll has 2,285 mg of sodium, compared with 962 mg for a Big Mac and 909 mg for a Whopper. Shredded Wheat has just 1 mg per ounce, while there are 304 mg in an ounce of corn flakes. Alka-Seltzer has 500 mg per tablet, but Tums has practically no sodium. In addition to advising hypertensive patients to stay away from prepared foods, many doctors tell them to throw away their salt shakers or fill them with salty-tasting but sodium-free potassium chloride. (Incidentally, if you don't already have high pressure, salt may not give it to you. An analysis of diet data from 10,372 persons in the Health and Nutrition Survey conducted by the National Center for Health Care Statistics found that those with lower blood pressure actually had higher intakes of calcium, potassium, and—yes—sodium.)

If changes in diet fail, there are always drugs. There were 27 million new prescriptions written for the diuretics, beta blockers, and vasodilators to treat hypertensives in 1981, part of a $3.5 billion market in cardiovascular medications. Used singly or in combination, these drugs can bring almost anyone's blood pressure down, reducing the risk of stroke and retarding the progression of coronary disease. A study of 11,000 patients in the federal Hypertension Detection and Follow-Up Program showed that hypertensives treated with drugs had a mortality rate 20 percent lower than patients who did not receive them. However, other studies have found that, while blood pressure medicines cut the death rate from heart attacks nearly in half, deaths from other forms of heart disease actually rose. Beta blockers can also increase cholesterol levels, reduce the benefits of exercise, and aggravate diabetes. Diuretics can throw the body's potassium level out of whack, which can throw the heart's rhythm out of whack. Vasodilators may not prevent the sharp and potentially harmful rise of blood pressure that occurs during exercise.

Because of this, the pendulum may be beginning to swing

back to nondrug therapy that emphasizes weight loss, relaxation, exercise, and restriction of coffee and alcohol in addition to sodium. In May 1984, a committee of experts convened by the National Heart, Lung, and Blood Institute urged that such non-drug therapies be "pursued aggressively" in treating milder cases of hypertension.

Diabetes

The risk of coronary artery disease is twice as great in diabetic men as in nondiabetic men and three times as great in diabetic women as in those free of the disease. Why does diabetes eliminate the protective effect of gender, leaving diabetic women at as great a risk as nondiabetic men the same age? We don't know. Nor are we even sure what the link is between coronary disease and the glucose intolerance of diabetes. We do know that diabetics have higher than normal levels of blood fats called triglycerides, elevated levels of LDL cholesterol, and depressed levels of HDL cholesterol. There is also evidence that diabetes stimulates the blood-clotting mechanisms that play a major role in the atherosclerotic scenario.

In juvenile-onset diabetes, which usually shows up before age thirty, the pancreas is incapable of producing enough insulin to drive the glucose, or sugar, from the bloodstream into the body's cells so that it can be used as fuel. Daily injections of insulin are required. Adults who become diabetic are able to produce a large supply of insulin, but not when they need it. They can often get by by taking sugar-lowering pills. Since adult diabetics tend to be obese and hypertensive, losing weight is important both in improving insulin responsiveness and in lowering coronary risk.

Physical Inactivity

The Framingham study made a convincing case against physical inactivity. The 16 percent of the males and 21 percent of the females judged to live virtually motionless lives had 3.5 times the rate of coronary heart disease of active persons. Physicians would love to believe that the converse is true—namely, that vigorous exercise helps prevent heart disease—but the jury is still out. Naysayers point to tragic evidence—the death of "the complete runner," James F. Fixx, while striding down a Vermont lane at the tender age of fifty-two. All three of his coronary arteries were blocked by atherosclerosis.

Did running do in the best-selling author or enable him to live as long as he did? His father, after all, died of a heart attack at forty-three. Some studies show a connection between fitness and cardiovascular health, with the most active participants having half the risk of heart disease and a death rate two thirds lower than the least active. Others do not. Then there are studies that confuse the issue, such as one that shows moderately active Finns had a coronary heart disease rate 2.5 times higher than both the most and least active Finns. Or another that shows that while fitness reduces the incidence of sudden cardiac arrest during a lifetime, the risk rises slightly *during* a workout.

Does that mean the 50 percent of a sample population who told pollster George Gallup they exercise regularly are wasting their time working out? Hardly. For one thing, being fit promotes a sense of well-being, as even the anti-exercise camp concedes. And even if exercise doesn't lower coronary risk directly, it helps to lower blood pressure, is associated with a decline in LDL and a rise in HDL (high levels of which have been found in marathon runners), and helps alleviate stress. It also reduces the heart rate, lets the heart pump more efficiently, and possibly increases the size of coronary arteries and encourages the growth of collateral vessels, enhancing the supply of oxygen to the heart muscle. In monkeys, exercise has even been shown to shrink atherosclerotic buildup in the coronaries. Unfortunately, their blockages are different from ours, and there isn't any evidence that we too can run away from atherosclerosis.

The ideal dose of exercise, according to a study of 17,000 Harvard men, burns 2,000 kcal (kilocalories) a week, which is the equivalent of walking twenty miles during a seven-day period.

This comparatively modest regimen was enough to cut the heart disease risk to half that of sedentary males and prolong life by four to five years. One need not train for marathons, only undertake a workout that raises the heart rate to 70 percent of its maximum—this can be estimated by subtracting your age from 220 and multiplying the result by 0.7—and keep it elevated for twenty minutes three times a week for four to six weeks, then twice a week thereafter. It should be a continuous-movement, aerobic activity like running, walking, cycling, or rowing, all of which require a sustained supply of oxygen, rather than a sporadic, anaerobic activity such as weight lifting, in which demand for oxygen comes and goes. (Isometric exertion against an immovable load, or pumping iron, raises the blood pressure and strains the heart. Dynamic activity reduces the resistance against which the heart sends the flow of blood, allowing the heart to get a good workout.) One article goes so far as to propose an ideal training regimen, right down to an 82 degree water temperature for swimming laps and a 68 degree air temperature for running them.

Fatigue is nature's way of saying, "Stop." In some people with a genetically abnormal heart, too much exercise can lead to a muscle-bound left ventricle, which is associated with sudden cardiac arrest. Autopsies of high school and college football players who have collapsed on the practice field often find this condition, sometimes known as the athletic heart syndrome. Because unsupervised vigorous activity has been shown to cause sudden death among the physically unfit, deconditioned males over forty should be tested on the treadmill before going gungho on the track.

Smoking

"Unless the smoking habits of the American population change, perhaps 10 percent of all persons now alive may die prematurely of heart disease attributable to their smoking behavior." So said the United States Surgeon General, C. Everett Koop, in 1983, nineteen years after the first surgeon general's report on smoking and lung cancer. Smoking is believed responsible for 30 percent of all heart disease deaths in the United States and could be the most important of the modifiable risk factors.

Twelve million person-years of epidemiological experience in the United States, Canada, Great Britain, and Sweden have provided the grim evidence of this man-made public health disaster. The coronary artery disease mortality among male cigarette smokers is 1.6 times that of nonsmokers. (Pipe and cigar smokers have only slightly increased risk.) The risk is directly related to the number of cigarettes smoked a day; a male between forty-five and fifty-four who smokes more than a pack has 2.15 times the normal risk; one who smokes less than a pack has 1.29 times the normal risk. Women smokers are thought to be at the same peril as males, but those who also use oral contraceptives have ten times the risk of heart attack as nonsmoking women who don't use birth control pills.

Cigarettes induce heart attacks, hardening of the arteries, and strokes by a variety of means. The high concentration of carbon monoxide in cigarette smoke damages cells in arterial walls, leads to rises of catecholamines (the "fight or flight" hormones that make platelets stickier), and increases levels of LDL. HDL, in contrast, drops. Nicotine and carbon monoxide interfere with the heart's blood supply and increase its need for oxygen, thus lowering the threshold for cardiac arrest. Smoking has also been shown to provoke coronary spasm.

The good news in all this is that the risk from cigarettes begins to recede almost as soon as a smoker quits, no matter how long he smoked. After a year or two, an ex-smoker isn't much worse off than a nonsmoker. Since the first surgeon general's report, about 30 million Americans have stopped smoking. The 50 million who persist in the habit need not fear that the inevitable consequence of quitting is flab. According to a study conducted by the Kaiser-Permanente health organization in California, the average weight gain among quitters was just two to three pounds. A study of British doctors who quit found an average gain of 4.3 pounds. In yet another study, 68 percent of 224 male ex-smokers gained weight, but for two thirds of them it was fifteen pounds or less.

Like other physicians, I find treating patients with coronary artery disease who continue to smoke most frustrating, and I know surgeons who hesitate, or even refuse, to operate on patients who smoke. Along with alcohol abuse, this self-inflicted disease contributes so substantially to the nation's health care costs that some have suggested a $3-a-pack tax to help foot the bill.

Obesity

Obesity—for the record, being 10 percent heavier than the ideal weight for a particular height and frame—is commonly associated with other risk factors such as hypertension, diabetes, high cholesterol levels, and inactivity. Eating too much, after all, goes hand in hand with exercising too little. But all by themselves, those extra pounds increase the strain on the heart and can be, in one of the favorite phrases of epidemiologists, a significant predictor of cardiovascular disease, especially in the young. The risk rises with the weight in both males and females, although the ascent is sharper for males. In an extremely obese patient, the heart muscle itself may be infiltrated with fat, impairing its ability to contract.

Though there is ample incentive, change does not come easily for many obese people. Eating habits are linked to our sense of self, and cutting down is contrary to basic psychological impulses nurtured from infancy. Even an objective analysis of an individual's reasons for overeating does not always lead to success, especially if a diet is the only tool. It is almost impossible to lose weight—and keep it off—without a judicious exercise program as well.

Cholesterol

Cholesterol has been the subject of one of the longest-running controversies in medicine. Since 1913, when Russian pathologist Nikolai Anitschkow fed rabbits a diet rich in the yellow waxy substance and produced atherosclerotic plaque, the confusion about whether we are what we eat has persisted. From the Framingham study, we learned that people with about 260 milligrams of cholesterol per deciliter (a tenth of a liter) of blood have four times the incidence of cardiovascular disease of those with levels at or below 220 mg. That jibed with the observations of researchers like Ancel Keyes, who noted that coronary disease steered clear of cultures that steered clear of cholesterol.

A twelve-year study in Finland found that men who followed a cholesterol-lowering diet for six years cut their coronary death rate in half. When they resumed their former diets, the death rate went back up. In Norway, meanwhile, more than 1,200 men eating a low-cholesterol diet cut their heart attack rate nearly in half over about the same period. These were small studies, however, and they involved men in mental institutions (Finland) and men with abnormally high cholesterol levels (Norway). They failed to convince a chorus of cholesterol naysayers, a group that at one time even included authorities such as Christiaan N. Barnard, who said in 1975: "People tell you to stop eating fats, stop doing all sorts of things. They make your life miserable but they don't know what they're talking about."

The biggest bunch of naysayers turned out to be the members of the Food and Nutrition Board of the National Academy of Sciences, the nation's Supreme Court of research, who in 1980 threw out the case against cholesterol altogether. Overruling numerous health organizations and federal agencies, the board concluded that the average American had nothing to fear from a richly marbled sirloin or an extra-thick shake. It recommended no restriction of cholesterol intake and, with a twist of the butter knife, noted that low serum cholesterol levels are associated with an increased risk of cancer.

"It is necessary to be aware that food contains many substances other than cholesterol that can affect the serum cholesterol level," wrote Victor Herbert, professor of medicine at the State University of New York's Downstate Medical Center and a member of the academy's panel, in *The New York Times.* "Whole milk contains cholesterol, and yet if you drink whole milk, your serum cholesterol falls rather than rises. The reason for this is believed to be that whole (and skim) cow milk contains two substances that reduce the production of cholesterol by the human liver to such an extent that they more than counterbalance the amount of cholesterol absorbed."

How did this confusing state of affairs develop? We are born with an innocently low level of cholesterol, but life is indeed cruel, for LDL, that troublesome conveyor of cholesterol throughout the body, increases in the blood with age. When males reach puberty, they also suffer the added blow of a drop in HDL, the substance that scoops up cholesterol from the bloodstream and carries it to the liver for removal from the body. This may partly account for why males have 60 percent more heart attacks than females.

According to Michael S. Brown and Joseph L. Goldstein, known as the Gold Dust Twins because of the prodigious flow of research money into their laboratory at the University of Texas Health Sciences Center, the keys to disarming LDL are receptors clustered on the surface of cells that soak up the lipoprotein molecules like a sponge. The cholesterol globule the LDL is carrying is then drawn into the cell, causing a shutdown of the cell's own cholesterol-producing machinery—the body produces two or three times more cholesterol than a person is likely to consume in food—and halting the synthesis of new LDL receptors, at least until the cell needs more cholesterol.

The fortunate among us have more of these receptors, or better ones, than most people. Thus more cholesterol is sequestered safely inside cells, leaving less floating around in the bloodstream, ready to wreak atherosclerotic havoc by caking up the pipes. A wealth of these receptors may explain why the Pima Indians of Nevada, who eat a diet of foods fried in fat and have one of the world's highest obesity rates, have only one quarter the heart attack rate of Americans in general. For those unlucky enough to be born with a shortage of receptors, "it's like a shower with a partially blocked drain," says Brown.

The National Academy of Sciences said, in effect, that with so much going on internally, the external cholesterol from food scarcely mattered. The academy's study drew support from the American Medical Association, which had long been skeptical of the diet-heart disease hypothesis, and the food industry, which turned out to be well represented on the board—two of its fifteen members had received research support from the egg industry while another was a paid consultant for the egg board. But anticholesterol forces—the American Heart Association, the Harvard School of Public Health, and the U.S. departments of Health and Human Services and Agriculture among them—held firm. As it happened, the National Heart, Lung, and Blood Institute had already launched its own ten-year, $150 million cholesterol study. It tracked 3,806 men between the ages of thirty-five and fifty-nine who had serum cholesterol levels of at least 265 mg, substantially higher than the national average of 215 mg. Half were given six daily doses of cholesterol-lowering cholestyramine in orange juice—"orange flavored sand," one participant called it—while the control group polished off a similarly gritty placebo. The results, announced early in 1984, indicated that those on the drug had an 8.5 percent drop in serum cholesterol, experienced 21 percent fewer bypasses, suffered 19 percent fewer heart attacks, and, most important, had a 24 percent lower death rate. The rule of thumb: For every 1 percent drop in serum cholesterol, there is a 2 percent drop in heart disease.

If the average cholesterol level of Americans could be lowered by 10 to 15 percent, coronary disease could be reduced by 20 to 30 percent, saving hundreds of thousands of lives as well as perhaps $20 billion in lost wages each year.

Still, some were skeptical, among them Joseph Vitale, associate dean of the International Health Program at the Boston University School of Medicine, who noted that those who took cholestyramine had a slightly higher incidence of gastrointestinal cancer. Why this was so isn't clear, since the drug is generally regarded as safe. (This is reminiscent of the controversy surrounding a World Health Organization study that found that men taking another ballyhooed cholesterol-lowering drug, clofibrate, were 25 percent more likely to die from a range of maladies including cancer, stroke, respiratory disease, and heart attack.) Nevertheless, the Heart, Lung, and Blood Institute study does provide the most solid connection yet between reduction in dietary fats, lower serum cholesterol, and a decline in heart disease. On balance, I think the benefits of a low cholesterol level are considerable, especially when it can be achieved without drugs.

That means cutting down on eggs, each of which has about 250 mg of cholesterol, all in the yolk, and red meat, which has about 100 milligrams per three ounces. Three ounces of liver has 300 mg, three ounces of kidneys 375 mg, and three ounces of brains a whopping 2,675 mgs. Turkey and chicken, on the other hand, have just 65 mg for a similar portion. Cholesterol comes exclusively from animal sources, so there's not a speck of it in grains, fruits, or vegetables.

Other components of the diet can modify the way the body handles cholesterol. Saturated fat, for example, stimulates the production of LDL, effectively raising the cholesterol level. Polyunsaturated fat, on the other hand, lowers the total cholesterol level, while monounsaturated fat, which can be found in olive oil, corn oil, and certain varieties of safflower oil, seems to lower only the amount of LDL in the blood without altering the beneficial HDL.

Although a steak's load of cholesterol and saturated fat is double trouble, a dinner of lobster, shrimp, or salmon, all of which contain cholesterol and have long been blacklisted, may actually be beneficial. According to William E. Connor of the Oregon Health Sciences University in Portland, seafood is rich in Omega-3 fatty acids, which help keep blood cholesterol levels low. That is why Eskimos in Greenland can eat a diet of fish, seal, and whale, and seldom get coronary disease, and why men on a diet of salmon and shellfish experienced drops in serum cholesterol that rivaled those of a control group on a low cholesterol diet. Vegetarians have still lower levels of cholesterol (although lactovegetarians—those who eat dairy products and eggs—have higher levels than stricter vegetarians who don't). A study of 25,000 Seventh Day Adventists in California, half of whom were lactovegetarians, found that those who ate meat six times a week were six or more times as likely to die from heart disease as those who abstained.

Fiber seems to lower LDL—a cup of oats has been shown to cut it by 20 percent. Alcohol apparently does, too; social drinkers have LDL levels 33 percent lower than teetotalers. (Heavy alcohol consumption, on the other hand, raises cardiovascular mortality.) A Norwegian study indicates that those who drink nine or more cups of coffee a day have 14 percent more cholesterol in their blood than one-cup-a-dayers. Evidence is accumulating that the soybeans so common in Oriental diets play a role in lowering cholesterol and perhaps in keeping it low. When 127 men and women at nine European medical centers replaced animal proteins with soybean products for eight weeks, their cholesterol levels dropped about 25 percent. Even when 500 mg of cholesterol was added to their daily diet, serum cholesterol levels did not rise.

Though it still seems downright un-American to trade steaks

for soybeans, there have been substantial changes in the nation's diet over the past thirty years. Beef consumption is up 90 percent per capita, but eggs are down more than 30 percent, milk and cream down 26 percent, butter down 52 percent, and lard down 84 percent. Chicken and turkey, meanwhile, are up 132 percent and fish 8 percent. Fat in pork has declined 30 percent in the past decade or so. Fat in beef is down 7 percent, and producers are seeking the Agriculture Department's permission to lower it further.

All this has resulted in a drop in dietary cholesterol from an average of 800 mg or more a day in 1963 to about 500 mg today. But despite twenty-five years of nagging from the American Heart Association, the average male consumes the equivalent of a stick of butter in saturated fat and cholesterol each day and eats 187 pounds of meat per year, as against 71 pounds of fowl and fish. We get 40 percent of our calories from fat, 30 percent more than our grandparents and three times more than the Japanese. In a country where about half the population still dies of cardiovascular disease, the national average serum cholesterol level of 225 mg is clearly too high.

What is the ideal level? At a risk factor seminar in the packed auditorium of the Annenberg Building one day in spring 1984, W. Virgil Brown, the medical center's cholesterol expert and chairman of the American Heart Association's nutrition committee, interpreted the cholesterol numbers game:

> If a person's blood cholesterol level is below 200 mg, our belief is that simply reminding him of the heart association diet is sufficient. What about people over 200? The people in this group should have the components of their total cholesterol, the LDL and HDL, measured. Individuals with LDL levels of less than 100 mg are at low risk. Individuals with LDL levels of 200 mg or more have a high risk.
>
> What about the 90 percent of the population with LDL between 100 and 200 mg? Here is where the ratio of LDL and

the protective HDL comes in. The data on people who have a ratio of 2 [that is, twice as much LDL as HDL] or less show they have very low risk. Those with ratios between 2 and 3 are at modest risk and should be placed on a diet that restricts cholesterol and saturated fat. Once you pass 3, the risk increases, and there is a significant increase in risk between 3 and 5. This group, about 25 to 30 percent of the population, should be placed on the diet and reminded that cholesterol intake of less than 100 mg a day is perfectly compatible with health.

About 10 percent of the population is in a very high risk group with ratios about 5. These people should also be placed on the diet, and those with an inadequate response after several months should be considered for drug therapy.

By diet, Brown means a daily limit of 300 mg of cholesterol for men (or about an egg yolk's worth) and less for generally smaller females. No more than 30 percent of the day's calories should come from fat, with no more than one third from saturated fat. The less cholesterol, and more unsaturated fat, the better. It's also a good idea to limit red meat to no more than once a week, and try not to eat more than one or two eggs and a single glass of whole milk during that period. But help yourself to fish, pastas, fruits, and vegetables. One of the major advantages of this approach is that there are no forbidden foods. You just may not be able to eat as much of everything as you want.

At the same seminar was a man with a vastly different message. What Carrie Nation was to alcohol, Nathan Pritikin was to cholesterol. His diet allows just 100 mg a day, making other nutritionists look like libertines. He scorned all fat—saturated, polyunsaturated, and monounsaturated. It clogs us up, he said, and allowed just 10 percent of caloric intake in fat and only 13 percent in protein. The mainstays of the Pritikin diet are the complex carbohydrates, especially the grains that are the basis of diets in the Third World, where atherosclerosis is virtually nonexistent. Good enough for the Bantus, good enough for those who come to Pritikin's longevity centers or buy his books.

The following is a typical Pritikin menu: a breakfast of half a grapefruit and a bowl of cooked whole-wheat grain cereal with sliced banana, skim milk, cinnamon, and bran; a lunch of lentil soup, whole-wheat pita bread stuffed with salad, vegetables sprinkled with vinegar and bran, and a glass of water with a lemon wedge; and a dinner of defatted oxtail soup, steamed broccoli and squash, brown rice, sourdough bread, and applesauce with skim milk yogurt. Pritikin's patients arrive at the centers with an average serum cholesterol of 235 and leave four weeks later at 175. Still, Mount Sinai's Brown and others question how long the improvement holds up once a patient leaves what some of them call "the religious experience" of the Pritikin environment and tries to stay on what, by American standards, is a very unpalatable diet. "It's like giving up cars," Brown says, "to avoid auto accidents."

There's even more disagreement about the ultimate payout Pritikin talked about: not just retarding the atherosclerotic process but reversing it. Researchers have managed to shrink blockages in primates fed a low cholesterol diet, and all cardiologists have seen deposits in humans disappear, too. But so far, neither Pritikin nor anyone else has proved he can make them go away on command.

Coronary Prone Behavior

Why do we seem to have a corner on the market in coronary prone behavior? Perhaps it is because of the reluctance of many American parents to respond when their children cry. Japanese parents are more consoling, and their babies, though they start life with personalities similar to those of American infants, become more placid and calm within a few months. To Meyer Friedman, one of the pioneers of the Type A concept, the hard-driving, hurry-up, never-say-die impulse grows out of childhood feelings of insecurity and the belief that parental love is dependent upon what one does rather than upon who one is.

In any event, it isn't hard to see how the rewards we bestow on the Type As among us can overshadow the coronary price many of them eventually pay. As they are climbing to the top, the evidence indicates, their blood-cholesterol level is also rising, and their blood-clotting mechanism is shifting into high gear. The mental stress they endure raises blood pressure and narrows arteries, and they can also have forty times the normal level of steroids in their circulation, along with three times the adrenalin and greater amounts of testosterone and insulin.

"If you see a lot of these people," said Melvin Stern, a psychiatrist in Silver Spring, Maryland, who helps many bypass patients and heart attack victims learn how to change, "you begin to understand that they are so cognitively oriented that they don't deal with feelings. They have the capacity to deal with them, but by and large they don't. They run from intimacy and, more specifically, from anything having to do with confrontations. Work enters into it because, when pushed, they have found that the way they can avoid people being dissatisfied with them is to work harder.

"They avoid anger like the plague, and so they build up a lot of frustration and rage. I had one patient who would crush things in his house. He was very embarrassed about it. He was going to build a quiet room in the basement and go in there and close the door. I called it his bomb shelter."

Of all the characteristics of the Type A personality, some researchers are honing in on this subsurface anger as the active ingredient. Using what they called a hostility scale—or Ho scale —derived from the Minnesota Multiphasic Personality Inventory used in schools throughout the country, they found that the angriest, least trusting, and most cynical subjects were 50 percent more likely to have coronary artery disease than those at peace with the world and five to six times more likely to have heart attacks. The study, one of the first to include women, found that the dangers of Type A behavior crossed the gender gap.

There are many methods to gear down Type As—biofeedback, relaxation training, meditation, tranquilizing drugs—but it may require psychotherapeutic counseling to get to the roots of some of their destructive behavior patterns and help patients replace aggressiveness with assertiveness and hostility with affection. Through a combination of individual and group therapy, patients build a picture of their reactions and relationships. Seeing bits of themselves in others, they begin talking—about their fears of confrontation at work, their difficulties with family and friends, and the frightening feelings that their coronary events have made them second-class citizens. Eventually, they become more conscious of their behavior, and that makes it easier to change.

"I don't think it's necessary for a Type A person to undergo a total personality transplant," says Harold Eist, a Washington-based psychiatrist with experience in treating coronary prone behavior. He focuses on what he calls "reactive intensity"—the people who overreact to stress, an especially dangerous commodity when exacerbated by a sense of powerlessness. Other psychiatrists have singled out the hostility-anger component as the active ingredient in the Type A personality, while still others concentrate on time urgency and compulsiveness.

Probably the largest study of the effectiveness of modifying Type A behavior was recently undertaken by the Heart, Lung, and Blood Institute. After videotaped interviews in which the extent of coronary behavior was quantified, two thirds of the 800 participants met regularly in small groups with a therapist to discuss their lives and problems, act out troublesome situations, and practice being more Type B (which is defined as not being a Type A). One exercise involved standing in a line—nothing short of torture to these restless souls—and learning how to use the time for contemplation and reflection. The other participants in the study received no special counseling. Friedman, who directed the study, found that after three years of psychological guidance, 9 percent of the men had suffered recurrent heart attacks. In the control group, the rate was 19 percent.

For their part, private psychiatrists like Stern and Eist say the transition from Type A to Type B can take anywhere from six months to two years, but the odds are better than even money that a well-motivated patient can make the psychological journey, especially if he seeks help soon after a coronary event or a first bypass. The fear of having the chest cut open a second time can be a powerful incentive to change, as can the soothing benefits of Type B life.

Sometimes, however, a patient can change too much. "One of the problems is that patients can attack the issue of resolving their Type A behavior with Type A intensity," says Eist. "I'm thinking of a man who ran 10 miles a day, watched his diet and wouldn't eat an egg, monitored his blood pressure, and meditated, but nothing relieved the underlying intensity and tension. He was in the process of killing himself through his rigorous attention to risk factors. He was as lean as a whippet, and he still dropped dead of a coronary event.. So changing modifiable risk factors, while it can be helpful, can be nevertheless worked at with such relentless fury that the individual will kill himself doing it."

THE PAYOUT

In the early 1970s, the National Heart, Lung, and Blood Institute set out to calculate the value of a systematic program of risk-factor modification. The Multiple Risk Factor Intervention Trial (or "MR. FIT") enlisted 12,866 male volunteers, aged thirty-five to fifty-seven, in twenty-two treatment centers around the nation, each volunteer with two of the following three risk factors: high blood pressure, elevated serum cholesterol, and a history of cigarette smoking. Half were given counseling and behavior-modification therapy; half were left alone. After ten years and $115.8 million, the study failed to show that those who underwent treatment specifically designed to reduce coronary risk actually lived longer. One subgroup in the special treatment category—those with slight EKG irregularities—even had a higher death rate. Does this mean risk-factor modification doesn't work? Absolutely not. It turned out that while the counseled men changed for the better—half the smokers quit, for example—men in the other group did, too, and almost as much. Just joining the study was enough to get them to alter their habits. Both groups in the study had death rates that were 40 percent lower than the mortality for white American males during the same period.

So you might say that MR. FIT's failure was society's gain. Nevertheless, it is unlikely that coronary heart disease can be controlled as easily as, say, polio, at least until we have a cardiovascular Drāno. Although smoking, cholesterol, and hypertension have been linked with coronary artery disease for decades, they don't necessarily cause it. They are merely discrete pieces of a complex puzzle we only partly understand. Cleaning up your act will lessen your risk but not eliminate it. The depressing reality is that there's just too much cardiac risk around. I've seen patients who, like James Fixx, have stopped smoking, lost weight, and changed their diets, only to drop dead while jogging in the prime of life. And then there was Winston Churchill, who ate, drank, and smoked cigars with enthusiasm, had a stressful line of work, and got his exercise, he said, by attending the funerals of friends who exercised. He lived to be ninety.

11

Cardiac Cripples
The Back-to-Work Problem

---

*O God our Father, whose mercy is boundless and whose
wisdom contains the answer to all our human needs, I humbly
pray for recovery from illness. If it be Thy will, breathe healing
into my stricken body. Patiently quiet the fears that have
assembled in my mind, and increase my faith in Thy everlasting
love, until I know Thou doest all things well. Amen.*

—Prayer for recovery of The Mended Hearts,
an organization of cardiac patients

THE ELEVATOR OPENED ON the twenty-fourth floor of the Annenberg Building, and a middle-aged couple stepped out. He was dressed in a red-striped polo shirt, khaki trousers, and brown penny loafers—the uniform of the country club on a day ordinarily reserved for the office. With his wife at his side, he walked with a slow, stiff-legged gait, back arched and shoulders motionless, past the plaques commemorating the Samuel Bronfman Department of Medicine and the Irving Geist Thrombosis Center, past the laboratories of the Division of Atherosclerosis and Metabolism, past the poster for a revival of *The Cherry Orchard* that somehow looked at home on the gleaming white walls of the hospital corridor. He stopped, turned into a room marked "Caution: Radiation Hazard" to get directions, then

205

resumed the trek down the hall to Suite 24–42 for his postoperative appointment with the cardiothoracic surgeon. After countless assaults on body and mind, what other tortures have they in store for me? he may have been thinking as he took his seat. Or perhaps he was simply allowing the eerily familiar sights, sounds, and smells of the medical center to bombard him, innumerable reminders of the days before and after the surgeon opened his body like a carton of eggs. Slowly, gingerly, he settled in among his coronary comrades, united by hidden scars and pale, expressionless faces that looked a bit like worn furniture in the sidewalk sunlight, waiting for the movers.

They have come from Smithtown, Port Washington, and Malverne on Long Island, from Wilton, Greenwich, and Darien in Connecticut, from the New Jersey towns of Teaneck and Basking Ridge, and from Nyack clear to Utica in New York. As a renowned academic medical center, Mount Sinai also draws an international clientele from North and South America, the Caribbean, and Europe. Three or four months after surgery, they are gathered in the very examining rooms where many first confronted the decision to submit to bypass surgery for what is, in effect, a 5,000-mile checkup. For most of those in Suite 24–42— as for most patients recovering from coronary artery surgery— the months since discharge have been a time of healing and a return to wholeness. There may still be nagging aches and pains —maybe a catheter has left a lasting irritation, or an incision needs extra attention from a plastic surgeon. Although the clinical consensus is that bypass takes six months to a year to get over, most of these patients are already well on their way.

But some patients, perhaps a third or more if the studies only now emerging are correct, will travel a bumpier road. Though doctors may have promised that the operation would enable them to continue, or resume, working, for a surprising number of patients it is the first step to a retirement that is not always welcome. The ordeal can also strain marriages and shatter friendships. Bypass surgery is a confrontation with one's mortality, with human nature. Once someone has held your heart in his hands, its beat will forever have new meaning. Anxiety, depression, fear, guilt, confusion, and lapses of memory—the symptoms, some of which took root in the operating room, commingle with each other and feed on life's everyday difficulties. Patients are robbed of their sense of well-being or infused with self-doubt. Others cope with the realization of having suddenly grown frail and old. Given the more than one million people who have already undergone the procedure, and the 200,000 or more who join them every year, this post-bypass syndrome is taking on the dimensions of a public health problem in its own right. Decades ago, before the era of open-heart surgery, patients with diseased and malfunctioning heart valves were consigned to live as invalids, and became known as cardiac cripples. Now it seems as though bypass surgery, a cornerstone of medicine's spectacular counterattack against coronary disease, is creating a new generation of cripples.

Consider the case of Julius Gould as he waited in Examining Room 3. An accountant, he wore a gray suit, white shirt, blue-patterned tie, shiny black oxfords, and, unlike many in the suite, a wristwatch. All dressed up with nowhere to go. His first three postoperative months, he began, "had been hell."

"I was a very aggressive individual, working all the time, and suddenly I'm thrown into a situation where I can't do anything. I was dependent on myself, and now I find myself dependent on other people. It's very depressing, the most depressing thing I've ever come across. I can't concentrate. I can't even read a newspaper. I'm distracted. I feel like jumping out of my skin. I have to be with people or I'm fit to be tied.

"I don't feel as strong—that's what really bothers me. I feel like a weakened kitten. I've been walking in the hallways of my building for an hour, hour and a half a day, and at a brisk pace. But I just don't feel the strength returning. Whether it's mental or physical, I don't know. And my sleeping is poor, too. I wake up around five o'clock in the morning and take half a Valium, then get maybe another hour's sleep. My appetite is way down. And I find that I get tearful where I wouldn't have before. I've lost my ability to cope with things and people. And stress. I've been in my office a few times. I've gotten some things done, but not anywhere near what I used to do.

"I knew people that went through it, and most of them seemed to make a good go of it. But I guess I haven't followed that course. My wife has been terrific. She's taken the brunt of this. I just hope that one day I get over this apprehension, this depression, and make it back."

The unique and often devastating emotional impact of cardiac surgery plays itself out in as many ways as there are patients. The minister who finds himself crying in the pulpit, his fire and brimstone gone up in smoke. A factory foreman, once the most popular guy on the shop floor, finds himself isolated and alone at his new desk job, with little work to do and no desire to do it. The traveling salesman who can't drive more than a few hours or lug his suitcase of samples up a flight of stairs. Or an accountant named Julius Gould, whose obsession with his limitations threatens even the hope of further progress.

Bad as it is, the inability to bounce back is made all the worse because of all the bypass patients who do bounce back, their resurrections often chronicled in newspapers and magazines. Society exerts other pressures, offering disability benefits to tempt patients into premature (and potentially health-threatening) retirement while at the same time placing roadblocks along the path back to work. Some bypass patients fail to accomplish their goals not so much because of what the operation has done to them as because of the way others now perceive them.

The pressure on surgeons and cardiologists to concentrate on the next patient sometimes leaves their last patient with no one to turn to when, months after surgery, difficulties emerge. To be fair, the strain that bypass, the most commonly performed major surgery, exerts on the nation's medical system is fearsome. Nor is it within a doctor's power to undo the incentives the disability system stacks in favor of retirement. Still, some patients understandably become disillusioned with health care professionals who promised to write them a new lease on life but, they feel, have written them off instead.

There have been countless examinations of coronary bypass surgery, and not one of them has made a convincing case that it doesn't work. Symptoms and signs of ischemia disappear in most cases, and performance on the treadmill improves. For safety and effectiveness, it's hard to argue with an operative mortality rate of 1 percent and an anginal relief rate near 90 percent. But making patients feel better is not the same as making them feel useful, much less be useful. This dilemma is crystalized in the treadmill irony: Some people function well in daily life, only to be tripped up when their disease is revealed on the cardiologists' conveyor belt; after bypass surgery, cardiologists are discovering, patients sometimes function well on the treadmill, only to be tripped up by life.

In an informal study of bypass patients in the weeks after hospital discharge, Mount Sinai social worker Linda Rodgers followed the progress of ten cases. All were first-time bypass patients, with an average age of fifty-eight and without major medical complications. Nine were men; seven were married, two were single, and one was widowed. Six had been employed prior to surgery and expected to return to work, one was unemployed, and two were retired. During their hospitalizations, Rodgers found that three of the patients were reasonably calm, one was a "proficient denier" (and an alcoholic to boot), another was mildly anxious, and five were "overtly anxious with varying degrees of depression." All in all, they were a fairly typical group. "In no way," she writes, "was I prepared for the avalanche of overwhelming psychosocial problems related by nine of the ten patients."

One patient, so unsteady from surgery that he appeared drunk, was picked up by the police during his first walk after he returned home. He was taken to a local hospital, where he was asked to sign himself into the psychiatric ward. "I don't know what I'm afraid of," he said later, when the incident was behind him. "I went through a lot in my life with a back operation, but this is different. Times I'm so scared, I feel my heart pounding and shaking my whole body."

Said another: "I wonder if I'll ever get back to where I was before."

And another: "I am uncertain about what my future is going to be. What will I do with myself? Will I ever be able to work again? I feel so tired all the time, and I think 'What is it? Why is this?' "

Even the patients who were calm before surgery seemed to suffer psychological aftershocks. One complained of severe anxiety, lack of appetite, and a "fear of firsts"—the first visit with friends, the first dinner out, the first time driving a car. He walked three miles a day without leaving home because he was afraid to go outside. Another of the preoperatively cool patients was reluctant to work despite an apparent return to health. And the third, whom Rodgers described as an intelligent and well-adjusted individual with an excellent marriage and a high-paying job waiting, said: "I just don't seem to care much—it's all too much effort somehow." And those were the calm ones.

Most of the patients Rodgers followed had a pathological preoccupation with their hearts, their symptoms, and their surgery, and some suffered anorexia, insomnia, depression, irritability, and had difficulty concentrating. Anxiety followed them home, where it grew like a cancer into a major obstacle to recovery.

Such discouraging findings are not unique to Mount Sinai patients. A study of thirty patients conducted by the University of North Carolina School of Medicine a few years before Rodgers' survey sounded a similar alarm. One to two years after surgery, 69 percent reported they felt better, but 83 percent were unemployed (most had blue-collar jobs), and 57 percent were described as "sexually impaired." The North Carolina patients also showed a drop in self-reliance, were less aggressive, and reported a lack of pleasure from close relationships. A third were troubled by depression and withdrew from social activities. What made the study especially worrisome was that all the patients had the advantage of participating in a rehabilitation program and were relatively young for bypass veterans, with an average age of fifty-one.

He was a minister and looked the part. White-haired, plump, rosy-cheeked, with a reassuringly rich, soft voice and a formal bearing. A little chest pain, a routine physical, a treadmill, a catheterization, and at sixty-five years of age, Harold Meienhafft found himself on the way to the operating room for a triple bypass. He made a smooth recovery, but just before he was ready to go home to Pennsylvania, he had a crying spell. He sensed that someone had pulled out his hinge pins, and he wasn't sure how the doors to his future would open. In retrospect, that was the first sign that he was failing. Over the next months, my case notes reveal a man whose body was healing but whose sense of self was eroding.

February 8, 1983: One month after surgery, M. reports freedom from angina and shortness of breath. Can walk for an hour. Appetite returned. Finds himself crying without good reason, and is bothered by wide swings of mood. Has fits of coughing when he tries to talk [particularly significant considering his occupation]. Insomnia—afraid to go to sleep for fear he won't wake up. When he does fall asleep, nightmares are frequent. Visited his congregation, but hasn't yet taken the pulpit.

April 5: Recovering nicely except for recurrence of hypertension. But depression limits sense of well-being. Weight going up. States he has been taking nadolol three times a day, instead of once, as prescribed. When he ran out of the drug, he asked the advice of a member of his congregation, who gave him vitamins, and then he became dizzy. [He seems to be playing out some kind of role reversal, asking for help instead of providing it.] Also very upset about a lawsuit—someone fell on the steps of the church and sued everyone in sight, including him. He is afraid this will reflect poorly on his leadership, that the parishioners will use it as a way of getting him out of the pulpit, as some have been trying to do, he now insists, for a while. [His depression is taking on a distinctly paranoid edge.] Rebuffs suggestion that he seek professional counseling.

May 24: Slightly cheerier and less fatigued. Seems to have regained some emotional steadiness. Is finally back in the pulpit.

February 7, 1984: One year after surgery—no pain, but blood pressure, obesity, and inactivity worrisome. Having trouble coping with the emotional pressures of the ministry and plans to give it up. Feels himself being squeezed out of his job, but clearly has the sympathy of his congregation. Still troubled by lapses in memory and by depression. [Mr. Meienhafft's self-esteem has plummeted.] Talks about moving to the country and spending his days fishing and walking through the fields.

"My faith will carry me through," Reverend Meienhafft once told me. But somehow, the ordeal of heart surgery eroded that faith and sapped his confidence. He went back to work but couldn't handle the emotional demands of his congregation and sought escape. He had become a taker, rather than a giver. Bypass surgery relieved his pain but left a scar that has not healed.

In April 1981, the National Center for Health Care Technology, a division of the Public Health Service, gathered doctors, executives, union leaders, insurance officials, lawyers, nurses, psychologists, economists, and even philosophers near Washington for a two-and-a-half-day conference. Their focus: the perplexing prevalence of postoperative depression, disrupted family and sexual relationships, and lower than expected employment rates of coronary bypass patients.

Consider a report from the Columbia-Presbyterian Medical Center in New York City on the experiences of one hundred consecutive patients after bypass surgery, a slice-of-life approach that can be especially revealing. Of those who survived three and a half years, 60 percent said they were pleased with the results of the operation, and only 4 percent said they were displeased, which is understandable. After all, 53 percent reported that they were completely free of pain, another 28 percent said pain was minimal, 16 percent said it was moderate, and only 4 percent said it was severe. The Columbia patients also reported substantial improvement in the "quality of life" indicators—general level of pleasure, reduction of anxiety and depression, feelings of improvement in job and family roles, and sexual satisfaction. The last item is rather curious, however, since the frequency of their sexual relations actually decreased. Before surgery, 67 percent were sexually active at least once a week, 22 percent were less active, and 11 percent were inactive. Nine months after surgery, 38 percent were active at least once a week, and 31 percent reported no sexual activity at all. One fourth reported continued difficulties with sex after three and a half years. In other words, the Columbia patients were more satisfied with life even though they enjoyed one of its central pleasures far less after surgery than before. Compare this to a study in Britain, where 73 percent reported satisfactory sex lives before surgery and only 47 percent did so afterward, with 57 percent of the men developing impotency. Surprisingly, 69 percent of these patients were able to exercise well on a treadmill.

At the same conference, a team from the University of Wisconsin Medical School reported tracking 358 bypass patients for about a year. Before surgery, 69 percent were employed full- or part-time, 10 percent were not working, and 21 percent were retired; after surgery, 58 percent were working, 11 percent were unemployed, and 29 percent were retired (these figures were a little worse than those reported by the Columbia team). Although 82 percent of those previously employed returned to work, only 7 percent of those not working went back to their jobs after bypass. In other words, if you have continued to work and decide to have surgery to preserve your career, you stand a good chance of succeeding, though it is not automatic. On the other hand, the Wisconsin researchers found that practically no patients who had been forced to leave their jobs because of coronary pain went back to them after bypass surgery. The message: *Patients who expect bypass surgery to make them wage earners again are almost always disappointed.*

The longer a patient was out of work before surgery, the longer it took for him to resume work after discharge, perhaps because prolonged unemployment damages self-esteem more than surgery can repair. Patients who weren't working tended to be older than fifty-five, had had more chronic illness in the past, and reported less improvement in cardiac symptoms through bypass surgery than those who resumed working. More than 70 percent of the professionals among the Wisconsin patients returned to work, as against 68 percent of clerical workers and 44 percent of factory workers. Professionals also resumed working sooner than the others. Looked at another way, men with incomes greater than $25,000 a year were more likely to return to work than those making less than $25,000.

In yet another study presented at the meeting, the Montreal Heart Institute came up with its own list of factors affecting employment after following more than 1,500 patients for several years. In order of importance, they were length of preoperative inactivity, income, type of occupation, education, age at surgery, duration of symptoms, severity of angina, noncardiovascular illness, and associated vascular disease.

Why focus on work? As the Wisconsin researchers noted, "the prevailing work ethic of our western culture implies that individual identity and social status are defined to a large extent by occupational status. Gainful employment is not only a means to an end, but an end in itself." In short, we are what we do. But the decision to return to work can be agonizingly complex to make and difficult to analyze. Do people retire because they can't work, or because their employers won't let them, or because they simply don't want to?

From his vantage point in Boston, Thomas J. Ryan isn't alarmed by the return-to-work experience of bypass patients. He believes many have made a positive decision to change their lives, slow the pace, spend more time with their families, or just watch the sunsets. They've bought a little more time for themselves, and they'll be damned if they're going to share it with the boss. "Although the quality of life is unquestionably better for the surgical group than the medical group, every study that has looked at it has found employment status has not changed," said Ryan. "I think there's no disgrace in quitting if you've undergone the major assault of a heart operation and paid your price on the altar of the surgeon's table. And there's a personal component, too. A patient says, 'I've gone to the well and I'm only six years away from retiring anyway, so now that I'm healthy again I think I'll take advantage of it.'

"I think knowing some doctors are going to operate on your heart is a hell of a lot scarier than having your gallbladder out. It comes back on patients in ways that they haven't expected. A certain small percentage are devastated by surgery. But a bigger percentage of those who don't return to work have a whole new lease on life. They don't have to go back to the gristmill. They can get their jollies out of smelling the flowers."

Then again, illness can provide a very practical answer for leaving an unsatisfying job or, for that matter, a difficult marriage. There is a lot of "secondary gain" for a patient who doesn't return to work. Heart surgery, like heart disease, can offer a convenient way out.

Whatever is going on under the surface after surgery, there don't appear to be many doctors looking at it. Our institutions are based on illness models, not health models. Centers like Mount Sinai are designed to deliver acute care and acute care only. Its physicians don't have the time, or the space, to care for patients beyond the week and a half it takes to get most of them medically stable, and there's little follow-up to see how they are adjusting on the outside. When Linda Rodgers asked a social worker at another New York City hospital whether she kept track of bypass patients after their discharge, she was told that "two out of two thousand cases have been followed."

To make matters worse, some physicians, apparently lacking either information about postoperative convalescence or sophistication about the psychological problems it can stir up, often try to reassure patients by suggesting they take it easy a while longer than the six to ten weeks that recuperation usually takes. Instead of calming a patient, such suggestions may lower his self-esteem and raise anxieties about his health and ability to earn a living and maintain family and social relationships. In some cases it seems evident that the local physician encourages invalidism by overestimating the physical impairment of surgery and causing patients to think of themselves as damaged. Thus the operation may not so much cure heart disease as confirm its existence—and this sends to the patient a subliminal message that he might have to go through it all over again.

One measure of the failure of the doctor-patient relationship is the growth of The Mended Hearts. From a handful of open-heart patients who met to discuss their problems at Boston's Peter Bent Brigham Hospital in 1951, the organization has swelled into the nation's second largest self-help group (next to Alcoholics Anonymous, on which Mended Hearts seems in some ways patterned), with 18,000 members—20 percent medical patients, 80 percent surgical, of which 90 percent have had by-passes—in fifty states, the District of Columbia, and Puerto Rico, in Canada, West Germany, Italy, and even New Zealand. The 160 chapters hold monthly meetings at which cardiologists, thoracic surgeons, rehabilitation specialists, psychiatrists, psychologists, and sex therapists share their views. These are typically followed by what in essence are group-therapy sessions, where members and their families share problems, compare notes, and commiserate.

In one recent year, the organization's members also visited 50,328 patients in three hundred hospitals a total of 127,147 times, offering help and encouragement to those heading for the operating room. Their message was succinctly summed up by Joseph R. Amato, the executive vice president, head of the District of Columbia chapter, and himself a bypass veteran: "We are the living proof that heart surgery can be successful, and that you can pick up your life as you knew it before surgery. We tell people almost any major surgery is followed by depression. I can remember going through it myself. And people prone to depression before surgery can have worse bouts with it afterward. It depends on whether they've been worrywarts, whether they get support from their families."

Amato, who went back to his job in the federal government for three years before his doctor persuaded him to retire, now works out of an office down the hall from the operating rooms in the Washington Hospital Center. He got the space, plus a grant for office equipment, because hospital officials were impressed with what Mended Hearts did for their patients. The hospital, which schedules five or six heart operations every day, does its part, too, holding daily seminars at which the next morning's crop of patients and their families are told what to expect, both in the operating room and in the intensive care unit. It isn't that way at all of the hospitals in town, however. "The clinic at the National Institutes of Health is notorious for not giving enough support," says Amato, savoring some of the irony. "The Mended Hearts who come from there say they weren't properly prepared beforehand, and there was no follow-up. And at the Walter Reed Army Hospital the patients want to be discharged after surgery, not from the hospital but from the military. We have to convince them they're still productive. Our understanding is that the patients get little or no orientation, so they're grateful to us for whatever help we can give."

The case of Walter Stein, the salesman from Westchester whose bypass was chronicled in Chapter 7, is a good example of the ambivalence surrounding the issue of retirement for many bypass patients. When we left him, he was being wheeled out of Operating Room Number 2 on his way to the CICU. He was sent home about ten days later, and there he continued the smooth and uneventful recovery that would lead him, he thought, back to work. But we'll let him tell it:

"I was doing great, or at least I thought I was. I was cutting the grass, climbing trees and sawing off branches. Occasionally, the area of my chest where the bone was cracked got a little sore. That took a little while to knit together, I guess. Otherwise, I was feeling fine. I was just waiting for the day to go back.

"As a first step, I had to go to a company doctor. Then he said I had to get a letter from a cardiologist, and I did that. Next thing you know, the company said I needed another physical from the cardiologist. So I went back to him, and he put me on the treadmill. I was really pounding away, and I guess my blood pressure went up a little bit. Anyway, the doctor told me he didn't want me lifting anything heavy.

"Well, it just so happened that the company did away with my job while I was recuperating, so if I wanted to go back, I would have had to go back into a job that at times meant doing physical work, which I hadn't done much of before. When the doctor found out about this, he said, 'No way, not if they want you to go around carting stuff during the day.' Then he said to me, 'If you want disability, I'll back you up, because you can't do what your company says is required of you.'

"I might have been able to go into a rehabilitation program and get myself in shape to do this kind of work, but it would have taken me a while, and I'm almost sixty-two. And as far as starting something new, I don't think there's too much chance of doing that. And if I wound up without a job, I'd lose profit sharing, and I'd lose medical benefits. Christ, they were practically forcing me to take disability. But in the end, I told the doctor okay, because at least I'd have sixty percent of my salary coming in.

"I had no idea this would happen. I expected that, when I was ready to go back to work, I would go back. They could have made room, I guess. Everybody said it was okay for me go to back to work, but not under the conditions they had set up." He laughs bitterly. "So I sold the house and invested the money in CDs. That'll pay my rent on my new apartment. It's in a complex with tennis courts, outdoor and indoor swimming pools, an exercise room, and a steam room and a sauna. I figure I'll try to make the most of the next couple of years. I'll get in some exercise and get myself in shape. Still, it's disappointing. When you get down to it, I'd rather be working. I've never been out of work, not since I was sixteen. Now all of a sudden I find myself moping around here. I guess it takes a little getting used to."

So here is a man who had triple bypass surgery with the expectation of returning to work, and who now finds himself struggling to fill the free time of unwanted retirement. Was he seduced by disability benefits or blackmailed by them? And what role did his physicians play in determining his fate?

"Our entire health care, insurance, and compensation system generically does not encourage people to return to work," says Richard Gorlin, chief of medicine at Mount Sinai. "There's Social Security for some, disability insurance for others, worker's compensation for others, and so on down the line. There are a whole series of policies available to our employed population that make them quite willing to take this form of financial reward rather than return to the work place. Organized labor says, 'No, they've paid their dues, they should have an easy life.' Management says, 'We'd love to get them back to work,' but they are afraid it would produce litigation if anything happens. The result is that very often a person takes disability or takes retirement.

"It's healthy, if you have been palliated—I won't use the word *cured*—that you go back because of all the positive aspects of work, how individuals often live longer as a result of work. A physician can be helpful in making representations, when asked —to employers, to unions, to state boards, to federal boards— of how rehabilitatable and how employable a given individual is, but when you get to a certain point it's out of their hands. Society has created all these rewards for not working. I don't think we're in a position to negate those."

It's much the same story from those on the other side of the time clock—the corporate medical directors. Of the eighty-four Consolidated Edison employees who had bypass surgery between January 1980 and August 1983, 62 percent went back to work, 18 percent retired, and 20 percent were still on the fence. That's not a bad record, but Thomas J. Doyle, medical director of the New York utility, thinks it could have been better had not disability benefits been such tough competition. Under Con Ed's triple-tiered compensation system, employees get a week of full pay for each year of service. When this is exhausted, there is an insurance program that union members can opt for (the company pays part of the costs) that will provide 80 percent of the employee's salary for another twenty-six weeks. After that, there are additional disability-retirement benefits based on age and length of employment.

"Benefit designs have seriously hampered in many ways the return-to-work situation," said K. D. McMurrain, the medical director at Procter & Gamble, where a combination of corporate and other benefits entitles long-term employees to about half of their salaries for the rest of their lives. And, he went on, "disability benefits receive special tax considerations so the take-home pay often is not too far off of what they were bringing home on a regular basis, and they are doing this without working. So as long as they are considered disabled, the incentive to return to work is minimal."

Much as companies would like to get patient-employees back to work—it is cheaper, after all, than putting them out to pasture—bypass surgery can pose special problems, particularly for blue-collar workers who need to make a gradual reentry and may even require less physically demanding jobs. Like other companies, Con Ed is willing to keep returning employees on restricted duty—no heavy lifting, driving, or climbing ladders—for at least a year and perhaps longer. If an individual cannot manage to go back to his old job, the company tries to find another job, preferably in the same location. So far, says Doyle, it has largely succeeded. But it's getting harder all the time. "Everyone must have a productive job, since we're not a social service organization. Especially with long-service people, we prefer to find something they can do, either with talents they have or new talents they can pick up in our training course. But we have been shrinking over the last ten years, so each year it gets more and more difficult to tailor-make jobs for handicapped people."

"I've worked my way up from a laborer to a supervisor, going to night school and all that," said Jordan Roberts, who was a foreman for a New Jersey company before his triple bypass. "I had thirty or thirty-five people working for me. I never collected a penny of unemployment in my life. Then, all of a sudden, I was told I needed a bypass. It was very hard to accept.

"After the operation, I had an irregular heartbeat for a while.

Our company has a disability program, but it is predicated on Social Security, and with Reaganomics, they were putting people off, not putting them on. So I got turned down. I could have appealed and maybe even won. But my lawyer told me all the company has to do is offer you another position and that would knock out Social Security later if I got worse. Maybe it was psychological, but I was afraid I couldn't handle my old job, which required me to be on call around the clock. I certainly didn't feel like an invalid; I just wasn't sure I could still handle that kind of stress.

"Eventually, they gave me a temporary position at another plant keeping track of productivity and standards. It was a good job, but it was forty miles away from my home, not five minutes like the old plant, and after about nine months I found I just couldn't take it physically. So I went back to the old plant, and they gave me a desk job, but nothing really to do. My bosses gave me the feeling that they didn't care what I did. After twenty-five years with the company, I felt I had a lot to offer, but if I had an opinion, they would ignore it. That part I could accept. What bothered me was that the people I worked with seemed to lose respect for me. These are the people I've worked with, gone to picnics and Christmas parties with. I guess the fact that I didn't die threw them. They must have thought, this guy can't be that sick. One guy even said to me, 'I suppose one day you'll have a heart attack in front of us, and we'll have to carry you out.' I guess he was being sarcastic.

"They kept paying me, but it was hard, very hard. I know that a lot of people have psychological problems after their bypass, but I just wasn't prepared for any of this. Nothing annoys me more than to see someone like Rock Hudson, who went through bypass, propped up in a chair with eight-hundred-dollars worth of clothes on saying, 'It was nothing.' Anyway, since I got out of the hospital I suppose I've been drinking more than I should —mostly beer—and that's one of the reasons my weight is so bad. If I was older, say fifty-five, I would have taken early retirement. But I'm only forty-eight, and I'm feeling much better physically. Sometimes I begin to feel sorry for myself. I wake up at night and wonder how things got so turned around. If I didn't have a pension to lose, I think I would just pack it in. But I'm just too young to sit and look out the window. I'm down to a few more years until I can retire. It looks like a prison sentence, but I'm going to try to make it."

And so it went. Every six months or so, Roberts would come in for an examination. He complained of sweating, sensations of suffocation, palpitations, and irritability. He was drinking beer —his weight was over 260 pounds—and smoking cigarettes. But mostly, he was angry about his job. First he insisted on a limited work schedule, and the company went along. Then he demanded full-time work, but the company doctor didn't think he was ready. Roberts feared they were pushing him to retire. Eventually, company officials, their considerable patience exhausted, pressed him to go back to his old job. Instead, he arranged a deal for early retirement. But after it was all approved, he changed his mind. The final twist came a year later when the company, which had fallen on hard times, laid him off. He was the only employee in his category to be dumped, he told me over the phone a few months shy of the third anniversary of his bypass surgery and just a few years away from his pension.

There are no good guys or bad guys in this tale, just one tragic figure. Following bypass surgery, Roberts lost his grip on the ladder of success, and this was as much a function of his own personality as of corporate exigencies. He was unable to control his drinking and smoking, or his anger and frustration, and ultimately he couldn't achieve the mental transition from the symptomatic state to full recovery. His entanglements with the company were more the product of his own maladjustment than of an insensitive employer.

Sometimes the employer needs more rehabilitation than the

patient, especially when the boss regards a worker who has had bypass surgery as "damaged goods." According to J. Fred Lucas, former corporate medical director for Electronic Data Systems in Houston and a participant at the 1981 forum, bypass patients make many employers jittery. "Individuals running a department get nervous about them dying on the job, so they would just as soon see them retired or disabled, and out of the area they are responsible for. If they die in someone else's care, that's fine by them."

How far can a bypass patient bounce back? Are there jobs they shouldn't be allowed to take? Should discrimination against them by employers and society be permitted? What are the limits of recovery?

When Philip Johnson, the distinguished architect, had triple-bypass surgery in 1975, some feared his career would be at an end. Far from it. Since then, he has completed the corporate headquarters of American Telephone and Telegraph in New York City, arguably his finest work. In 1982, at age seventy-five, he received the Heart of New York Award for "the splendid example he has set for other heart patients by resuming an active and productive life."

Less recognized but certainly a success in his own right was Jacob Landers. An assistant superintendent of the New York City public school system, Mr. Landers underwent quadruple-bypass surgery in 1975. In May 1982, at age sixty-nine, he became perhaps the oldest graduate in the history of New York University Law School.

On April 1, 1980, Alexander M. Haig underwent triple-bypass surgery. Less than a year later, the fifty-six-year-old retired general was confirmed as Secretary of State.

Bypass veterans run Fortune 500 companies, manage baseball teams, write best-sellers, make movies, star in movies, and even run marathons. Indeed, forty-three-year-old Joe Michaels of

Bayside, New York, has run eleven *ultra* marathons since his 1980 double bypass.

But one of the most difficult cases, from a medical and legal perspective, was that of Edward O'Neil. A former Air Force fighter pilot, O'Neil flew a Delta Airlines 727 up and down the East Coast between Miami and Montreal. In 1970, at age forty, he took a routine six-month physical, which showed "borderline" irregularities on his EKG. Subsequent catheterization showed an occluded right coronary artery, but since there was adequate collateral circulation from the left side of his heart, he needed no operation. Banished from the cockpit, he set about to work his way back, quitting his thirty-cigarette-a-day habit, jogging, watching his diet, and dropping thirty-five pounds from his six-foot one-inch frame. By 1976, an EKG and coronary angiogram reflected the benefits of these changes, and he was granted a limited certificate that allowed him to resume flying, but only as a copilot or flight engineer. Three years later, O'Neil noticed that telltale anginal chest tightness and was soon carted into the operating room at Massachusetts General Hospital, where surgeon Cary W. Akins sewed segments of saphenous vein to his left anterior descending, circumflex, and right coronary arteries. When he arrived home, he again vowed he would get back to the cockpit. But he knew that would be no easy matter.

At the time, the Federal Aviation Administration had the right to disqualify a pilot only if it could find evidence that an applicant could "reasonably be expected" to have a heart attack. But even though this clearly gave flyers who underwent bypass an opening to prove that they weren't at risk, the agency routinely denied them flight certificates anyway. No doubt looming large in the administration's memory was a string of disasters and near-disasters traced to coronary artery disease (though not to pilots who had bypasses). In 1962, a Flying Tiger plane crashed in California killing three crewmen and two passengers when the pilot had a heart attack. In 1966, seventy-eight passengers and a crew of five died when an American Flyers Airline jet nose-dived into an Ardmore, Oklahoma, cornfield when the pilot had a heart attack. Indeed, a month after O'Neil had his bypass, a Pan American pilot who left his 747 cockpit while flying from Honolulu to Los Angeles was later found in a rest room, dead of a heart attack.

Under the law, O'Neil had another chance—an appeal to the National Transportation Safety Board. Until the mid-1970s, the board backed up the FAA because bypass patients weren't able to marshal enough evidence for their cause. Then, with the advent of diagnostic tools like thallium and gated blood-pool scans, the tide turned. Cardiologists could testify with great precision about what was going on inside a heart that had been operated on, and many of the finest in the country did, including Richard Gorlin.

That was what happened in September 1981, when O'Neil's case came before Administrative Law Judge William E. Fowler, Jr., in Boston. For two days, physician after physician testified as to the state of O'Neil's coronary anatomy, vessel by vessel and graft by graft. The FAA called Milton J. Sands, director of the catheterization laboratory at Connecticut's New Britain General Hospital, Hendrick B. Barner, a professor of surgery at St. Louis University School of Medicine, and James R. Hickman, Jr., who specialized in aerospace medicine. Their message, in essence, was that surgery, far from curing the underlying disease, at best merely forestalled its toll. O'Neil's risk of having a heart attack, they argued, was greater than that of the population at large. And while it was one thing to risk one life, the person at the controls of a commercial airliner had more than a hundred in his hands.

Appearing on the pilot's behalf were Akins, O'Neil's surgeon, Peter C. Block, director of the Massachusetts General catheterization laboratory, Michael Lesch, chief of cardiology at Northwestern University, and Emil P. Taxay, a specialist in aviation medicine. They contended that all O'Neil's bypass grafts were open and were expected to stay that way, and that what had been wrong with him was corrected. The FAA, they said, was biased against bypass.

"It was a good show," O'Neil joked when the hearing was over. "I didn't know whether I would live through the weekend when they got through with me." In December, Fowler reversed the FAA and ruled that O'Neil should be recertified as a pilot. The FAA appealed, but in May the transportation safety board affirmed the judge's decision. Within a few months, O'Neil was back in the air and in the captain's seat.

As it happened, four days after O'Neil's successful appeal, FAA regulations that had been in the pipeline for years finally went into effect. Instead of requiring proof that a pilot's heart disease "may reasonably be expected to lead to myocardial infarction," the new rules said a pilot must have "no established medical history or clinical diagnosis of myocardial infarction, angina pectoris, or coronary heart disease that has required treatment or, if untreated, that has been symptomatic or clinically significant." This placed coronary heart disease in the same category as epilepsy, insulin-dependent diabetes, psychosis, and drug addiction.

"The key is the disqualification by history alone," said O'Neil's attorney, Mark T. McDermott, of Washington, D.C., "which means there is no chance for a risk assessment. That knocked the NTSB completely out of the picture. All they can do is look to see if the pilot has a history of surgically treated disease and then disqualify him.

"It's a stupid rule, because a major part of our safety system is based on voluntary disclosure by pilots. Often the pilot is the only one who knows he's having symptoms, and the only one who can make himself seek treatment before disaster occurs. If he's making $110,000 a year and he knows he's going to be disqualified for the rest of his life if he seeks treatment, he's not going to seek treatment. So it's a dangerous rule that harms safety rather than helps it. It's hard to find a qualified doctor anywhere in the United States that supports the FAA's position. At a time when there's so much hope that cardiac patients can be rehabilitated, it's incredible to me that we have a rule that says symptoms and treatment are disqualifying entities in themselves. It flies in the face of science."

On behalf of O'Neil and two other pilots who had won their certificates but were at risk of losing them at their next six-month recertification, McDermott tried and failed to persuade the federal appeals court to scrap the new rule. Unless the FAA changes its mind—and it has hired the American Medical Association to review all its medical standards—McDermott's only hope is the Congress. Meanwhile, O'Neil and a few other pilots who have had bypasses are flying, but only through the good graces of the FAA, which has given them special exemptions based on periodic examinations.

If O'Neil were the only person aboard a 727 who could handle the controls, it might not be wise to let him back in the cockpit. But there are several among the crew who would be ready to take the stick in the unlikely case of a coronary event. Still, the case of Edward O'Neil sends an optimistic message to those bypass patients fighting to regain jobs and self-respect. Just as Ed O'Neil got back at the controls, bypass patients can get back into control. Bypass went on trial, and it won. It fell to the surgeon who performed O'Neil's bypass among a thousand others to sum up the meaning of the verdict: "Should Alexander Haig not be allowed to be Secretary of State because he had a bypass?" Cary Akins asked. "Should we allow truck drivers and train engineers to resume their duties or a surgeon to continue operating? Where do we draw the line?"

Successful bypass patients have pushed the line back and, in doing so, proved that society's perceptions and prejudices can be overcome and that bypass surgery, more than merely rebuilding hearts, can rebuild lives.

12

The Bottom Line
The Economics of Bypass

EVERY TIME A TEST is carried out, a drug is given, an intravenous line is connected, or a patient is moved from one bed to another at Mount Sinai, a billing slip finds its way to a bare brick structure two blocks north of the Annenberg Building. There, in the fourth floor control room of the financial division, dozens of keypunch operators, working in shifts around the clock, enter the codes from the slips, along with patients' identification numbers, into twenty-five terminals linked to an IBM 4341 mainframe computer, which tracks every dollar flowing into and out of the medical center. Twelve thousand slips arrive at the control room each day. All are entered by code numbers, not dollars, so the hospital can instantly update (read raise) prices when inflation demands.

About 125 patients leave Mount Sinai each day, and the computer makes sure their bills soon follow. In fact, some patients prefer to pay on their way out, stopping by the Patients' Accounts office on the first floor of the Metzger Pavilion, just past the ceremonial entrance hall lined with plaques proclaiming the gifts from the city's leading families of "free beds founded in perpetuity." The hospital accepts credit cards, and it's not unheard of for some patients, especially those from overseas, to charge the whole tab. But most of the time the office sends the bill to the patient's home. In the case of our Mr. Stein, the four-page statement arrived two weeks after his discharge. This is what it looked like:

The Mount Sinai Medical Center
One Gustave L. Levy Place
New York, New York 10029

$700.00—RM/BRD 2 at $350.00 from 6/4/83

Room and board charges were $350 a day on Housman 3, an amount that rivals the most expensive hotel rooms in Manhattan. Some hospitals, including Mount Sinai, are working with hotel chains to develop residences that will save patients money. Despite the price, beds in the better New York City hospitals are hard to come by. Occupancy rates are always near 100 percent, and there are long waiting lists for admission, the result of a state policy that discourages hospital construction.

$64.00—BLOOD—SMA-6 6/4/83

$117.00—BLOOD—SMA-12 6/4/83

Sequential multiphasic analyses. Blood tests in which two or three milliliters of serum are placed in the tubing of a machine that automatically processes six or twelve routine assays that are the mainstay of laboratory screening for systemic disease. These eighteen tests measure the blood sugar, blood urea nitrogen (BUN), creatinine, sodium, potassium, chloride, bicarbonate, calcium, magnesium, phosphate, uric acid, alkaline phosphatase, bilirubin, cholesterol, the transaminase enzymes (SGOT and SGPT), total protein, and albumin. They are performed on everybody admitted to a hospital, and they are repeatedly checked during a stay for major surgery. If a physician just wanted to know the magnesium concentration, he would still order an SMA-12, and eleven unwanted tests.

$18.00—ROUTINE URINE 6/4/83

One of the better bargains in medicine. This test involves a plastic strip holding little sections of filter paper, each impregnated with chemicals that change color in the presence of certain substances in the urine, including sugar, acid, blood, ketones, protein, and bilirubin. Then, a test tube of urine is spun in a centrifuge, which concentrates any solids at the bottom. Normal urine should contain virtually no cells; if significant numbers of red blood cells are found in a sample from a male or nonmenstruating female, or if white blood cells, kidney cells, bacteria, or mineral crystals appear, it means that infection, stones, tumors, or other urinary disease may be present. The vast majority of routine urinalyses performed in the hospital laboratory are normal, but abnormal results could have great importance, especially for a patient about to undergo heart surgery.

$79.00—EKG 6/4/83

Electrocardiograms are money-makers for the hospital. They are taken by technicians who

operate consoles connected by telephone to a
central computer in the basement, which prints
out the tracing, interprets it, and generates a
report within seconds. To obtain the
"professional" fee from third-party payers, the
EKG must be reviewed by a cardiologist, who
can read a hundred normal tracings an hour (but
may spend much longer on a single abnormal
one). Mount Sinai collected more than $2 million
processing 60,000 EKGs in 1983.

$107.00—CHEST—2 FILMS 6/4/84

Back-to-front and left-to-right X-ray pictures of
the chest, which were on view in the operating
room during Mr. Stein's surgery. It is hard to
calculate the cost of the equipment, labor, and
silver used to produce the film, though the
latter can ultimately be recycled. Still, this
charge seems steep.

$176.25CR—RED CELL P/F 6/5/83

Packed and frozen red cells. Someone had
donated blood in Mr. Stein's name, and a credit
was entered on his bill.

$27.00—BLOOD TYPING 6/6/83

$22.00—BLOOD COMPAT TEST 6/6/83

This and the three items that follow refer to
blood matched in the hospital blood bank with
Mr. Stein's type and tested by mixing the blood
of donor and recipient to make sure no reaction
developed. Even so, combinations of blood that
get along well in the test tube sometimes cause
a transfusion reaction in the patient. Four units
were set aside for Mr. Stein's operation.

$22.00—BLOOD COMPAT TEST 6/6/83

$22.00—BLOOD COMPAT TEST 6/6/83

$22.00—BLOOD COMPAT TEST 6/6/83

$916.00—OPERATING ROOM 6/6/83
> This was the hospital's cut of the OR expenses
> and is used to pay for personnel and
> maintenance. It is based on the average time
> required for bypass surgery.

$90.00—SURGICAL SUPPLIES 6/6/83
> This covers the gases, drugs, tubes, needles,
> syringes, and other equipment on the
> anesthesiologist's cart, but not his services.

$1040.00—SURGICAL SUPPLIES 6/6/83
> The perfusion kit, including the disposable
> membrane oxygenator, clear plastic tubing,
> clamps, stopcocks, and other paraphernalia used
> with the cardiopulmonary bypass pump.

$580.00—SURGICAL SUPPLIES 6/6/83
> The basic open-heart kit containing many of the
> instruments needed for a cardiac operation. Most
> are sterilized and reused.

$695.00—SURGICAL SUPPLIES 6/6/83
> The coronary bypass kit, containing special
> clamps, forceps, sutures, and retractors.

$32.00—PACING WIRES 6/6/83
> This is the charge for the thin epicardial
> electrodes implanted toward the end of the
> procedure.

$1,220.00—RM/BRD 2 at $610.00 from 6/6/83
> The day rate for the CICU is probably a
> bargain, since the technological resources of the

Unit are not duplicated anywhere else. Much of the equipment used in treating intensive care patients is not billed separately. It's not that the hospital administration wouldn't like to; it's just that it's too great a burden on the CICU staff to worry about billing slips when tending to the critically ill.

$60.00—PLEUREVAC 6/6/83

The canister that hangs over the footboard of the bed to collect and measure fluid draining from the chest tubes. An ingeniously designed piece of hardware (actually, plastic) that nevertheless could have been replaced by two ordinary bottles, one of them partly filled with water.

$13.00—EGG CRATE 6/6/83

A slab of corrugated foam rubber placed over the mattress to help patients avoid bedsores while they are immobilized. For sanitary reasons, the pads are not reused, so each patient takes it with him, like a teddy bear, when he's transferred to Housman 3.

$107.00—CHEST—BEDSIDE 6/6/83

This was the first X ray after Mr. Stein arrived in the CICU. The portable machine wheeled to his bed produced a picture of vastly lesser quality than the one taken in the radiology department upon admission, but it's the best we can do when the patient can't leave the Unit.

$41.00—COULTER COUNT CBC 6/6/83

The Coulter Counter is an amazing machine that takes a drop of diluted blood, counts the red cells, white cells, and platelets, and determines the amount of hemoglobin. A technician used to count the cells using a microscope.

$34.00—BLOOD HEMATOCRIT 6/6/83

This reading of the volume of packed red cells in the blood helped us decide when to give Mr. Stein a transfusion. Unlike the CBC, which is performed in the hospital's main laboratory, the hematocrit can be measured quickly in a satellite laboratory next to the CICU.

$14.00—BLOOD-DIFFERENTIAL 6/6/83

This test requires that a technician smear a drop of blood on a glass slide and stain it to reveal the distinguishing features of the various white blood cells. Then he counts out 100 cells to determine the percentage of each kind. Automated methods to handle this task are becoming available.

$49.00—SERUM ALBUMIN 6/6/83

A protein extract of blood given to Mr. Stein, which served as a volume expander, much as plasma was once used. It has not been shown to be more effective than salt water and is a lot more expensive.

$98.00—SERUM ALBUMIN 6/6/83

$64.00—BLOOD SMA-6 6/6/83

If ordered STAT in the CICU, these results can be available from the hospital laboratory in a few hours.

$117.00—BLOOD SMA-12 6/6/83

$119.00—ARTERIAL BLOOD GAS 6/6/83

This measures the amount of oxygen, carbon dioxide, and acid in blood obtained from the arterial line. The results were used to adjust the ventilator and, when the time came, help us wean Mr. Stein from it. Like many other blood tests in the CICU, we leave the timing of blood gases to the nurses, a policy not in effect elsewhere in the hospital.

$40.00—URINE—SODIUM 6/6/83

$40.00—URINE—POTASSIUM 6/6/83

Urine sodium and potassium levels reflect how the kidneys are working. Mr. Stein probably could have done without these tests.

$30.00—BLOOD—OSMOLALITY 6/6/83

This is a measure of the richness of the blood plasma. The more molecules dissolved in the blood, the higher the osmolality. Though it is one of the ways we can tell if a patient needs more fluid, it's not very useful in the CICU if kidney function is good. Another fairly routine but unnecessary expenditure in Mr. Stein's case.

$34.00—URINE—OSMOLALITY 6/6/83

This tells if Mr. Stein's kidneys are producing a concentrated urine, one measure of their function. It makes no sense that it should be $4 more expensive than the same test performed on blood serum, especially since the urine needs less preparation for testing.

$40.00—BLOOD—POTASSIUM 6/6/83

Blood potassium concentration is one of the most important items monitored in the early hours after surgery. A potassium level too high or too low can have catastrophic effects on cardiac rhythm and turn a routine case into a disaster. Almost every patient initially has a low potassium reading, which requires prompt and careful attention by the nurse to keep it in the normal range. One of the main justifications for having a laboratory adjacent to the CICU is to get potassium results quickly.

$40.00—BLOOD—GLUCOSE 6/6/83

Sugar measurements were important since Mr. Stein was a "borderline" diabetic by his account. It turned out that he crossed that line when insulin was needed in the early postoperative period.

$119.00—ARTERIAL BLOOD GAS 6/6/83

$119.00—ARTERIAL BLOOD GAS 6/6/83

$40.00—BLOOD—SODIUM 6/6/83

$40.00—BLOOD—POTASSIUM 6/6/83

$40.00—BLOOD—GLUCOSE 6/6/83

$119.00—ARTERIAL BLOOD GAS 6/6/83

$79.00—EKG 6/7/83

The morning-after electrocardiogram. Actually secondary in importance to the one taken by the CICU nurse shortly after surgery, which was a freebie since it was not recorded by the technician and never found its way into either the EKG-reading or billing computers. Just as well, as the computer frequently misreads these early tracings.

$40.00—BLOOD—SODIUM 6/7/83

$40.00—BLOOD—POTASSIUM 6/7/83

$30.00—BLOOD—OSMOLALITY 6/7/83

$119.00—ARTERIAL BLOOD GAS 6/7/83

$34.00—BLOOD—HEMATOCRIT 6/7/83

$64.00—BLOOD SMA-6 6/7/83

$117.00—BLOOD SMA-12 6/7/83

$40.00—BLOOD—POTASSIUM 6/7/83

$119.00—ARTERIAL BLOOD GAS 6/7/83

$34.00—BLOOD—HEMATOCRIT 6/7/83

$119.00—ARTERIAL BLOOD GAS 6/7/83

$40.00—BLOOD—POTASSIUM 6/7/83

$40.00—BLOOD—GLUCOSE 6/7/83

$119.00—ARTERIAL BLOOD GAS 6/7/83

$34.00—BLOOD—HEMATOCRIT 6/7/83

$40.00—BLOOD—SODIUM 6/7/83

$40.00—BLOOD—POTASSIUM 6/7/83

$40.00—BLOOD—GLUCOSE 6/7/83

$30.00—BLOOD OSMOLALITY 6/7/83

$119.00—ARTERIAL BLOOD GAS 6/7/83

$34.00—BLOOD—HEMATOCRIT 6/7/83

$40.00—BLOOD—POTASSIUM 6/7/83

$119.00—ARTERIAL BLOOD GAS 6/7/83

$34.00—BLOOD—HEMATOCRIT 6/7/83

$40.00—BLOOD—POTASSIUM 6/7/83

$119.00—ARTERIAL BLOOD GAS 6/7/83

$34.00—BLOOD—HEMATOCRIT 6/7/83

$235.00—RED CELL P/F 6/7/83

> Transfusions. The billed amount is more than Mr. Stein's insurance might have paid, but the hospital gave him credit for a "deposit" left in his name in the blood bank. Mr. Stein was fortunate that the blood was available, since shortages are common at the beginning of the summer. Even elective heart surgery takes priority over many other kinds of operations—not always a sensible policy—but we are still occasionally forced to cancel a case when the blood bank runs dry.

$119.00—ARTERIAL BLOOD GAS 6/7/83

$119.00—ARTERIAL BLOOD GAS 6/7/83

$40.00—BLOOD—POTASSIUM 6/7/83

$119.00—ARTERIAL BLOOD GAS 6/7/83

$34.00—BLOOD—HEMATOCRIT 6/7/83

$40.00—BLOOD—POTASSIUM 6/7/83

$119.00—ARTERIAL BLOOD GAS 6/7/83

$40.00—BLOOD—POTASSIUM 6/7/83

$119.00—ARTERIAL BLOOD GAS 6/7/83

$40.00—BLOOD—POTASSIUM 6/7/83

$119.00—ARTERIAL BLOOD GAS 6/7/83

$34.00—BLOOD—HEMATOCRIT 6/7/83

$40.00—BLOOD—POTASSIUM 6/7/83

$119.00—ARTERIAL BLOOD GAS 6/7/83

$40.00—BLOOD—POTASSIUM 6/7/83

$40.00—BLOOD—GLUCOSE 6/7/83

$34.00—BLOOD—HEMATOCRIT 6/7/83

$84.00—BLOOD—PT 6/7/83

$41.00—BLOOD—PTT 6/7/83

$34.00—BLOOD—FIBRINOGEN 6/7/83

$60.00—PLATELETS—FACTOR 3 6/7/83

> This and the three preceding entries are tests of blood coagulation. PT stands for prothrombin time, PTT for partial thromboplastin time—both measures of how long it takes certain components of the blood to clot. Fibrinogen and platelet factor 3 are substances in the blood that also participate in clotting. They were ordered because of concern that Mr. Stein was bleeding too much through his chest tubes.

$40.00—BLOOD—POTASSIUM 6/7/83

$98.00—SERUM ALBUMIN 6/7/83

$40.00—BLOOD—POTASSIUM 6/7/83

$40.00—BLOOD—GLUCOSE 6/7/83

$119.00—ARTERIAL BLOOD GAS 6/7/83

> Altogether, Mr. Stein had sixty-nine separate blood tests on a single day, at a cost of $3,449. Almost all were carried out in the CICU laboratory at the discretion of the nursing staff. About the only good part was that not one needle puncture was required, since the arterial

line could be tapped whenever a sample or specimen was needed. In a way, though, we were not really testing Mr. Stein's own blood but rather a conglomeration of fluids infused or transfused into his vessels during and after surgery.

$119.00—ARTERIAL BLOOD GAS 6/8/83

$34.00—BLOOD—HEMATOCRIT 6/8/83

$64.00—BLOOD—SMA-6 6/8/83

$117.00—BLOOD—SMA-12 6/8/83

$41.00—COULTER COUNT CBC 6/8/83

$14.00—BLOOD DIFFERENTIAL 6/8/83

$196.00—SERUM ALBUMIN 6/8/83

$34.00—BLOOD—HEMATOCRIT 6/8/83

$119.00—ARTERIAL BLOOD GAS 6/8/83

$107.00—CHEST—BEDSIDE 6/8/83

$107.00—CHEST—BEDSIDE 6/8/83

The second X ray of the day followed removal of the chest tubes. We wanted to make sure there were no complications, such as a collapsed lung, before Mr. Stein left the intensive care unit.

$13.20—DRUGS 6/8/83

$7.70—DRUGS 6/8/83

Here's where the hospital saved Mr. Stein some money. Many of the institutions in town have banded together to order pharmacy supplies collectively, getting a better deal and passing

some of the savings along to their patients.
Even so, an institution the size of Mount Sinai
spends well over a million dollars a year on
antibiotics alone.

$51.70—IV SOLUTIONS 6/8/83

Each time the nurse hangs a bottle of salt water
or sugar water on the hook above a patient's
bed, she enters it on a log in his hospital record.
A carbon is sent to the billing office, which then
tacks this on as the total charge.

$79.00—EKG 6/8/83

$3,150.00—RM/BRD 9 at $350.00 from 6/8/83

The day rate on Housman 3.

$23.00—RESP. THERAPY IPPB 6/8/83

Translation: respiratory therapy using
intermittent positive-pressure breathing. Second
translation: the charge for the plastic gizmo that
Mr. Stein blew into to help expand his lungs.

$41.00—COULTER COUNT CBC 6/9/83

$14.00—BLOOD DIFFERENTIAL 6/9/83

$41.00—COULTER COUNT CBC 6/10/83

$33.00—PROTHROMBIN TIME 6/10/83

This appears to have been ordered in error,
perhaps by an overworked resident or
physician's assistant. Mr. Stein had no
blood-clotting abnormalities and was not among
the many postoperative patients given
anticoagulants, who would have needed this test
to measure how their blood was affected.

$107.00—CHEST—2 FILMS 6/10/83

> At this point, Mr. Stein was well enough to travel by wheelchair down to the radiology department for his first top quality X rays since surgery. With no delivery charge, he got two for the price of what one cost in the CICU.

$64.00—BLOOD SMA-6 6/10/83

$117.00—BLOOD SMA-12 6/10/83

$41.00—COULTER COUNT CBC 6/12/83

$64.00—BLOOD SMA-6 6/12/83

$117.00—BLOOD SMA-12 6/12/83

$13.00—EGG CRATE 6/13/83

> He either wore out the first one or the hospital double-billed him.

$41.00—COULTER COUNT CBC 6/14/83

$107.00—CHEST—BEDSIDE 6/14/83

> Once again, and for reasons unclear, the X-ray machine came to him.

$64.00—BLOOD SMA-6 6/14/83

$117.00—BLOOD SMA-12 6/14/83

$41.00—COULTER COUNT—CBC 6/15/83

$8.20—DRUGS 6/15/83

$45.10—DRUGS 6/15/83

> The digitalis, vitamins, iron, and other medicines he was taking on Housman 3. Again, a good deal compared with the cost at his neighborhood drugstore.

$107.00—CHEST—2 FILMS 6/16/83

$41.00—COULTER COUNT CBC 6/16/83

$10.70—TAKE HOME DRUGS 6/16/83

$5.78—TAKE HOME DRUGS 6/16/83

$4.17—TAKE HOME DRUGS 6/16/83

$3.45—TAKE HOME DRUGS 6/16/83

$3.76—TAKE HOME DRUGS 6/16/83

$3.98—TAKE HOME DRUGS 6/16/83
> The hospital sends him home with a week's supply.

$9.00—IV SOLUTIONS 6/16/83

$64.00—BLOOD SMA-6 6/16/83

$117.00—BLOOD SMA-12 6/16/83

$46.75—DRUGS 6/16/83

$8.80—DRUGS 6/16/83

$2.30—DRUGS 6/16/83

$6.00—DAILY TELEPHONE 6/17/83

$27.00—DAILY TELEPHONE 6/17
> Like a hotel, the hospital takes a cut.

TOTAL DAYS IN HOSPITAL—13

TOTAL CHARGES—$16,589.34

COVERED BY INSURANCE—$16,524.50
> Mr. Stein's insurance paid for everything except the drugs he was sent home with and the

telephone. The hospital's benefit analyst made sure of this even before he was admitted. If his insurance wasn't adequate to cover the costs likely to arise, a deposit would have been requested, and bills would have been issued weekly.

PAYMENT DUE FROM PATIENT—$64.84

Even before Mount Sinai's statement arrived at the Stein household—indeed, even before Mr. Stein arrived—his wife received a bill from the One East One Hundredth Street Physicians, P.C.

$1,500.00—ADMINISTRATION OF ANESTHESIA 6/6/83

The professional services of the anesthesiologist and his assistant, including the preoperative evaluation, the passing of gas in the operation room, monitoring during the procedure, and a postoperative visit. There's a joke around the medical center that patients wake up after surgery to find these bills pinned to their pillows.

A few weeks later, after a more decent interval, Mr. Stein received a bill from the Division of Cardiothoracic Surgery for Mindich's fee and related charges.

$4,750.00—CORONARY ARTERY BYPASS, AUTOGENOUS GRAFT, THREE ARTERIES 6/6/83

The division has a corner on the market. No one is allowed to do cardiac surgery at Mount Sinai besides its members. The hospital believes heart surgery should be performed only by the full-time academic staff. This fee represents a pretty hefty take for what was about an hour of Mindich's time. The medical center keeps most of it.

$1,100.00—HEART-LUNG MACHINE, ASSEMBLY AND OPERATION 6/6/83

This pays for the perfusionists who run the $125,000 bypass pump, a complicated piece of equipment that requires careful and continuous monitoring by two experienced technicians prepared to operate it by hand if the power fails. At Mount Sinai, they are among the best in the business.

$80.00—SPIROMETRY—PULMONARY FUNCTION STUDY 6/6/83

$80.00—SPIROMETRY—PULMONARY FUNCTION STUDY 6/7/83

He had one lung test on the day of surgery and another the day after, to adjust the respirator and wean him from it.

$45.00—COMPREHENSIVE SERVICE, ESTABLISHED PATIENT 8/24/83

The follow-up visit in Annenberg 24-42.

$60.00—X-RAY EXAM OF CHEST, TWO VIEWS, LATERAL AND POSTEROANTERIOR 8/24/83

Note: They bill more for X rays than for a follow-up visit with the doctor.

$40.00—ELECTROCARDIOGRAM, COMPLETE 8/24/83

The surgeons charge $39 less than the hospital for an EKG. They also charge half as much for the chest X rays.

TOTAL CHARGES—$6,155.00

The last statement to arrive—through inefficiency, not decency—was from Cardiology Associates, for my bill.

$225.00—COMP HISTORY & PHY IN HOSP 6/5/83

This is the fee for my clinical evaluation before surgery—an interview and physical exam by both the cardiology fellow and myself, our review of the reports, and interpretation of the electrocardiogram and chest X ray. I should have billed $125 for reviewing the angiograms made in Westchester, but it slipped through the cracks.

$585.00—SUBSEQUENT HOSPITAL VISITS 6/6/83

I spent more time with Mr. Stein before and after surgery than any other physician—about a dozen visits in all, which works out to about $50 per visit. Insurance picked up the whole cost, as it did for the surgeon's and anesthesiologist's fees.

TOTAL CHARGES—$810.00

These bills bring Mr. Stein's balance to $25,054.34. Throw in a hematology consultation at $225, rehabilitation at $175, and about $3,000 for the diagnostic workup (Holter monitor, exercise test with nuclear study, and catheterization), and the grand total comes to about $28,500. (All Mr. Stein paid for were the telephone and the prescriptions, a one-week supply of digoxin, iron, acetaminophen with codeine, aspirin, dipyridamole, and Colace.) That's about average for an uncomplicated triple bypass at a major teaching hospital in New York City. If he had had his operation in the Midwest, charges may have been 10 or 20 per-

cent cheaper and the hospital stay that much shorter. At the time
of Mr. Stein's surgery, the University of Florida in Gainesville
reported that the average cost of a coronary bypass operation
was $21,155 for their patients under the age of sixty (with a
mortality rate of 1.3 percent), while for those over sixty-five
costs averaged $36,918 (and the mortality rate was almost six
times higher). Whatever the differences induced by geography
or demography, the price of bypass surgery is going up, fueled
by a medical inflation rate that has soared 520 percent in the last
sixteen years. Just six months after Mr. Stein's operation, another typical bypass patient at Mount Sinai was charged
$19,935.50 for his uncomplicated ten-day hospital course, a 20
percent increase.

The fact that an item like a $13 egg crate is billed separately,
a $500 disposable bypass pump oxygenator is tucked away
under "surgical supplies," and some of the high-tech equipment
used in the CICU doesn't appear at all makes Mr. Stein's bill
almost impossible for a doctor, much less a patient, to understand. In large part, it's the nature of the beast. Hospital bills
are an auditor's nightmare. There are now several dozen companies in the country specializing in the scrutiny of hospital bills,
and the consensus is that more than 90 percent of the big ones
contain overcharges ranging from 5 to 15 percent. The issue
isn't fraud, the auditors agree, but simply sloppy bookkeeping.
"You'd be amazed how many times the decimal point is put in
the wrong place," Richard Mandel, president of Republic Service
Bureau, a nationwide auditing service, told *The New York
Times*. "The remarkable thing is that it is always too far to the
right."

All this was on my mind when I showed Mr. Stein's bill to
Samuel Davis, then president of the Mount Sinai Hospital. He
agreed that the hospital's accounting system left something to
be desired but wasn't sure all the mistakes were in the institu-

tion's favor. "The charge for an X ray is always greater than the cost of an X ray," said Davis, sitting in his office in front of a blackboard crammed with cost-flow diagrams. "If you were a student of American history, you may remember how tariffs on the railroads were established in the early days: 'all the traffic could bear.' Charges are not in all cases a function of costs. There is a certain amount of Robin Hoodism. But there are lost charges, which benefit the patient on whose behalf the charges are being paid, so that explains the missing charges."

In other words, the things that were done but didn't appear on Mr. Stein's bill make up for the hospital's somewhat arbitrary markup on things that were done and billed.

In any event, Davis insisted, a Mount Sinai bypass is a good buy. "All in all, $16,000 is not a lot of money given our CICU and the intensity of labor there. We pay nurses $23,000 a year to start, and look at how many nursing hours there are per day in the CICU—I think the number is something like 14.5 nursing hours per patient day. My guess is that the real cost of a day in the CICU comes to more than $1,000. If you add it all up, I think that it's not a bad buy."

But what if certain bypass patients qualified for a 50 percent discount on their hospital bill? Then Mr. Stein's $16,000 bill wouldn't seem like such a good deal. In effect, most Mount Sinai patients—or, more precisely, their insurers—are given such a discount. Their bills are paid not by ordinary private carriers, as Mr. Stein's was, but by one of the Big Three: Medicare, the federal government's insurance plan for the elderly; Medicaid, the state-administered plan for the poor; and Blue Cross, the nation's largest private health insurer. In order to clamp down on health care costs in New York, all three pay hospitals not for the specific charges racked up by individual patients but simply according to the number of days the patients were hospitalized. These third-party payers use different formulas, but the idea is the same: They compare a given hospital's books with those of similar institutions nearby, add a little for inflation, and subtract a little (and sometimes not so little) for a low occupancy rate, a longer-than-average stay, or higher-than-average costs, and *voila!*, come up with a single per diem rate. The formula is adjusted to account for particularly sick patients requiring extra care, the kind familiar to tertiary-care teaching institutions like Mount Sinai, many of whose patients are passed up the line from the primary provider, the physician, and health care's second tier, the community hospital. So, when all is said and done, Medicare, Medicaid, and Blue Cross pay Mount Sinai about $600 a day for each of their patients, no matter what's wrong and what is or isn't done during the stay. Since 40 percent of its patients are covered by Medicare, 15 percent by Medicaid, and 30 percent are under Blue Cross, Mount Sinai gets that reimbursement rate for 85 percent of the people it serves.

For five out of six patients, then, the hospital bill, mistakes and all, is irrelevant. Little wonder Davis says the amount of effort necessary to keep track of all the charges is disproportionate to the increased revenue that would be collected. Under its contract, the hospital agrees to accept as full payment whatever the Big Three pay; as a result, says Davis, Mount Sinai writes off over $60 million of unpaid charges each year. In a way, Mr. Stein's company and other private insurers are helping defray this loss, which is why some carriers are getting out of the health care business in states like New York.

New York is one of several states where hospitals are coming under increased pressure to bring down costs. But in many areas of the country, Blue Cross, the organization that picks up much of the bill for coronary bypass, simply pays what hospitals charge, case by case. In 1983, the organization's average hospital payment ranged from $11,500 to $16,500, and sometimes went much higher. In Dallas, for example, the average Blue Cross hospital payment for coronary bypass was $23,500. Some areas are shifting to a prospective payment system based on diagnosis-related groups (DRGs), under which Blue Cross (or Medicare and Medicaid) pay a fixed amount based on a particular procedure (rather than the length of stay), whether or not the case in question is straightforward or complicated. Had Davis been head of a hospital in Topeka, Kansas, for example, he would be looking at a DRG reimbursement rate for coronary bypass that averaged $15,858 in 1983—still almost twice what Blue Cross was paying for a bypass operation in New York.

In Dallas, Topeka, and other locales blessed with relatively generous reimbursement rates, bypass can be a money-maker. In institutions that perform a great many procedures—better known as bypass mills—the operation can be a major source of revenue, especially if many of the patients are low-risk cases. What does bypass surgery mean to an institution like Mount Sinai? Davis pauses, then sighs. "Our classification system tells us our patients are very sick. That's also true for bypass patients. Therefore, from an economic standpoint, bypass surgery under present reimbursement in New York State is not a winner. As a hospital administrator, I scratch my head and say, this is probably necessary surgery; a lot of pain and discomfort has been eased by this surgery, but a lot of discomfort has been caused for hospital administrators."

So much for the hospital. What about the corporations that sell the tubing, monitors, scalpels, egg crates, and all the sundry paraphernalia of modern medicine? Heart drugs alone, a $400 million a year business in the early 1970s, now cost Americans nearly $4 billion annually. And the annual costs for hospital and nursing-home care for heart patients during this period rose from $2.2 billion to $28.7 billion. The portion of that attributable to coronary bypass is already over $4 billion and climbing. Consider, for example, the oxygenators (at $250 to $350 each) that must be slipped into the bypass pump before each of the hundreds of thousands of open-heart operations (not just bypass but valve repair, correction of congenital defects, and other problems), not to mention all the other disposable devices used during the procedures. It's a $196 million a year market worldwide. American manufacturers are usually satisfied with a markup of about 50 percent, but the markup common in the hospital supply trade is 60 to 70 percent (for drug companies, it's more like 80 to 90 percent). The beneficiaries of the medical-industrial complex's notorious insensivity to price are such companies as American Bentley, which controls 32 percent of the market and is owned by American Hospital Supply, the General Motors of health care, Bard Cardiopulmonary, with a 16 percent share, and Travenol, with 10 percent.

Still, given the dimensions of medical expenditures—almost a quarter of a trillion dollars a year in this country and growing —the profits from coronary bypass are merely a rounding error. Even from the hospital administrator's point of view, only 15 percent of the cost of a surgical procedure goes for supplies, as against at least 60 percent for labor. The rest goes to pay the mortgage, the electric bill, and the like.

There is still one more set of outstretched latex-gloved hands —those of the physicians who charge for their services separately from the hospital. In Mr. Stein's case, Mindich's fee was $4,750 for the three bypasses. Here, again, the landscape is dominated by third-party reimbursers. In contrast to the way they seem to have roughed up hospitals such as Mount Sinai, Medicare, Medicaid, and Blue Shield (Blue Cross's counterpart that covers professional fees) have treated some doctors with kid gloves. True, Medicare has forced participating physicians to freeze their fees until October 1985, but many feel those fees have already risen far too high. In Washington, D.C., for example, they soared 75 percent from 1975 to 1979. Many blame the "usual, customary, and reasonable" system the reimbursers relied on previously—third parties unquestioningly paid up to the 90th percentile of the average fee in a given area, no matter how high that average went. What is "usual, customary, and reasonable?" This was the subject of a 1981 commentary in *The New England Journal of Medicine* by Benson B. Roe, a cardiothoracic surgeon at the University of California in San Francisco.

In the process of becoming financially dependent on third-party payers, physician lobbyists recognized the likelihood of being locked into a schedule of fixed fees which they feared would not keep pace with costs and new development. To forestall that problem, the American Medical Association campaigned successfully for a new method of payment that would retain flexibility and avoid a ceiling on fees. The A.M.A. also argued strenuously, and successfully, for "free choice": the principle that patients should be able to choose any physician they like without bureaucratic constraint. It was argued that if reimbursement were restricted to a fee schedule, the "best" doctors would not be available to the economically disadvantaged. What the lobbyists got written into Federal law was a system that mandates insurance payments on the basis of the regular [*usual*] fee of any physician whom the patient cares to choose [assuming it to be within the range of *customary* fees in that area, or, if precedent is lacking, to be *reasonable*]. The U.C.R. movement—to pay each physician at that physician's own price—was supported by strong economic pressure from large purchasers of health care packages, whose constituents were demanding protection against fees that might exceed their coverage.

Although the U.C.R. concept may have been reasonable and workable as a basis for billing individual patients, it has been a failure as a basis for reimbursement from insurance funds. Because it contains none of the limits or standards that are applied to other services covered by insurance, the charges for medical services have escalated, with little or no restraint, to the point at which current fee levels in several medical and surgical specialties are simply indefensible and deserving of public censure. In effect, usual, customary, or reasonable [UCR] has become a boondoggle. . . .

Thus the spiral began. The magnitude of the problem varies among the specialties and among geographic areas; my own field of cardiac surgery and my own state of California are possibly among the worst offenders, but they may portend a pattern for the whole profession.

The surgical operation that now heads the list in dollar cost in this country is coronary-artery bypass grafting for angina pectoris. Recent surveys have established that more than 100,000 coronary-bypass operations were performed in this country in 1979. A total of 125,000 operations is a reasonable estimate for 1980. In a three-month period in 1979, the California Blue Shield paid surgeons $709,000 for this operation—20 percent more than the next most expensive procedure [total hysterectomy].

Blue Shield has verified that the average fee paid for this operation during June 1980—to the principal surgeon alone—was between $3,500 and $4,200. Additional professional fees were usually paid for two assistants, a cardiologist, an anesthetist and an intensive-care physician, plus technician's charges for a pump perfusionist, adding at least another $2,500 to $3,500 per case [excluding the hospital's charges]. If those aggregate charges were applicable nationwide, it would total between half to three-quarters of a billion dollars in fees alone and well over $1.5 billion when hospital costs are included—all for just one specific type of operation to treat 0.04 percent of the population.

Nearly all these coronary-bypass operations in the United States in 1979 were performed by some 700 surgeons, according to one survey. This total divides up into an average workload of less than three cases per surgeon per week and provides an annual income of $350,000 from this single operation [assuming a fee of only $2,500, which is well below the average]. Since most cardiothoracic surgeons also do many other operations, and since complicated adjuncts add to the fee in many cases, it is conservative to estimate that their average gross income exceeds $500,000. It should be stressed that these numbers do not reflect the top of the field or the highest fees; they are a reasonable guess at the income of the average surgeon performing this procedure.

This line of reasoning leads inescapably to the conclusion that if there is money being made on bypass surgery, the surgeons are making it. There is a catch, though. In most teaching hospitals such as Mount Sinai, cardiothoracic surgeons don't keep their fees. In fact, they are paid a relatively small percentage; the rest goes to finance the activities of the medical school and pay for research and residency programs. So a big-league surgeon such as Mindich, who does perhaps five hundred bypass operations a year at an average of $5,000 apiece, could generate an annual revenue of $2,500,000, only a small fraction of which winds up in his paycheck. It is conceivable, in fact, that there is enough surgical surplus to make up for most, if not all, of the losses incurred from that $600 per diem reimbursement rate. Just think of the gravy a slice of the surgical fee represents to a medical center in another state already in the black as far as bypass is concerned. Even if it collects a slightly smaller surgeon's fee, say $3,000, it receives a far more generous hospital reimbursement—say, $12,000 of a $14,000 bill—and is still way ahead of Mount Sinai. Now take a "bypass mill" that handles fifteen or more cases a day. Factor in the economies of scale and specialization, and it's not hard to imagine annual profits approaching $10 million, which isn't bad in an industry accustomed to operating on razor-thin profits.

For the big bypass centers, however, the key to success is volume, and they are increasingly meeting competition from community hospitals trying to capture a share of the business of bypass. Even in New York, where bypass surgery is at best a marginal source of revenue, hospitals are motivated to offer the procedure to keep their beds filled and their occupancy rates high, avoiding the heavy penalties assessed for below average utilization. This is why, from time to time, surgeons are the subject of bidding wars that rival those waged for centerfielders. Hospitals will seemingly give away the store, because any losses from bypass will be more than balanced if they can avoid the occupancy penalty and keep per diem rates high for all their patients. Ultimately, however, Medicine (with a capital M) pays. The real danger of the physician reimbursement system is the free-agent surgeon who keeps most of his fees—and there is at least one in New York City pulling in well over seven figures annually—since this money could be used by deserving medical institutions to train doctors and conduct research.

The rise of the surgeon in the hierarchy of the medical industry is evident when the other physicians' fees on Mr. Stein's bill are examined. My group, Cardiology Associates, charged $810 for my services in Mr. Stein's treatment, and I didn't get to keep it either. At that rate, ninety-five visits would be needed to charge what Mindich charges for a triple bypass, a procedure that takes him about an hour. From the point of view of the institution that hired us both—and collects the lion's share of our fees—treatment by Mindich generates more revenues than treatment by me. True, I can order procedures like stress tests, nuclear scans, and angiography, which are reimbursed at a much higher rate than my time. But this flexing of diagnostic muscles, apart from narrowing the gap between surgical and medical revenues, leads many patients down the corridor to the operating room. (The fact that I get paid more for a pacemaker evaluation, which takes a minute or two, than for spending thirty to forty minutes examining a patient and exploring with him the nature of his problem speaks volumes about the priorities of American health care reimbursement.)

Nor is there an economic disincentive for a cardiologist to let a surgeon relieve a patient's pain, since bypass patients usually still need a cardiologist's services after surgery. In fact, a randomized study of unstable angina patients conducted in the early 1970s by the National Heart, Lung, and Blood Institute indicated that surgical patients continued to spend as much on medical care as angina patients who managed without surgery. The study compared a group of about one hundred patients with unstable angina who were under age seventy and had at least one coronary artery with a 70 percent blockage. According to economic data based on rates at the University of Alabama Medical Center in Birmingham, one of the busiest bypass centers in the country, at the end of the study's first year the mean cost of treatment was $7,666 for medical patients, as against $12,674 for surgical patients. But after two years, nearly 44 percent of patients initially randomized to medical therapy "crossed over" to surgery, and they paid a total of $23,500. In the third year, the difference in cost between the groups disappeared, indicating that, despite the higher initial investment in surgery, bypass patients faced the same expenses down the line as medical patients. In other words, subsequent medical costs were not diminished by having an operation and, at least for patients with unstable angina, fees for cardiologists didn't change.

The study was less clear about the patients' return on their investment. When asked, 21 percent of the medical patients, 35 percent of the surgical patients, and 52 percent of the late surgical patients reported their health to be good or excellent. But when asked how many days they were unable to carry out their usual activities because of heart disease, the medical patients reported only thirty, as against forty-eight for the surgical patients and seventy-two for the late surgical patients. Paradoxically, the late surgical patients thought they were doing better while they lost more days due to illness. Although a greater percentage of them were employed than either the medical patients or the patients initially sent to surgery, they lost $8,010 in annual income, adjusted for inflation and expressed in 1981 dollars, as against $5,487 for the medical group and $5,764 for the surgical group. So it seems that bypass surgery failed to reduce the Alabama patients' subsequent medical expenses and also failed to enable them to earn more money.

Studies such as this have important ramifications for national health policy. If the patients who failed medical therapy and ended up in the late surgery group could have been ferreted out and sent to the operating room initially, the cost of treatment would have been reduced by $3,933 for each of the one hundred patients in the trial.

The economic consequences of selecting the right patients for surgery were also apparent in a more ambitious and highly theoretical cost-benefit analysis compiled in 1981 by the Center for the Analysis of Health Practices at the Harvard School of Public Health. Using some fancy statistical footwork to factor in the improvement in quality of life (so much pain relieved per dollar of cost), it estimated that the "cost" of bypass surgery for patients with severe angina and blockage of the left main coronary artery, the worst form of the disease, worked out to $3,800 a year. By contrast, for a patient with minimal symptoms and only single-vessel coronary disease, the cost per "quality-adjusted year of life gained" went up to nearly half a million dollars. In short, the milder the case, symptom for symptom, the higher the cost of relieving the patient's distress.

The researchers based their work on an imagined population of fifty-five-year-old males, the typical bypass patients. The first step was to gather data from studies on survival after bypass and medical therapy and compile averages. But to use survival figures alone would ignore the principal reasons many patients have for choosing bypass surgery: "relief of pain, disability, and psychological burden of angina pectoris." The trick was figuring in the trade-off between symptom relief and life expectancy. The authors wrote:

The time-tradeoff approach seeks a balance between some number of years with angina and some fraction of the number of years that a patient would accept to be free of angina. For example, a patient might be willing to trade ten years with his severe angina for seven years without it. For this patient, one year at his level of angina would be worth 0.7 quality-adjusted years. . . . For a patient with milder angina or a more sedentary lifestyle, the weight assigned to one year with angina might be higher—for example, 0.9. For one with very severe angina or extreme psychological distress from it, a weight of 0.5, reflecting a willingness to give up half of his remaining life expectancy to be rid of the angina, might be plausible.

There is a risk-aversion factor, as well. A study of lung cancer treatment found that some patients considered a guaranteed life expectancy of less than 12.5 years preferable to only a 50 percent chance of living twenty-five years.

Punching these assumptions into their computer, the researchers estimated that quality-adjusted life expectancy improved 6.2 years with surgical therapy, compared to medical therapy for patients with left-main disease. For those with triple-vessel disease, the gain was 3.2 years, for double-vessel disease only 1.1 years, and for patients with single-vessel coronary disease selection of surgical therapy added just 0.5 years.

Next, they figured in the net cost of bypass, including the operation and hospitalization at an average of $17,500, and subtracted what it would cost to treat the same patients medically. Adjustments were made to reflect the authors' not necessarily valid assumption that surgical patients tend to have fewer heart attacks after their operations than medical patients (at a cost roughly estimated at $7,500 a heart attack). They also assumed that the number of surgical re-ops was balanced by the number of medical crossovers to later surgery. When all was said and done, the "net resource cost" of bypass surgery was estimated to be $14,000 for patients with severe angina and $15,500 for those with mild angina, a higher figure because the drug expenses averted would be lower.

Finally, the quality-adjusted life-expectancy calculations were combined with the resource cost calculations. The more favorable the ratio of net cost (which is higher for healthier patients and lower for sicker ones) to gain in life expectancy and symptom relief (which is lower for healthier patients and higher for sicker ones) the more economically attractive surgery became. Thus, the authors could calculate the relative dollar costs of bypass surgery for each pain-free year a patient survived. For patients with single-vessel disease bothered by only mild angina, the net cost of surgery was $470,000, as compared with $17,000 for those disabled by severe pain. For patients with triple-vessel disease, the cost effectiveness was $7,500 for patients with mild symptoms, only $500 more than if they had severe angina. Still, this was twice as costly as the bottom line for surgery for patients with left-main disease.

What are we to make of such numbers? There are too many unfounded assumptions to lean too heavily on cost-benefit analyses of this sort, but the conclusions underscore the importance of operating only on patients who really need surgery. This decision should depend on anatomy and symptoms. Judging from current hospital rosters, however, we seem to provide bypass more in relation to demographics than disease. Both the Coronary Artery Surgery Study of 24,000 patients at fifteen centers and the Hospital Discharge Survey conducted by the National Center for Health Care Statistics agreed that an overwhelming proportion of bypass patients are white. In fact, in 1982, the latest year for which the figures are available, 160,000 bypass patients were white, while only 4,000 were nonwhite (7,000 were not classified). And yet coronary artery disease is just as prevalent among blacks. What's more, although Medicaid accounts for 20 percent of all hospital stays, it pays for just 5 percent of all bypass operations.

13

Beyond Bypass
The Angioplasty Alternative

AT NIGHT, AFTER HIS stint treating coronary patients at the University of Zurich had ended, Andreas Gruentzig would slip off to the animal laboratory and the hospital morgue to perfect his new device on canines and cadavers. At first glance, the long, narrow tube looked like the catheters then used to squirt dye into the coronary arteries so they could be x-rayed. But at its tip Gruentzig had fashioned a sausage-shaped plastic balloon that could be inflated on command. He would guide the tube through his subject's body toward the heart and carefully position the tip at the point of an atherosclerotic blockage. Then he would expand the balloon, hoping to crush the plaque against the artery wall, clearing an opening for the precious blood to flow through. The idea of balloons in the circulatory system was not new. Intra-aortic balloon pumps were widely used even then. But rather than push the blood through the vessels, Gruentzig's balloon pushed the plaque out of the way. If such a technique could work how many hearts could be restored to health? How many lives could be saved?

Charles Dotter had been the first to push wires and catheters through blockages in the leg arteries of patients a decade earlier in 1964, poking through the clogged vessels and reaming them out as though he were twisting a pipe cleaner through the stem of a meerschaum. Like many pioneers, he was laughed at. No one believed "dottering" would do any good, much less fulfill its inventor's high hopes. But in 1971, while he was a medical resident, Gruentzig visited a clinic near Cologne where patients underwent the procedure. He came away impressed. Mastering the leg-vessel technique on his own patients, he set out to refine the crude coaxial catheter to suit his ultimate target. "The legs were only my testing ground," he recalled. "From the very beginning, I had the heart in mind."

In 1977 Gruentzig, who would later become professor of medicine at Emory University in Atlanta, startled cardiologists at the American Heart Association's 50th Annual Scientific Sessions meeting with the news that he had tried the balloon in human coronary arteries, and it had worked. Percutaneous transluminal coronary angioplasty (PTCA) was born. In 1983 alone, an estimated 30,000 angioplasties were performed—many with catheters bearing Gruentzig's name—at an average cost of $5,300 per procedure. Many cardiologists believe angioplasty will one day rival coronary bypass surgery. Some believe it already does.

Compared with surgery, angioplasty has considerable advantages. It is far less traumatic. Instead of general anesthesia and a long, deep chest incision, there is only a Novocain shot and a single small puncture. Instead of a week and a half in the hospital, patients are generally out the next day. And it's about a quarter the price of bypass surgery.

But even in experienced hands, snaking a catheter through the winding pathways of the circulation safely into the midst of a coronary obstruction is no easy feat. The ideal blockage is regularly shaped, without crags that could snag the guide wire, and is located near the entrance to the artery, where it can be easily reached by the catheter. If a blockage occurs at a fork in an artery—and many do—there is a risk that compressing it will close off the branch vessel. What's more, not all deposits are equally crushable. The old, hard ones break nicely, like cracking a crust of ice on top of soft snow. But newer ones common in patients with suddenly worsening angina tend to come back quickly, like snow drifting across a freshly plowed road. Although experts claim they can successfully open single vessels 80 percent of time (it is much lower for less experienced practitioners), long-term recurrence is the Achilles heel of angioplasty. A quarter or more of the dilated deposits grow back; often patients have to return to the catheterization laboratory for a second or even a third angioplasty—and receive a second or third bill. And with angioplasty, strike three is usually out. These patients end up with bypass surgery.

Unlike the fail-safe world of cardiopulmonary bypass, the heart is unprotected by cardioplegia during angioplasty, though some practitioners use an intra-aortic balloon pump as an added margin of safety in worrisome cases. Sometimes merely the catheter's touch sends an artery into spasm, or knocks off a chunk of atherosclerotic debris, which tumbles downstream. Sometimes the vessels tear or rupture. For these reasons, a surgeon and a pump team are kept standing by (with their meters running, of course). Five percent of the time, the OR crew must swing into action, and with a mortality rate of 6 percent and a nonfatal heart attack rate of 41 percent, the combination of angioplasty and emergency bypass surgery is a much more risky proposition than either procedure is alone. So angioplasty, which is billed as less traumatic to the patient and his pocketbook, can occasionally end up being just the reverse.

Furthermore, PTCA's underlying effectiveness is uncertain. According to the National Heart, Lung, and Blood Institute, which has been keeping track of about 3,500 angioplasty patients, about half have remained asymptomatic without medication. But nuclear images indicate some of the hearts of these pain-free patients have small oxygen-starved areas. And like bypass patients, people undergoing angioplasty also seem to have problems returning to work.

No wonder Gruentzig has a healthy respect for his brain-child's limits. "I know that damn balloon catheter," he said. "I invented it. It has problems. You can cause problems with the guide wire, with the catheter. You may disrupt the artery. You may close the artery. You may dissect the artery. You may dissect other arteries that were not diseased before. You can really mess things up. I have seen too many complications in the past not to be cautious. I have gotten excited and jumped in to do dilatation. Then we put the catheter in and, boom, the artery closed immediately when I just touched it with the guide wire. The patient got a reinfarction. 'Oh, God,' I said, 'if only I had stepped back.' "

The Food and Drug Administration also is cautious, recommending that angioplasty be performed only on patients with a single obstruction. Most cardiologists also prefer a patient with stable angina, who is otherwise a candidate for bypass surgery. Still, the number of two- and even three-vessel angioplasties is rising, despite the greater risks with multiple dilatations. Geoffrey O. Hartzler of the Mid-America Heart Institute in Kansas City, Missouri, has done as many as ten inflations in as many parts of a single coronary tree.

Few cardiologists are as enthusiastic about angioplasty as Hartzler. Will angioplasty replace bypass? Should it? Given the safety and effectiveness of both procedures, it would take a study of more than a thousand patients—and that would require many millions of dollars—to find the answer. Anyway, says K. Peter Rentrop, who, as director of interventional angiography at Mount Sinai, performed more than two hundred angioplasties in 1983, the two aren't competitive but rather complementary. "If I can transform somebody who has triple-vessel disease into somebody who has single-vessel disease without operating, I think I've achieved something," he told an audience of cardiologists at a recent seminar. "We think that probably most of our younger patients will eventually need surgery, but we're thinking about decreasing or postponing the need for repeat operations."

Angioplasty might make further inroads into the bypass market if new techniques fulfill their promise. Ultrasonic catheters, with high frequency vibrations emanating from their tips, could make the blood in an artery vibrate enough to break through the most stubborn atherosclerotic encrustation. Laser beams may prove even more effective. In cases where a balloon catheter can't squeeze by, a light gun could simply burn through the plaque. In theory, the beam vaporizes the clog in seconds, eliminating the problem of particles washing downstream. But first we have to control its penetration. As Rentrop says, "Laser is like playing with a knife in a dark hole." Obviously, a wound in the heart would be disastrous, but even a small scratch on an arterial wall could become the nidus of another atherosclerotic deposit. And what do you do with the byproduct of this incendiary treatment, the smoke?

For these reasons, the Food and Drug Administration has yet to approve laser angioplasty. But that hasn't stopped a half-dozen American teams from using light guns on animals, nor in March 1983 did it stop a Stanford University group from using a catheter fitted with an argon laser to burn through an obstruction deep in the leg artery of a sixty-two-year-old man facing amputation. It succeeded, and the patient left the hospital the next day. A second patient given laser treatment a month later wasn't as lucky. His vessel closed, and bypass surgery for the limb was required.

A few months later at the University of Toulouse in France, an American team used an argon laser developed and patented by Daniel S. J. Choy, a New York City oncologist, on the coronary arteries of five patients. Two had their left anterior descending arteries "lased," the other three their right coronary arteries. (The patients had other blockages and were going to bypass surgery anyway.) The experiment worked in four cases; in the fifth, performed with a modified laser, the artery was torn. Although all five patients were doing well a month later, angiograms showed that only one of the lased arteries was still open.

Along with lasers, the marriage of catheterization and fiber optics has also given us angioscopy—a tiny lens that can peer from the tip of a catheter down a coronary artery to let us actually see the blockage. To guide this coronary camera to the trouble spot, we may someday call on hematoporphyrin derivative, a substance that has a propensity for finding atherosclerotic plaque in animals and, researchers hope, in humans. When exposed to ultraviolet light, this chemical glows, lighting up the deposit. And if a substance can be found that responds to ultraviolet wavelengths, perhaps a chemical cousin can be uncovered that responds to laser light, allowing the plaque to be vaporized without damage to neighboring tissue, completing the search-and-destroy mission.

For many years, angiographers maintained a hands-off policy toward heart attacks. Once an attack began, they let it happen and hoped for the best. Bypass surgery and angioplasty are still deemed too dangerous for most patients in the midst of myocardial infarction, but now we aren't always passive when heart attacks strike. With interventional angiography, we can limit their damage and sometimes even halt them.

Like many new therapies, this one was born of desperation. Its father was Peter Rentrop. During the years when Gruentzig was developing his balloon catheter at Zurich, Rentrop was running the catheterization laboratory at the University of Göttingen in West Germany. One day in 1978, while a catheterization was being performed on a truck driver with unstable angina, the patient began suffering severe chest pain. His right coronary artery had been closed by a blood clot, a heart attack had started, and a routine procedure was fast turning into a disaster. Called to the scene by his resident, Rentrop recalled another patient who had suffered a similar complication and been rushed to bypass surgery, only to end up with devastating heart damage. Though probing clotted coronary arteries with catheters was still taboo, he had become convinced this was the only solution. For forty-five minutes he paced up and down the room, his own heart racing. Then, over the objections of a colleague, Rentrop took the tiny guide wire and poked a hole in the newly formed clot. The blocked artery opened. The heart attack stopped.

Today, Rentrop and others have traded the clumsy and often dangerous wires and tubes for drugs like urokinase, a product of urine, or streptokinase, a product of bacteria. Like modern-day chemical leeches, these agents eat away at the fibrin that holds the clots together, reopening the clogged passageways of the coronary circulation. There are two difficulties, however. The drugs have to be administered quickly, in the very first hours after a heart attack begins, and they tend to cause bleeding, which can be calamitous for a patient with a dormant ulcer, an undiscovered tumor, or even a mild bruise. The bleeding can be contained by injecting the drugs directly into the coronary arteries, thus insuring that most of the dose gets where it is needed. But to find the right artery, an angiogram has to be performed first. That takes time, often enough to render the drugs worthless. So some cardiologists simply give the drugs intravenously when heart attack victims arrive in the hospital. They believe the time advantage outweighs both the higher risks of bleeding and the smaller dose reaching the coronary blockage.

The solution to this cardiological quagmire would be a clot-dissolving drug that could be injected into a peripheral vein without exposing the rest of the body to the risk of hemorrhage. In fact, such a substance exists. It goes by the cumbersome name of tissue plasminogen activator (T-PA), and it works only when it is in contact with the fresh blood clots we believe are

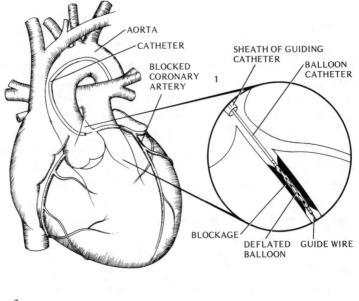

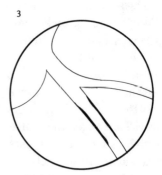

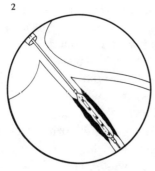

THE ANGIOPLASTY PROCEDURE

1 Inserted in an artery in the groin or arm, the catheter is slid through the circulatory system into the aorta, stopping at the mouth of the left main coronary artery.
The balloon tip is positioned at the site of the blockage.
2 The balloon is inflated, crushing the atherosclerotic plaque against the artery wall.
3 The catheter is withdrawn, leaving a wider path for the blood.

responsible for most heart attacks. Injected into the arm, T-PA searches the circulation for the scene of the atherosclerotic crime, then solves it.

A large protein—527 amino acids long—T-PA is hard to come by. The body normally produces it only in minute quantities. Cancerous melanoma cells produce more, but not enough to let us use the product of one disease to treat another. The most promising source of T-PA is the California-based firm of Genentech, whose researchers are using recombinant DNA technology to manufacture the substance in greater quantities. It is already in use experimentally, and the indications are that it may be a tremendously valuable weapon. But it will be a while before we can determine the range of safe and effective doses.

In medicine, detection is the better part of valor. The importance of early diagnosis in a progressive disease goes without saying. New techniques and technologies nearing clinical application could provide answers to problems that have been vexing physicians since Heberden, such as why some people have no symptoms despite severe triple-vessel disease while others are immobilized by a single atherosclerotic deposit.

Computers are already helping make angiography simpler and safer by reducing the two main sources of complications: the jostling of the coronaries by the catheter; and the X-ray dye, which can sometimes be toxic. Using a technique called digital subtraction imaging, X-ray angiograms are electronically enhanced many times over, enabling us either to use very small amounts of the dye injected in the aorta or to avoid the catheter entirely and inject the dye intravenously. The implications of this technical wrinkle are deceptively profound: Angiography could become so quick and safe that it could make other cardiac diagnostic tools like some nuclear scans obsolete and come to rival the electrocardiogram as a mass-screening aid.

Another device, computerized axial tomography, or the CAT scanner, has for years furnished wondrously detailed X-ray slices of other organs but was too slow to capture the beating heart. By gaiting today's speedier electronic components to a patient's electrocardiogram, however, CAT scans of the heart are coming into focus. Even more promising, perhaps, is a new generation of nuclear imaging techniques that not only let us peer inside the heart but tell us about the organ's metabolism at the same time. Researchers are developing an arsenal of radio-active isotopes, substances that tag along with various biochemical components as they go about their business in the body. Because they give off detectable radiation, they let us follow the play-by-play, too, enabling us to measure the blood flow to different parts of the heart, monitor the various enzymes in cardiac muscle, tell whether a drug is working, and expose the secrets of platelets and plaques. Positron emission tomography, PET scanning, takes the slicing approach of a CAT scan one step further, using radionuclide probes to go beyond the cell and explore the very atoms of the heart.

One of the newest frontiers is nuclear magnetic resonance imaging (NMR). Here, a patient is placed in the midst of a powerful magnetic field, which alters the configuration of the hydrogen atoms that make up the molecules of the heart. These atoms are then pelted by radio waves, and the resulting reactions are recorded. The information is computed to produce an image that gives doctors a look at not only the structure but also the function of cardiac cells.

Is NMR safe? It seems to be, though there are stories of Kelly clamps magnetically pulled from white-coat pockets and flying through the air. The biggest problem may be its expense: With the special housing required to protect and properly isolate the intense magnetic field, a single machine costs up to $3 million. Only a handful of hospitals across the country has them. When the Memorial-Sloan Kettering Cancer Center, one of the most advanced research and treatment centers in the world, tried to join that select club in 1983, its application for an NMR machine was initially turned down by New York State health care regulators, who wanted the doctors to cart their patients to the unit at neighboring New York Hospital. Approval came only after *The New York Times* reported that a group of private radiologists who did not fall under the regulators' control were installing their own machine a few blocks away.

We are also finding new uses for old technology. A case in point is echocardiography. For years, cardiologists have sent sound waves through the chest wall toward the heart and recorded the echoes, capturing images of the valve leaflets and other structures. Now, microphonelike sonar probes are found in the operating room, where they are passed over exposed hearts during surgery to produce pictures of the interior of coronary arteries and even to clock the speed of the blood flowing through them. As ultrasound technology improves, we may one day be able to visualize the coronary arteries sonically through a closed chest wall, a magic more appealing than either radiation or magnetism.

Computers are also helping us wring more information out of that old workhorse of cardiac diagnosis, the electrocardiogram. Electronic brains can combine the EKGs of hundreds of heartbeats and amplify them to disclose hidden abnormalities. Another microprocessor-based device, called a Cardiointegraph, can analyze a single-beat EKG that looks normal to the eye of even a seasoned cardiologist and find clues to disease. Its motto: "Who knows what evil lurks in the hearts of men? The Cardiointegraph knows."

When the first pacemaker was installed almost four decades ago, its proud recipient was tethered to a console as big as a trunk by wires leading out of his chest. Now there are pacemakers the size of silver dollars containing computers and power stations that maintain contact with the heart through antenna-like electrodes and communicate by telemetry to doctors on the outside. Patients can simply hold a device connected to a telephone receiver to their chests and the pacemaker transmits a signal to a distant computer, which makes a diagnosis. It is even possible using today's technology to adjust pacemakers by satellite, beaming corrective signals down on patients. (Intriguingly, there was talk that an American-made, programmable pacemaker was worn by Leonid Brezhnev while he was in power in the Kremlin.)

There are even more advanced models that are, in effect, implantable electronic cardiologists. Using an expanding array of tiny sensors that measure the temperature, blood pressure, and chemical and electrical activity of the cardiovascular system, these electronic marvels are able to spot irregular rhythms that can lead to cardiac arrest and treat them by triggering built-in defibrillators or dispensing drugs—and there are several promising antiarrhythmic agents being tested—from pumps that have been installed in the patient's body. These pumps could also release medications to strengthen a failing heart or disarm marauding platelets.

There are also new drugs designed to improve the elasticity of the red cells, allowing the blood to squeeze by plaque more easily. Slippery blood would be easier for the heart to push around the body, and the organ's need for oxygen would be lower. Researchers have also developed a fluorocarbon substance that can deliver oxygen to needy tissues, augmenting the supply carried by hemoglobin—in effect, artificial blood. And the science of prosthetic cardiovascular materials may advance to the point where one day we may also have artificial vessels for the artificial blood to flow through, eliminating the need to harvest saphenous veins and reducing the trauma of bypass surgery. Or perhaps we will be able to clone natural veins from our genetic stock. It may also be possible to isolate the gene responsible for HDL, manufacture it using recombinant DNA techniques, and supply it to people with unhealthy cholesterol levels. There may be other natural protective factors as well, substances that, when given in sufficient quantities, may enable us to increase the heart's ability to live without oxygen—what cardiologists call an ischemia-resistant myocardium—or render the coronary arteries immune to the atherosclerotic process.

In the meantime, heart transplant programs are multiplying, thanks to cyclosporine, a powerful antibiotic that bolsters immune systems weakened by the drugs needed to keep the body from rejecting foreign tissue. In 1968, only 20 percent of the heart transplant recipients at Stanford University lived a year. Now 80 percent do. And the Stanford transplant program has grown from 60 patients in 1981 to 250 just two years later. A major problem remains: the dearth of donor organs. Some believe that animals can provide the solution; others are betting on machines. Some put their faith in Baby Fae, who lived for twenty days after the heart of a baboon was transplanted into her tiny chest at Loma Linda University Hospital in California in 1984; others choose Barney Clark, the Seattle dentist who received the first artificial heart at the University of Utah Medical Center two years earlier.

As coincidence would have it, Baby Fae's struggle for life coincided with the 57th Annual Scientific Sessions of the American Heart Association. For four days, the cardiologists who gathered by the thousands in Miami Beach picked and chose among 1,800 original papers, culled from more than 5,700 abstracts submitted to meeting organizers and presented by researchers from around the world. There were sessions on diet, antiarrhythmic drugs, ultrasound techniques, the molecular biology of lipoproteins, apolipoproteins, radionuclide tomography, endothelium-platelet interactions, cardiac imaging, laser angioplasty, and, of course, coronary bypass surgery. And in the vast exhibition hall, the medical-industrial complex displayed its wares. Heart valves, catheters, and pacemakers were set out on velvet under glass, like jewels at Tiffany's. Physicians could stroll through a capsule of long-acting Inderal the size of a first-class lounge in a Boeing 747, or view a 360-degree movie on the wonders of the drug Procardia. Computer screens were everywhere, flashing the results of angiograms, nuclear scans, and ultrasound examinations to anyone who would stop and look.

None of this would have been possible twenty years ago. Indeed, such a technology fair could not even have been imagined. And it is undoubtedly no coincidence that during the past two decades the death rate from heart disease has dropped more than 30 percent, a decline that translates into half a million lives saved every year. It is possible that the end of the twentieth century will also mark the end of the cardiac century. But we are still a long way from cardiology's Holy Grail, a drug capable of dissolving atherosclerotic plaque and washing it from our bloodstream. That will require an even greater research effort, and we still spend more each year on bypass surgery than we do on basic investigation into the mystery of heart disease. Is our society willing to make such an investment? Can we afford not to?

Glossary

Adrenalin See Epinephrine.

Aerobic exercise Any strenuous, dynamic physical activity such as running, cycling, or swimming that requires a continuous supply of oxygen.

Anaerobic metabolism Chemical processes in the body's cells that take place in the absence of oxygen, using different enzymes and producing different byproducts than aerobic metabolism.

Aneurysm A bulging segment of blood vessel or heart muscle resulting from a weak spot caused by atherosclerosis, heart attack, trauma, or genetic defect. Aneurysms of arteries can rupture when they become too large; aneurysms of the heart rarely burst but can cause chest pain, shortness of breath, fatigue, or abnormal heart rhythms.

Angina pectoris Cardiac chest pain, usually due to disease of the coronary arteries. Typically provoked by exercise or emotional stress, which increases the heart's need for oxygen, or vascular spasm, which decreases the heart's blood supply.

Angiography A diagnostic test in which X-ray films are taken while dye is injected into an artery through a catheter, outlining any blockages. Coronary angiography is required before bypass surgery.

Angioplasty The use of a catheter to open a blocked artery.

Aorta The trunk of the body's arterial tree. It begins in the left ventricle and distributes oxygenated blood to all organs and tissues of the body.

Arrhythmia A disturbance of the heartbeat.

Artery One of the vessels that carry blood away from the heart to the rest of the body.

Atheroma A tumorlike deposit of fatty material in the artery. Also called plaque.

Atherosclerosis A disease of the lining of the artery involving the buildup of cholesterol and fibrous tissue, which can narrow the vessel and block blood flow. Commonly called hardening of the arteries.

Atrioventricular node A pea-sized area of heart muscle between the upper and lower chambers that relays the electrical impulses controlling the organ's rhythm.

Atrium (auricle) One of the two upper chambers of the heart that collect blood from the veins and transport it to the ventricles for pumping.

Auscultation The act of listening to the heart through the stethoscope.

Blood pressure The force exerted by the blood against the artery walls.

Bradycardia Slow heart rate.

Bruit A noise that the blood makes as it passes through an artery, signifying turbulent flow.

CABG Coronary artery bypass graft surgery.

Calorie The amount of heat required to raise the temperature of 1 kilogram of water 1 degree centigrade. Often used to measure the energy value of foods and exercise.

Capillaries The smallest blood vessels linking the arteries and veins, which allow oxygen and nutrients to flow from the blood to the tissues in exchange for waste products.

Cardiac arrest Stopping of the heartbeat. Usually due to ventricular fibrillation and fatal unless cardiopulmonary resuscitation is performed.

Cardiac cycle One complete heartbeat, incorporating the electrical activation, contraction, ejection, relaxation, and reloading of the organ.

Cardiologist A physician specializing in diseases of the heart.

Cardiomyopathy A disease in which the heart muscle becomes abnormally stiff or weak. It can be caused by infection, toxic substances, or lack of oxygen due to coronary artery disease.

Cardioplegia The process of stilling the heart by injecting it with a cold potassium solution during cardiac surgery.

Cardiopulmonary bypass The establishment of artificial circulation in which a heart-lung machine temporarily replaces the natural organs.

Cardiopulmonary resuscitation A first-aid technique to supply oxygen to the lungs and keep the blood flowing in a victim of cardiac arrest.

Cardioversion   The restoration of normal heart rhythm, usually by the application of an electrical shock.

Catecholamines   Chemicals produced by the nervous system and adrenal glands that increase cardiovascular action.

Catheter   A thin, flexible tube that can be guided through blood vessels into the heart to make measurements, inject X-ray dye or drugs, or open atherosclerotic blockages.

Cholesterol   A fatty substance found in animal tissue that is an ingredient of atherosclerotic blockages.

Claudication   A pain or weakness, usually in the legs, due to impaired circulation.

Collateral circulation   Pathways formed by small blood vessels when main arteries are blocked.

Congestive heart failure   The failure of the heart to pump effectively, depriving the body of oxygenated blood and backing up fluid in the lungs, abdomen, or legs.

Coronary   The name of the arteries arising from the base of the aorta that supply the heart with oxygenated blood.

Defibrillation   The termination of atrial or ventricular fibrillation, usually by electrical shock.

Diabetes mellitus   A disorder of sugar metabolism, usually due to an inadequate supply of insulin from the pancreas.

Diastole   The period between contractions when the heart is relaxed.

Dilation   Widening of the blood vessels or an enlargement of the heart.

Dyspnea   Shortness of breath.

Echocardiogram   A noninvasive test in which a picture of the inside of the heart is made by bouncing high-frequency sound beams (ultrasound) off the organ from a transducer placed on the outside of the chest.

Edema Accumulation of excessive fluid in tissues.

Ejection fraction The percentage of the contents of the left ventricle expelled with each heartbeat. Fifty to seventy is normal.

EKG An electrocardiogram. A recording of the electrical activity of the heart using electrodes attached to the limbs and chest. Also called ECG.

Embolism The blocking of a blood vessel by floating debris, usually a blood clot.

Endocarditis The inflammation of the inside of the heart, usually caused by bacterial infection.

Endothelium The inner lining of blood vessels.

Epinephrine (adrenalin) A hormone produced by the adrenal glands that increases the speed and strength of the heartbeat, constricts small blood vessels, raises blood pressure, and opens airways in the lungs.

Erythrocyte Microscopic disc-shaped sacs containing the pigment hemoglobin. There are 5 million red blood cells in each cubic millimeter of blood.

Fatty streak A flat, yellow patch on the wall of an artery containing cholesterol; thought to be the earliest evidence of atherosclerosis.

Fibrillation A cardiac arrhythmia in which individual muscle fibers in the heart contract randomly, resulting in the loss of pumping power. Unlike atrial fibrillation, ventricular fibrillation causes death if not corrected.

Fibrin A strandlike protein involved in the formation of blood clots.

Gated cardiac blood-pool scan A test in which the blood is labeled radioactively by the injection of a short-lived isotope and a sensor placed over the chest records a motion picture of the heart's pumping action.

HDL High density lipoprotein that removes cholesterol from the bloodstream. It lowers the risk of atherosclerosis.

Heart attack See Myocardial infarction.

Heart block A disorder in which the conduction of electricity from one part of the heart to another is delayed.

Hemoglobin The iron-rich red pigment in the blood that carries oxygen.

Hemorrhage Bleeding.

Hepatic Of the liver.

Hypercholesterolemia Excess cholesterol in the blood.

Hypertension See High blood pressure.

Hypertrophy Overdevelopment or thickening of heart muscle.

Hypotension Low blood pressure.

Hypothermia Cooling of the body to reduce metabolism.

Intermittent Claudication See Claudication.

Intra-aortic balloon pump A device placed in the aorta that inflates and deflates with the cardiac cycle to help the heart pump.

Invasive A procedure in which the body is entered.

Ischemia A lack of oxygen in an organ or tissue.

LDL Low density lipoprotein that carries cholesterol through the bloodstream. It increases the risk of atherosclerosis.

Leukocyte One of a family of particles in the blood that are involved in immunity and inflammation and combat infection. Normally there are 5,000 to 10,000 per cubic millimeter of blood.

Lipid Fat.

Lipoprotein A protein molecule capable of binding lipids. Since fats do not dissolve in blood, they must be carried by lipoproteins.

Lumen The hollow part of a tube; the passageway through a catheter or blood vessel.

Mediastinum The area in the center of the chest, behind the breastbone and between the lungs, where the heart is situated.

Monounsaturated fat See Unsaturated fats.

Murmur A noise that the blood makes as it passes through the heart, which can be a sign of disease.

Myocardial infarction The death of a portion of heart muscle resulting from interrupted blood supply.

Myocardium Heart muscle.

Noninvasive A diagnostic test or procedure that is conducted without trauma to the body.

Obese More than 15 percent above ideal weight due to excess fat.

Pacemaker A natural or artificial timekeeper for the heartbeat. Normally this function rests in the sinoatrial node, but temporary or permanent electronic devices may be installed when the natural mechanism fails.

Palpitation Sensation of rapid, forceful, or irregular cardiac activity.

Pericardium The sac around the heart.

Plaque   See Atheroma.

Plasma   The liquid part of the blood.

Platelet   The smallest cellular element in the blood; important in blood clotting and atherosclerosis.

Polyunsaturated fat   See Unsaturated fats.

Potassium   A mineral that participates in the electrical processes of cells.

Prostaglandins   A family of substances produced by cells throughout the body that help regulate blood flow, temperature, inflammation, and metabolism.

Pulmonary   Of the lungs.

Râles   Crackling sounds heard during examination of the chest with a stethoscope, indicating fluid or secretions in the microscopic air sacs of the lungs.

Red blood cell   See Erythrocyte.

Renal   Of the kidneys.

Revascularization   A surgical procedure in which diseased blood vessels are repaired or replaced to restore blood flow to the limbs, kidneys, intestines, brain, or heart.

Rheumatic heart disease   Scarring of the inside of the heart, especially the valves, which progresses for years after acute rheumatic fever, a childhood disease that can follow a streptococcal throat infection.

Saphenous vein   A large, superficial blood vessel in the leg removed and grafted onto the heart during bypass surgery to deliver blood around blocked coronary arteries.

Saturated fats   Fats, usually of animal origin, loaded with hydrogen. When consumed in the diet, they can increase the level of cholesterol in the blood and increase the risk of heart disease.

Septum The muscular wall dividing the left and right chambers of the heart.

Serum The liquid portion of the blood, minus the proteins involved in blood clotting.

Sinoatrial node A thumbtack-sized mass located in the back of the right atrium that initiates the heart's electrical cycle; the heart's natural pacemaker.

Sodium A mineral plentiful in table salt that is associated with fluid retention and high blood pressure.

Spasm See Vasospasm.

Sphygmomanometer An inflatable device used to measure blood pressure.

Stenosis The narrowing of a conduit such as an artery.

Sternum The breastbone.

Stress test A procedure in which blood pressure, breathing, heart function, and the electrocardiogram are monitored while the patient exercises on a treadmill, bicycle, or stepladder.

Stroke Injury of brain tissue caused by impaired blood flow.

Systole The period when the heart is contracting.

Tachycardia Rapid heart rate.

Tamponade The compression of the heart by fluid or clotted blood in or around the pericardium.

Thallium scan A test in which a radioactive substance is injected into the circulation to make an image of the blood flow to heart muscle; often performed in conjunction with a stress test.

Thoracic Of the chest.

Thrombosis The process of blood clotting.

Triglycerides   A group of fats found in plant and animal products that may increase atherosclerosis.

Unsaturated fats   Fats capable of absorbing hydrogen that lower blood cholesterol. Polyunsaturated fats are believed to decrease both LDL and HDL; monounsaturated fats are thought to decrease the harmful LDL but not affect the beneficial HDL.

Vasospasm   The excessive contraction of a blood vessel, resulting in insufficient blood flow.

Vein   One of the blood vessels that carry blood from the parts of the body to the heart.

Ventricle   One of the two pumping chambers of the heart.

White blood cell   See Leukocyte.

Index